REINTERPRETING EXPLORATION

NATIONAL HISTORY CENTER

REINTERPRETING HISTORY
Wm. Roger Louis, *series editor*

Historiography is the art of conveying the ways in which the interpretation of history changes over time. The series Reinterpreting History is dedicated to the historian's craft of challenging assumptions, examining new evidence, and placing topics of significance in historiographical context. The vigorous and systematic revision of history is at the heart of the discipline.

Reinterpreting History is an initiative of the National History Center, which was created by the American Historical Association in 2002 to advance historical knowledge and to convey to the public at large the context of present-day issues. The books in the series usually have their origins in sessions organized by the National History Center at the annual meetings of the AHA.

REINTERPRETING EXPLORATION

The West in the World

EDITED BY

Dane Kennedy

OXFORD
UNIVERSITY PRESS

OXFORD

UNIVERSITY PRESS

Oxford University Press is a department of the University of Oxford.
It furthers the University's objective of excellence in research, scholarship,
and education by publishing worldwide.

Oxford   New York
Auckland   Cape Town   Dar es Salaam   Hong Kong   Karachi
Kuala Lumpur   Madrid   Melbourne   Mexico City   Nairobi
New Delhi   Shanghai   Taipei   Toronto

With offices in
Argentina   Austria   Brazil   Chile   Czech Republic   France   Greece
Guatemala   Hungary   Italy   Japan   Poland   Portugal   Singapore
South Korea   Switzerland   Thailand   Turkey   Ukraine   Vietnam

Oxford is a registered trademark of Oxford University Press
in the UK and certain other countries.

Published in the United States of America by
Oxford University Press
198 Madison Avenue, New York, NY 10016

A copy of this book's Cataloguing-in-Publication Data is on file with the
Library of Congress.

ISBN 978-0-19-975534-9; 978-0-19-975533-2 (pbk.)

1 3 5 7 9 8 6 4 2
Printed in the United States of America
on acid-free paper

For our students

CONTENTS

LIST OF FIGURES

CONTRIBUTORS

STEPHANIE BARCZEWSKI is a professor of history at Clemson University. She is the author of *Antarctic Destinies: Scott, Shackleton and the Changing Face of Heroism* (2007), *Titanic: A Night to Remember* (2004), and *Myth and National Identity in Nineteenth-Century Britain: The Legends of King Arthur and Robin Hood* (2000). Her current projects include a study of country houses and the British Empire for Manchester University Press and a study of heroic failure in British culture for Yale University Press.

DANE KENNEDY is the Elmer Louis Kayser Professor of History and International Affairs at George Washington University. His latest book is *The Last Blank Spaces: Exploring Africa and Australia* (2013). Prior publications include *The Highly Civilized Man: Richard Burton and the Victorian World* (2005) and *The Magic Mountains: Hill Stations and the British Raj* (1996).

HARRY LIEBERSOHN is a professor of history at the University of Illinois at Urbana-Champaign. His most recent books are *The Return of the Gift: European History of a Global Idea* (2011), *The Travelers' World: Europe to the Pacific* (2006), and *Aristocratic Encounters: European Travelers and North American Indians* (1998). He has been a fellow of the Wissenschaftskolleg in Berlin (2006–7) and a member of the Institute for Advanced Study, Princeton (1996–7).

CLARE PETTITT is a professor of English at Kings College London. She is a Research Director of a four year AHRC interdisciplinary project, "Scrambled Messages: The Telegraphic Imaginary 1857–1900" and author of *Dr. Livingstone, I Presume? Missionaries, Journalists, Explorers, and Empire* (2007), *Patent Inventions: Intellectual Property and the Victorian Novel* (2004), and other publications on the history of the book.

MICHAEL F. ROBINSON is an associate professor of history at the University of Hartford. He is the author of *The Coldest Crucible: Arctic Exploration and American Culture* (2006), winner of the 2008 Forum of the History of Science in America book prize. He is working on a book, *Lost White Tribe: Explorers, Scientists, and a Theory that Changed Africa* for Oxford University Press. He writes a blog about science, history, and exploration called "Time to Eat the Dogs."

STEPHEN J. ROCKEL is a professor of African history at the University of Toronto Scarborough. He is the author of *Carriers of Culture: Labor on the Road in 19th Century East Africa* (2006) and articles in the *Journal of African History* and *The Canadian Journal of African Studies*, among other publications.

JANE SAMSON is a professor of history at the University of Alberta. She is the author of *Race and Empire* (2004) and *Imperial Benevolence: Making British Authority in the Pacific Islands* (1998), as well as editor of three other books on British imperial history. She has also published numerous articles and book chapters on Pacific missionaries (both European and indigenous) and is currently working on the life of George Sarawia, the first Melanesian Anglican priest.

BERNY SÈBE is a lecturer in colonial and postcolonial studies in the Department of Modern Languages at the University of Birmingham. He is the author of *Heroic Imperialists in Africa* (2013), which examines the making of British and French imperial heroes in Africa between 1870 and 1939, as well as several articles and book chapters on related subjects. He has also coauthored several illustrated books on the Sahara desert, including, *Sahara, the Atlantic to the Nile* (2003).

PHILIP J. STERN is associate professor of history at Duke University. He is the author of *The Company-State: Corporate Sovereignty and the Early Modern Foundations of the British Empire in India* (2011), which won the Morris D. Forkosch Prize from the American Historical Association, in addition to a number of articles, essays, and book chapters. He is also coeditor of *Mercantilism Reimagined: Political Economy in Early Modern Britain and its Empire* (2013).

GORDON STEWART is the Jack & Margaret Sweet Professor of History at Michigan State University. His books include *Journeys to Empire: Enlightenment, Imperialism and the British Encounter with Tibet 1774–1904* (2009) and *Jute and Empire: The Calcutta Jute Wallahs and the Landscapes of Empire* (2009). He has also written about the British Everest expeditions between 1921 and 1953 in *Past & Present*, No. 149 (1995).

WILLARD SUNDERLAND is associate professor of history at the University of Cincinnati. He is the author of *Taming the Wild Field: Colonization and Empire on the Russian Steppe* (2004) as well as coeditor of two collections of essays: *Peopling the Russian Periphery: Borderland Colonization in Eurasian History* (2007) and *Russia's People of Empire: Life Stories from Eurasia, 1500 to the Present* (2012). His latest book, *The Baron's Cloak: A History of the Russian Empire in War and Revolution*, will appear in 2014.

REINTERPRETING EXPLORATION

INTRODUCTION:
REINTERPRETING EXPLORATION

DANE KENNEDY

Exploration, as it is commonly understood, is the product of a particular historical legacy. In English usage, exploration is a term that first came to refer to arduous journeys into unfamiliar territories in the mid- to late- eighteenth century, while the word "explorer" was only coined in the early nineteenth century.[1] The unprecedented efforts by Britain and other European states and peoples to probe the far regions of the globe for the purposes of trade, conquest, and colonization provide the backdrop for the association of exploration and explorers with adventures in distant lands. The subtitle of the volume, "The West in the World," signals its intent to concentrate mainly on European exploration and encounters with other peoples. This subtitle is not meant to suggest that other societies did not engage in what can be broadly construed as exploration. What it is meant to suggest is that exploration is a concept and a practice that carries a particular set of cultural, social, and political valences, and they originate in the European historical experience.

Exploration came to assume a mythic status in the European mind, serving as the harbinger of Europe's triumphal entry onto the world stage. Each of the states involved in this enterprise had its own explorers to honor and celebrate. The posthumous apotheosis of Christopher Columbus by Spain, Vasco de Gama by Portugal, Francis Drake by England, and other early adventurers established a pattern that would persist into the twentieth century, imbuing a long line of explorers—Bering, Cook, Lewis and Clark, Livingstone, Brazza, Amundsen, and countless others—with iconic importance to the countries that claimed them as their own. As Jane Samson, Berny Sèbe, Willard Sunderland, and other contributors to this volume demonstrate, exploration and explorers became emblematic of state power and national prestige.

Exploration and explorers also became bound up with European notions of the modern, which reached full flower with the Enlightenment, the influence of which is skillfully probed here by Philip Stern. Europeans and their colonial cousins came to view expeditions of discovery as missions in the service of modernity. This higher purpose was identified with the technological innovations that made it possible for European explorers to circumnavigate the globe and reach its most remote regions, to exert their will over many of the peoples they encountered along the way, and to map out the geographical coordinates of their routes as guides to those who followed.[2] It was identified, too, with the scientific knowledge drawn from the plant, animal, and mineral specimens the explorers collected, the meteorological, magnetic, and astronomical data they recorded, and the ethnographic artifacts and linguistic knowledge they acquired. All of these activities and accomplishments contributed to Europeans' growing conviction that they embodied and advanced the forces of modernity. With the great eighteenth-century voyages of discovery by Louis-Antoine de Bougainville, James Cook, Alejandro Malaspina, and others, scientific exploration became firmly fixed in the European cultural imagination as a key measure of modernity.

Henceforth, exploration would connote a combination of scientific and technological achievement, state power, and national prestige—connotations that endure to the present day, perhaps most notably in space exploration.[3] These connotations have come to differentiate exploration from other forms of travel, such as those motivated by trade, tourism, and migration. It may be anachronistic, as Michael Robinson points out in his essay, to regard Columbus and other vanguards of European overseas expansion as engaged in exploration in the modern scientific sense it subsequently acquired, but the label has stuck because it has served a larger purpose—to establish a genealogy of exploration that reinforced a sense of European exceptionalism. Exploration became a triumphalist symbol of the energy, enterprise, and inventiveness that Europeans and their overseas offspring regarded as the key markers of difference between their own societies and those found elsewhere around the world.[4]

Exposing, analyzing, and challenging these associations have provided the main impetus for the renewed attention scholars have given to exploration in recent years. One objective has been to excavate the epistemological foundations of exploration and critique its ideological agendas. The growing influence of postcolonial perspectives within literary studies, cultural history, and other humanities disciplines has helped shape this agenda. So too has the self-reflexive turn taken by anthropologists, geographers, historians of science, and other social scientists, who have been spurred to critically assess exploration's contribution to the development of their own disciplinary practices and institutions. A second objective has been to show that the experiences of explorers in the field were often at variance with the ways they portrayed those experiences for public consumption. Area studies specialists, including historians and anthropologists, have demonstrated that the operations and outcomes of many expeditions were shaped in crucial ways by local peoples and polities, and that they relied heavily on indigenous intermediaries. Recent research has given new insight into the contested encounters and complex engagements that actually took place during and after expeditions—between explorers and the native peoples with whom they came in contact, between explorers and the natural environments within which they struggled to survive, and between explorers and the domestic institutions and publics from which they sought fame and fortune. Much of the scholarship on exploration can be characterized as concerned with the mediation between expectation and experience, between observation and understanding, and between representation and reality.

The purpose of this volume is two-fold: it seeks to summarize the issues that have informed much of the previous historiography on exploration and to trace the innovative and important lines of inquiry that have taken this subject in new directions in recent years. It is informed by the conviction that these new lines of inquiry have resulted in a widespread reassessment of the historical significance of exploration, shifting attention away from its longstanding triumphalist associations and toward a more nuanced appreciation of the multiple forces that propelled it and the unintended outcomes it produced. The following essays, many of them written by key contributors to this reassessment, address some of the significant themes it has pursued, including cultural encounters, scientific knowledge, print culture, imperial conquest, and more.

*   *   *

The heroic individual has long loomed large in the literature on exploration. One important reason for this emphasis on the ordeals and triumphs of the lone explorer is that much of the available information about journeys to distant lands came from the firsthand accounts of those who made them. Marco Polo's *Travels* helped establish the European genre of travel writing. Its readers included Christopher Columbus, who made marginal notations in his copy of the book prior to setting out across the Atlantic to America, where he recorded his own observations of the strange places and peoples he found there. By the end of the sixteenth century, Richard Hakluyt was able to compile enough firsthand accounts of travels by Englishmen to far-away places to fill the three volumes of *The Principal Navigations, Voyages, Traffiques and Discoveries of the English Nation* (enlarged ed. 1598–1600). Soon after, Francis Bacon advised travelers in his essay "On Travel" (1615) to keep a daily record of their observations in a diary or journal, already a common practice, he noted, in sea voyages.[5] With the dramatic expansion of print culture in eighteenth-century Europe, the demand for travel literature grew rapidly, making bestsellers of Bougainville's and Cook's journals and giving rise to popular travel satires such as Jonathan Swift's *Gulliver's Travels* and Voltaire's *Candide*. Explorers and other travelers soon came to recognize that they could win profit and acclaim by writing books, preferably two-volume tomes, about their journeys. By the early nineteenth century, publishing firms like John Murray had begun to specialize in the production and promotion of travel and exploration books. Later in the century, the rise of the new journalism created a further source of synergy between print culture and exploration, with men like Henry Morton Stanley and Pierre Savorgnan de Brazza writing sensationalist accounts about their exploits in savage lands that sold a great many newspapers. Exploration as it is commonly understood in European culture is thus inextricably associated with writing, publishing, and reading.

Explorers wrote about their own observations and experiences, giving their chronicles an autobiographical character. Even when they were describing the topography, climate, flora, and fauna of the places they passed through, the choices they made about what merited attention and how to describe their responses reflected their sensibilities, revealing personal preferences, prejudices, desires, and fears. Above all, of course, they wrote about themselves: It was their adventures and ordeals that drove their narratives. Invariably, they cast themselves as the heroes of their own tales, often in collusion with the press and the public, as Berny Sèbe and Clare Pettitt demonstrate in their chapters.

Just as explorers' own narratives were inherently autobiographical, those narratives of expeditions written by historians and others generally adopted a biographical approach. Biographies of the "great men" who led high profile expeditions have enjoyed an enduring appeal, as Jane Samson and Stephanie Barczewski show in their chapters on the exploration of the Pacific and the Antarctic. Explorers were usually cast as exemplars of courage, self-sacrifice, and patriotism. Well into the twentieth century, prominent historians such as Samuel Eliot Morison, Reginald Coupland, and John Beaglehole wrote about Columbus, Livingstone, Cook, and other explorers in celebratory terms, stressing their struggles with nature and their contribution to the advance of civilization.[6]

As European empires collapsed and gave rise to new nation-states in Africa, Asia, and the Caribbean from the mid-twentieth century on, Western scholars had less incentive to write about exploration. It ceased to stir the same sense of moral purpose and patriotic pride that had given the subject meaning to historians during the period of imperial rule. At the same time, geographers, anthropologists, and other natural and social scientists whose predecessors had served as handmaids of exploration and empire began to distance their disciplines from those associations—increasingly unwelcome as critical voices arose against them. The rise of area studies during the Cold War created a further disincentive to devote attention to exploration, since it harbored such strong Eurocentric associations. Nonetheless, many Africanists and other area studies specialists did draw heavily on explorers' firsthand accounts for evidence about indigenous societies, especially those without literate cultures.

Books about explorers and expeditions continued to be written and read, to be sure, but they were increasingly the work of journalists and other non-academic authors. Biography remained the standard genre, though many were biographies with a difference: the explorer as anti-hero replaced the explorer as hero. Stephanie Barczewski shows in her essay how biographical revisionism reversed the previously heroic reputation of the Antarctic explorer Robert Falcon Scott, portraying him instead as an insecure and incompetent leader. David Livingstone, Charles Sturt, Henry Morton Stanley, and other famous explorers were similarly judged anew as deeply flawed figures—selfish, manipulative, ruthless, obsessive, and emotionally troubled.[7] These critical biographies were especially prevalent in the 1970s and 80s, a period that saw the certitudes of the past contested in the culture wars that broke out in the shadow of the Vietnam War. More recently, the pendulum appears to have swung back in favor of biographies that laud the achievements of explorers, indicative, perhaps, of the neo-imperial mood among a certain portion of Western public opinion.[8]

A common characteristic of most of these biographies—laudatory and critical alike—has been an emphasis on what set their subjects apart from contemporaries. Some are portrayed as sui generis, all as exceptional. Yet explorers were products of their times, shaped by the same social, cultural, political, economic, and ideological forces as were their contemporaries.[9] If there is a single thread that runs through the recently renewed scholarly interest in the subject, it is the conviction that explorers and exploration cannot be fully understood without identifying and explaining the multiple contexts within which they operated.

* * *

There has always been a body of opinion, Michael Robinson observes, that considers exploration an innate human instinct, an impulse that separates Homo sapiens from other species. The evolutionary geneticist Svante Pääbo, for example, has speculated that the "exploration thing" may be hard-wired into the human genetic code.[10] If true, perhaps its most enduring expression is the epic quest, the long and arduous journey that leads to self-discovery. This theme figures prominently in the traditions of many cultures. Its appeal derives in part from its promise that the individual who endures this prolonged physical and psychological ordeal is spiritually transformed by it. Even if exploration as the search for new lands has all but come to an end, its appeal as an epic quest lingers on, manifested in mountaineering, "extreme sports," and other endeavors that seek transcendence by testing the limits of endurance.

In his book *Pathfinders: A Global History of Exploration*, Felipe Fernández-Armesto characterizes exploration as coterminous with human history itself, an assertion that appears on first glance to endorse the view of Pääbo. But Fernández-Armesto historicizes his argument by defining exploration as the process by which peoples dispersed across the globe and then reconverged.[11] His intent is to escape exploration's Eurocentric associations by stressing its global dynamics and dimensions. Much the same agenda has informed the work of a number of other historians in recent years. They have directed our attention to the ambitious and often risky journeys that non-European groups and individuals made into regions unknown to them. As Jane Samson points out, much research has been directed at the Polynesians' remarkable voyages across the Pacific, which required shipbuilding abilities, navigational knowledge, and other specialized skills that archeologists, ethnographers, and historians are only beginning to understand.[12] Expeditions sent out by Europeans' rivals for global hegemony have received closer attention as well. The famous voyages of Admiral Zheng He, whose fleets ventured as far as the east coast of Africa on behalf of the Ming empire in the early fifteenth century, have been interpreted by some historians as an abortive attempt by the Chinese to achieve the global reach and influence that Europeans established soon thereafter.[13] Gordon Stewart observes in his contribution to this volume that Qing China had penetrated central Asia long before European explorers entered the region. Moreover, its agents employed cartographic and ethnographic practices that resembled those of early modern European explorers.[14] Similarly, the Ottoman Empire in this period has been shown to have countered expansion by the Portuguese and other European states with its own exploratory ventures.[15] And Stephen Rockel notes in his essay that the Arab trader Said bin Habib crossed the African continent long before Livingstone, Cameron, and Stanley did the same to great acclaim.

While these examples serve as important reminders that other societies engaged in endeavors that can be characterized as exploration, they have done little to dislodge the consensus that European exploration had a disproportionate historical impact on the modern world, which is in turn reflected in the way the term is itself embedded in a European suite of ideas and practices. Rather than simply dismiss or deny these effects and associations, most recent scholarship has sought to interrogate their cultural and political purposes and reveal the realities in the field that complicated and often countered those purposes. Some of the issues this scholarship has addressed include the intellectual premises, political pressures, ethnographic meanings, cultural consequences, and environmental implications of European exploration.

One of the first indications that this subject was ripe for renewed scrutiny came with the publication of Edward Said's *Orientalism* in 1978.[16] This influential work, which helped give rise to postcolonial studies as an academic field, was not concerned with exploration per se. It did, however, draw heavily on European explorers' writings in its examination of Western representations of the Orient, and Said used the term "imaginative geography" to connote the culturally constructed nature of those representations. Above all, he made the case that the knowledge the West claimed to have acquired about the Orient by means of exploration and other inquiries served—and still serves—its imperial ambitions.

The implications of Said's analysis of the relationship between knowledge and imperial power were not lost on literary and cultural studies scholars, many of whom followed up his lead by giving greater scrutiny to exploration and travel accounts. Two influential works were Paul Carter's *The Road to Botany Bay* and Mary Louise Pratt's *Imperial Eyes*. While Carter and Pratt employed different methodological strategies, they shared similar objectives. Both addressed aspects of European exploration, with Carter focusing on Australia and Pratt on South America and Africa, but neither told conventional stories about explorers' experiences. Instead, they highlighted the discursive practices that underwrote explorers' accounts of their journeys, using them to carry out postcolonial critiques of Western conceptions of non-Western cultures and societies. Carter opened his book by declaring that history as it was commonly written in the West was intended "not to understand or to interpret," but "to legitimate" conquest, thereby becoming, in effect, as "imperial history." He sought to replace this history with a new "spatial history" that revealed how language rhetorically served to transform space into place, a location imbued with a meaning.[17] Pratt, too, asserted that her purpose was to "decolonize knowledge," to deconstruct the "planetary consciousness" that she argued the West had produced in the process of conducting expeditions across the globe. But unlike Carter, who was concerned exclusively with the West's efforts to impose its own categories of meaning on other places and peoples, Pratt offered glimpses of a counter-discourse that opposed the totalizing claims of this planetary consciousness, detecting its traces in the "contact zones" of cross-cultural interactions where some degree of "transculturation" or cultural exchange took place.[18]

Taken together, the postcolonial approach adopted by Said, Carter, and Pratt had a profound influence on subsequent scholarship on exploration, especially in literary and cultural studies circles. That influence derived in the first instance from their exposure and critique of the premises that informed so much prior scholarship on the subject. They presented explorers' individual feats of heroism and exploration's contributions to scientific knowledge as culturally constructed claims that both cloaked and legitimated the imperial interests these activities served. It was not the purpose of these scholars, however, to foreground the political and economic aspects of imperial exploration. Rather, they sought to show how exploration constructed claims about the objects of its knowledge that revealed a far more insidious and enduring form of power, the power to influence the way we view the world, its regions and inhabitants.

This interest in exposing the ideological and cultural underpinnings of exploration has been especially prevalent in literary criticism. It has produced a flood of books on travel writing, as well as journals such as *Studies in Travel Writing*. While the vitality of this scholarship is undeniable, critics have voiced concerns about its limitations, derived in part from its theoretical preoccupation with discursive formations and its methodological emphasis on textual practices.[19] Despite Pratt's call for her colleagues to give greater attention to the "contact zone" and its possibilities for cultural interaction and exchange, most of them devoted their energies on close readings of a select number of published texts by Western travelers. The experiential dimensions of exploration, such as quotidian encounters with other peoples, were either neglected altogether or assumed to have been accurately represented in the narrative accounts explorers wrote for domestic readers. Moreover, the emphasis this scholarship gave to travel literature as a genre often obscured the important ways exploration as a practice diverged from tourism and other forms of travel.

On the other hand, research into the production and dissemination of exploration narratives as an aspect of print culture has opened up several new and useful lines of inquiry. One issue that has generated considerable interdisciplinary attention of late is the process by which explorers' original field diaries were transformed into published texts that conformed to narrative conventions. It has become increasingly clear that what explorers wrote during their journeys often went through multiple revisions before the works appeared in print, a process that substantially altered the texts, eroding their authenticity as a record of immediate observations and experiences. In addition to the explorers' own emendations, their reports were often reworked by sponsors, officials, publishers, and others with vested interests in their success. The controversy caused by John Hawkesworth's editorial changes to Captain Cook's journal for the Admiralty-commissioned book about its South Seas expeditions, *An Account of the Voyages Undertaken for Making Discoveries in the Southern Hemisphere* (1773), which cast the encounter with the peoples of the South Pacific in a more sensational light than the original journal suggested, is a notorious example. Explorers' accounts were revised to make them more readable, more saleable, and less likely to embarrass the author or offend readers.[20] In addition to the texts themselves, the maps and illustrations that accompanied them were designed to appeal to the publications' purchasers. How these works were marketed and consumed tells us a great deal about the meanings and uses domestic audiences drew from expeditions. In her essay, Clare Pettitt discusses the "active reader," cautioning against regarding this elusive figure as the passive recipient of exploration's self-proclaimed messages about its meaning.[21]

Publishers and their publics were part of a much larger network of domestic institutions and interest groups that gave exploration much of its shape and purpose, as a growing body of scholarship has demonstrated. These entities included branches of governments (armies, navies, colonial services), geographical societies, museums and botanical gardens, missionary groups, and merchant associations. As these organizations' diverse range of interests in exploration has become better understood, it has become more difficult to identify a single and direct line of causation between exploration and empire. Expeditions were sponsored by a variety of groups for a variety of purposes, and even though those purposes overlapped insofar as they entailed a shared interest in acquiring knowledge of and access to the wider world, they could collide as well as collude. If exploration was the avatar of empires, it provided ample evidence that those empires were capable of assuming multiple forms and directed to multiple, often contending, objectives.[22]

One element of Western society that played a particularly important role in shaping exploration as a distinct enterprise, governed by a special set of protocols and practices, was the scientific community and its research agenda. Recent work by historians of science and technology has shown that scientific disciplines such as botany, zoology, and geography did not assume their present forms simply as a result of experiments in the laboratory or insights in the study. They derived as well from observations in the field, and especially from observations carried out by specially trained members of expeditions.[23] The relationship between exploration and science reached full flower during the period that Michael Robinson (drawing on categories originally advanced by William Goetzmann) terms "the second age of discovery." If its impetus can be traced in part to the scientific revolution of the seventeenth century, it was the Enlightenment in the eighteenth century that gave it staying power, laying the intellectual and institutional foundations for the enduring bonds between these two enterprises. Philip Stern's essay on the Enlightenment and exploration examines this crucial collaboration. Among its characteristics was an emphasis on the collecting, classifying, and categorizing of specimens and the use of instruments to survey cartographic space and measure meteorological and other natural phenomena, practices that contributed to the development of various scientific disciplines.[24]

Both Stern and Robinson also underscore that exploration appealed as much to emotion as it did to reason. Exploration narratives were popular with readers, as literary critics have shown, because they produced the frisson of physical danger, the fantasy of erotic freedom, and a variety of other thrills. Explorers themselves were not immune to such emotions; they were integral elements of what drew these men to distant lands. Joseph Banks was both the sober collector of botanical specimens and the rakish aficionado of Tahitian women during his South Seas voyage. Alexander von Humboldt was both the rigorous advocate of scientific rationalism and the romantic celebrant of natural wonder during his journey through Latin America. German and Belgian explorers of Africa were proponents of self-control and sober judgment during their expeditions, but they were often "out of their minds" from fever, fatigue, fear, and drugs, drifting into what the African anthropologist Johannes Fabian has termed a state of "ecstasis."[25]

Fabian's important study points to another prominent theme of recent scholarship on exploration—the quotidian experiences of explorers in the field, especially their cultural encounters with indigenous peoples. Both Harry Liebersohn and Jane Samson identify these "first contacts" as one of the central themes of the new historiography of exploration. As Liebersohn observes, the analysis of first contacts opens up alternative narrative perspectives, offering a means of overcoming the Western-centered focus of earlier scholarship on exploration. Area studies specialists, such as those Samson discusses in the Pacific context and those Stephen Rockel references with regard to East Africa, have been assiduous in pursuing indigenous perspectives on these encounters. Even though the archives have left us with few direct traces of the voices of the peoples who came in contact with explorers, historians, anthropologists, and other scholars have found new ways to gain insight into the experiences and intentions of these peoples. What they have revealed is that the local inhabitants often held the upper hand in encounters with the Europeans who passed through their territories. Though explorers rarely acknowledged their dependence on native peoples in the published accounts of their expeditions, they frequently vented frustration at their own helplessness and bewilderment in unpublished reports. As Rockel shows, European expeditions in East Africa relied on preexisting trade routes, labor practices, political systems, and other institutional structures to make their way into the interior. The same was true of expeditions into most other parts of Africa, as it was almost everywhere explorers passed through well-populated territories.[26]

The crucial contribution that indigenous guides, translators, and other intermediaries made to expeditions is another aspect of exploration as cultural encounter that has only recently begun to receive the attention it deserves. Although explorers often praised their native assistants, they usually cast these individuals in the conventional role of loyal servants, dutifully carrying out their masters' wishes. In truth, most of them were quasi-independent contractors with wills and agendas of their own. The novice African explorer Joseph Thomson privately credited his caravan's "headmen" with "the success of the expedition," gratefully confessing that they were "imbued with the idea that I was specially under their care . . . to be taken carefully & safely round and shown the sights" in central Africa.[27] Gordon Stewart notes that the Indian Pundits who were sent to explore Central Asia on behalf of the British Raj did not do so as auxiliaries to Europeans; they ventured into the region as autonomous agents who had been specially trained to gather the cartographic and other scientific information so prized by the West. In cases such as these, the "native" could actually become the "explorer," thereby destabilizing the very categories that sustained exploration as a European endeavor. Although the independent journeys carried out by the Pundits were unusual, the indigenous go-betweens who took part in European expeditions clearly enjoyed far greater independence and exerted far greater influence than has been previously recognized or acknowledged.[28]

A final theme that has attracted considerable attention in recent years is the relationship between explorers and the environment. Many scholars have taken their cue from Bernard Smith's pathbreaking book, *European Vision and the South Pacific*, engaging in related studies of explorers' representations of the territories they passed through and the agendas that informed those representations.[29] Although explorers sometimes drew on domestic aesthetic categories like the picturesque to portray the places they passed through, more often they emphasized the strangeness of these landscapes. Striking examples include the characterization of Latin America and India as "torrid" or "tropical" zones that posed special risks to Europeans. Even more distancing was the representation of Africa as "the dark continent."[30] Perhaps the most original and intriguing line of inquiry concerns exploration's contribution to the rise of a modern environmental consciousness. Gordon Stewart notes in his essay that explorers' discovery of the buried cities of Central Asia heightened their appreciation of the impact of climate change on human societies. One of the first works to show that exploration could give rise to a conservationist impulse was John MacKenzie's *The Empire of Nature*.[31] More recently, Aaron Sachs has traced Alexander von Humboldt's influence on the environmentalist tradition that arose from the exploration of the American West.[32] These and other studies of exploration have stressed the various ways we are inextricably bound to the natural world.

* * *

This volume is divided into two sections. The essays in the first section will examine some of the key thematic issues raised in recent scholarship on European exploration, issues that transcend the variable circumstances that affected its aims and outcomes. Michael Robinson addresses the crucial issue of exploration's connections to science, demonstrating that it evolved over time into a relationship that was at once intimate and contested. The equally vital issue of "first contact" is the subject of Harry Liebersohn's study, which uses the cases of Christopher Columbus in the Americas and James Cook in the Pacific to show how historians have become more attentive in recent years to indigenous peoples' perspectives on encounters with explorers. The Enlightenment's formative influence on European exploration as a distinct idea and practice is examined by Philip Stern, who highlights how it forged exploration's associations with modernity. Clare Pettitt probes the relationship between exploration and nineteenth-century print culture, tracing the press's move toward a "logic of seriality" that shaped popular attitudes toward explorers. And Berny Sèbe shows how exploration was used by geographical societies and other interest groups to generate jingoistic enthusiasm for imperial expansion by Britain and France, which helped to turn explorers into national heroes. These essays, it must be stressed, do not exhaust the range of topics that could be addressed. More sustained and systematic attention might also have been given to the role of biography, cartography, gender, the environment, and other topics that loom large in the history of exploration. Nonetheless, some of the central thematic concerns that presently occupy the attention of scholars engaged in the study of exploration are addressed in these first five chapters.

The second section turns to the history and historiography of exploration in particular regions. This territorial focus permits attention to be paid to the variations as well as parallels in the patterns of exploration around the globe. Although common interests and concerns drew expeditions to widely varied regions, those regions' physical environments, native inhabitants, and prior levels of engagement with the wider world shaped the strategies and experiences of explorers in critically important ways. By the same token, the various states that took part in exploration shared certain methods and intentions, but were also motivated by forces distinctive to their own societies. It is impossible, of course, to include essays about every region of the world that was targeted for exploration or about every country involved in that endeavor, but this section provides five studies that illustrate some of the patterns at play. It begins with Willard Sunderland's essay on Russia, which shows that the explorations conducted by this European outlier were in some respects imitative of western European models and in other respects shaped by its own distinctive history and circumstances. Jane Samson surveys the history of South Pacific exploration, tracing the changes and continuities that have informed scholarship on that popular topic. Stephen Rockel reverses the conventional view of European exploration in East Africa by revealing how reliant it was on indigenous systems of trade and labor. Gordon Stewart pays attention to the explorers who ventured into Central Asia, where a "thick layer of prior discovery" obliged them to reframe their achievements in terms of the recovery of a buried past. Finally, Stephanie Barczewski brings the volume to a close with an analysis of the changing reputations of Antarctic explorers, a case study of the susceptibility of historiographical tastes and judgments to broader historical trends.

* * *

Exploration is a fitting subject for a series devoted to reinterpreting history. An enduring source of popular interest, it has been in and out of favor among academic historians over the years. Neglected for several decades after decolonization because of its associations with a discredited Western triumphalism, it has recently returned to favor as a topic of investigation. It is now seen as a central and perhaps defining aspect of the West's encounters with other peoples and lands, laying the groundwork for imperial expansion, setting in motion the great engine of globalization, and contributing to the rise to modern scientific knowledge and ideas of difference. For all these reasons, scholars have devoted renewed attention to exploration. Far from rehearsing the tired old themes of exploration as the expression of individual heroism and national prestige, they have instead pursued new ones that speak both to its ideological contribution to a Western sense of exceptionalism and its experiential contribution to the cultural engagement with other peoples. Although exploration as a distinct practice was for the most part a Western-driven enterprise, it was also aided, altered, and remade by the non-Western peoples whose lands it sought to investigate.

This resurgence of academic interest in the story of exploration can be traced to several broader intellectual agendas. One is the endeavor to excavate the ideological foundations of the imperial project and expose its lingering influence on the mental map of the world. Another is the desire to trace the sources and discern the patterns of cultural encounters and exchanges, which have become such a prominent feature of what we now call globalization. A third is the increasing need to understand how our planet's complex climate and ecosystem operated in the past, providing insights that might mitigate the destructive effects of our insatiable demand for its resources. All of these agendas speak to issues that are in certain respects traceable to exploration as a primary point of inquiry. The ideas and practices of empire arose out of the initial expeditions to discover new lands. The primal scene of cultural encounter and exchange was the first contact between explorer and indigene. And the scientific investigation and economic exploitation of the natural world were integral to the enterprise of exploration. As historians and others work to craft integrated narratives of our intersecting pasts as a human community, it is hardly surprising that they have rediscovered the theme of exploration, since it serves as such a ready avenue of access to so many of the central problems that have arisen from those intersections. To be sure, much of what passes for the popular history of exploration continues to be preoccupied with the heroic achievements or character flaws of individual explorers. But the contributors in this volume make it quite clear that exploration can no longer be seen in the simplistic terms, whether celebratory or denunciatory, that seemed so prevalent in the past.

NOTES

1. See the entries for exploration and explorer in the *Oxford English Dictionary*. The English word exploration derives from Latin and appears in nearly identical form in several European languages, including French (*d'exploration*), Spanish (*exploración*), Portuguese (*exploracão*), Italian (*esplorazione*), and Dutch (*exploratie*).

2. See the compelling new study by Joyce E. Chaplin, *Round about the Earth: Circumnavigation from Magellan to Orbit* (New York: Simon and Schuster, 2012).

3. A revealing example is the study prepared for NASA-Goddard Space Flight Center by the Program of Policy Studies in Science and Technology, *The Exploration Ethic: Its Historical-Intellectual Basis: Final Project Report* (Washington, D.C.: 1975). The best treatments of exploration in its most recent variants are Stephen J. Pyne, *Voyager: Seeking Newer Worlds in the Third Great Age of Discovery* (New York: Viking, 2010), and Simon Naylor and James R. Ryan, eds., *New Spaces for Exploration: Geographies of Discovery in the Twentieth Century* (London: I. B. Tauris, 2010).

4. See Michael Adas, *Machines as the Measure of Men: Science, Technology, and Ideologies of Western Dominance* (Ithaca, N.Y.: Cornell University Press, 1989).

5. Francis Bacon, "Of Travel," in *The Essays of Francis Bacon*, ed. Clarke Sutherland Northrup (New York: Houghton, Mifflin, 1908), 56.

6. Samuel Eliot Morison, *Admiral of the Ocean Sea; a Life of Christopher Columbus* (Boston: Little, Brown and Co., 1942), idem, *The Great Explorers: The European Discovery of America* (New York: Oxford University Press, 1978); Reginald Coupland, *Kirk on the Zambesi* (Oxford: Clarendon Press, 1928); idem, *Livingstone's Last Journey* (London: Collins, 1945); John Beaglehole, ed., *The Journals of Captain James Cook*, 4 vols. (Cambridge: Cambridge University Press, 1955–1967); idem, *The Life of Captain James Cook* (Stanford, Calif.: Stanford University Press, 1974).

7. Tim Jeal, *Livingstone* (New York: G. P. Putnam's Sons, 1973); Roland Huntford, *Scott and Amundsen* (London: Hodder and Stoughton, 1979); Edgar Beale, *Sturt: The Chipped Idol* (Sydney: Sydney University Press, 1979); Frank McLynn, *Stanley: The Making of an African Explorer* (London: Constable, 1989). Although more sympathetic to its subject than the preceding works, the

psychoanalytic approach adopted by Fawn M. Brodie, *The Devil Drives: A Life of Sir Richard Burton* (New York: W. W. Norton, 1967), laid some of the analytical groundwork for the subsequent spate of anti-heroic biographies of explorers.

8. See, for example, the most recent work by Tim Jeal: *Stanley: The Impossible Life of Africa's Greatest Explorer* (New Haven, Conn.: Yale University Press, 2007), and *Explorers of the Nile: The Triumph and Tragedy of a Great Victorian Adventure* (New Haven, Conn.: Yale University Press, 2011). In seeking to restore Stanley's reputation—sullied even in his own lifetime by his wanton use of violence during his expeditions and his role in the establishment of King Leopold's genocidal regime in the Congo—Jeal has stressed the need to overcome "post-imperial guilt," which he derisively dismisses as making "moral Brownie points" through the condemnation of "'crimes' committed by earlier generations" (Tim Jeal, "Remembering Henry Stanley," *The Telegraph*, March 16, 2011). Ironically, Jeal made a key contribution to the anti-heroic turn in the 1970s with his myth-shattering biography of Livingstone.

9. I address this problem with respect to Richard Burton in *The Highly Civilized Man: Richard Burton and the Victorian World* (Cambridge, Mass.: Harvard University Press, 2005), 5–6, 268–269.

10. Elizabeth Kolbert, "Sleeping With the Enemy: What Happened Between the Neanderthals and Us?" *The New Yorker* (August 15 & 22, 2011): 72.

11. Felipe Fernández-Armesto, *Pathfinders: A Global History of Exploration* (New York: W. W. Norton, 2006).

12. Geoffrey Irwin, *The Prehistoric Exploration and Colonisation of the Pacific* (Cambridge: Cambridge University Press, 1994).

13. Louise Levathes, *When China Ruled the Seas: The Treasure Fleet of the Dragon Throne, 1405–1433* (New York: Oxford University Press, 1997); Edward L. Dreyer, *Zheng He: China and the Oceans of the Early Ming Dynasty, 1405–1433* (Harlow: Longman, 2006).

14. Laura Hostetler, *Qing Colonial Enterprise: Ethnography and Cartography in Early Modern China* (Chicago: University of Chicago Press, 2001).

15. Giancarlo Casale, *The Ottoman Age of Exploration* (New York: Oxford University Press, 2010).

16. Edward W. Said, *Orientalism* (New York: Pantheon, 1978).

17. Paul Carter, *The Road to Botany Bay: An Essay in Spatial History* (London: Faber and Faber, 1987), xvi.

18. Mary Louise Pratt, *Imperial Eyes: Travel Writing and Transculturation* (London: Routledge, 1992), 2, 9.

19. See, for example, Aaron Sachs, "The Ultimate 'Other': Post-Colonialism and Alexander von Humboldt's Ecological Relationship with Nature," *History and Theory* 24 (December 2003): 111–135.

20. See Kathryn Barrett-Gaines, "Travel Writing, Experience, and Silences: What is Left Out of European Travelers' Accounts—The Case of Richard D. Mohun," *History in Africa*, 24 (1997): 53–70; David Finkelstein, *The House of*

Blackwood: Author-Publisher Relations in the Victorian Era (University Park: Pennsylvania State University Press, 2002); Charles W. J. Withers and Innes M. Keighren, "Travels into Print: Authoring, Editing and Narratives of Travel and Exploration, c. 1815–c. 1857," *Transactions of the Institute of British Geographers,* 36 (2011): 1–14.

21. Clare Pettitt, *Dr. Livingstone, I Presume? Missionaries, Journalists, Explorers, and Empire* (Cambridge, Mass.: Harvard University Press, 2007); Leila Koivunen, *Visualizing Africa in Nineteenth-Century British Travel Accounts* (New York: Routledge, 2009); Edward Berenson, *Heroes of Empire: Five Charismatic Men and the Conquest of Africa* (Berkeley: University of California Press, 2011).

22. Examples included Morag Bell, Robin Butlin, and Michael Heffernan, eds., *Geography and Imperialism 1820–1940* (Manchester: Manchester University Press, 1995); Richard Drayton, *Nature's Government: Science, Imperial Britain, and the 'Improvement' of the World* (New Haven, Conn.: Yale University Press, 2000); Felix Driver, *Geography Militant: Cultures of Exploration and Empire* (Oxford: Blackwell, 2001); John M. MacKenzie, *Museums and Empire: Natural History, Human Cultures and Colonial Identity* (Manchester: Manchester University Press, 2009).

23. See, for example, Michael S. Reidy, Gary Kroll, and Erik M. Conway, eds., *Exploration and Science: Social Impact and Interaction* (Santa Barbara, Calif.: ABC-CLIO, 2007); Jim Endersby, *Imperial Nature: Joseph Hooker and the Practices of Victorian Science* (Chicago: University of Chicago, 2008); Patricia Fara, *Sex, Botany and Empire: The Story of Carl Linnaeus and Joseph Banks* (Thirplow, Cambridge: Icon Books, 2004); David N. Livingstone, *Putting Science in its Place: Geographies of Scientific Knowledge* (Chicago: University of Chicago Press, 2003); David N. Livingstone and Charles W. J. Withers, eds., *Geographies of Nineteenth-Century Science* (Chicago: University of Chicago Press, 2011). An important precursor to this line of inquiry was William H. Goetzmann, *Exploration and Empire: The Explorer and the Scientist in the Winning of the American West* (New York: Vintage, 1966).

24. Marie-Noëlle Bourguet, Christian Licoppe, and H. Otto Siburn, eds., *Instruments, Travel and Science* (London: Routledge, 2002).

25. Johannes Fabian, *Out of Our Minds: Reason and Madness in the Exploration of Central Africa* (Berkeley: University of California Press, 2000). Also see the collaborative compilation of texts edited by the anthropologist Nicholas Thomas and the literary scholars Jonathan Lamb and Vanessa Smith, *Exploration and Exchange: A South Seas Anthology, 1680–1900* (Chicago: University of Chicago Press, 2000).

26. See Stephen J. Rockel, *Carriers of Culture: Labor on the Road in Nineteenth-Century East Africa* (Portsmouth, N.H.: Heinemann, 2006).

27. Joseph Thomson to the Secretary of the Royal Geographical Society, July 19, 1880, CB6/2173, Royal Geographical Society Archives, London.

28. Useful introductions to this subject include Felix Driver and Lowri Jones, *Hidden Histories of Exploration: Researching the RGS-IBG Collections* (London: Royal Holloway, University of London, 2009), and Simon Shaffer, Lissa Roberts, Kapil Raj, and James Delbourgo, eds., *The Brokered World: Go-Betweens and Global Intelligence, 1770–1820* (Sagamore Beach, Mass.: Science History Publications, 2009). Among the pioneering work on this subject is Donald Simpson, *Dark Companions: The African Contribution to the European Exploration of East Africa* (New York: Barnes and Noble, 1976) and Henry Reynolds, *With the White People* (Ringwood, Victoria: Penguin Books, 1990), which built on his earlier essay, "The Land, the Explorers and the Aborigines," *Historical Studies*, 19, 75 (1980): 213–226

29. Bernard Smith, *European Vision and the South Pacific*, 2d ed. (New Haven, Conn.: Yale University Press, 1985 [1960]). A recent example of this approach is John McAleer, *Representing Africa: Landscape, Exploration and Empire in Southern Africa, 1780–1870* (Manchester: Manchester University Press, 2010).

30. See Nancy Leys Stepan, *Picturing Tropical Nature* (Ithaca, N.Y.: Cornell University Press, 2001); Felix Driver and Luciana Martins, eds., *Tropical Visions in an Age of Empire* (Chicago: University of Chicago Press, 2005); David Arnold, *The Tropics and the Traveling Gaze: India, Landscape, and Science, 1800–1856* (Seattle: University of Washington Press, 2006); Dorothy Hammond and Alta Jablow, *The Myth of Africa* (New York: The Library of Social Science, 1977).

31. John M. MacKenzie, *The Empire of Nature: Hunting, Conservation, and British Imperialism* (Manchester: Manchester University Press, 1988).

32. Aaron Sachs, *The Humboldt Current: Nineteenth-Century Exploration and the Roots of American Environmentalism* (New York: Penguin, 2006). Also see Richard H. Grove, *Green Imperialism: Colonial Expansion, Tropical Island Edens and the Origins of Environmentalism, 1600–1860* (Cambridge: Cambridge University Press, 1995).

PART I

Themes

1

SCIENCE AND EXPLORATION

MICHAEL F. ROBINSON

As expeditions of discovery sailed from Europe in the 1700s, people spoke of exploration as a new "fascination," a vogue that illustrated the rational virtues of the age. By the late nineteenth century, the language had changed. Writers increasingly described exploration as a "fever": something rampant, contagious, and immune to reason. Explorers poured out of the Western world for regions remote and dangerous. Some raced to the ends of latitude, to stand first at the polar axes. Others set off for the equatorial regions seeking lost tribes, lost cities, and lost explorers. Survey expeditions mapped the American West, inventoried ocean depths, and paved the way for the "Scramble for Africa." States sponsored some of these efforts. Museums and universities sponsored others. Meanwhile private adventurers set off to write, photograph, and hunt their way through the world's remaining *terrae incognitae*.[1]

Taken together, these activities produced oceans of text: articles, technical papers, and personal narratives. One writer for the journal *Nature*, buried by stacks of expedition literature waiting to be reviewed, wondered what was driving the process. Did exploration grow out of a deeper love of science, a "craving for knowledge by stronger stimulants than can be obtained by books?" Or was it—as the metaphor of fever suggests—something beyond conscious control, an instinctive desire, "a remote ancestral habit which still clings to us." If it was the latter, then science would seem to be artifice, a veneer applied to expeditionary endeavors in order to mask true motives, deeper and atavistic urges that lured explorers up mountains and into malarial jungles.[2]

Questions about the relationship between science and exploration predate the modern concepts of science and exploration themselves.

After all, the pursuit of knowledge was part of the travel story long before "scientist" and "explorer" entered common use in the 1800s.[3] What did the traveler learn through the rigors of travel? Was the voyage an opportunity for gaining knowledge about the world, as the work of Pliny, John Mandeville, and Marco Polo suggested? Or did it function, as Plato, Siddhārtha Gautama, and St. Francis seemed to think, as a way of learning about oneself?[4] In practice, these two motives for travel—worldly knowledge and self-knowledge—were not mutually exclusive. Three thousand years of travel literature have combined elements of both. Yet the idea of science as an objective, worldly form of knowledge gained ascendance in discovery expeditions after 1700. Self-knowledge became its expeditionary shadow, appearing in the poetry and art of the age and read between the lines of the explorer's narrative.

This long "prehistory" of science and exploration raises a question that may trouble the cultural historian. Are the links between travel and knowledge best pursued through a study of culture and history? After all, the story of the traveler who gains wisdom through his arduous journey is common across cultures and historical periods. What do we gain, then, by looking at a relationship that seems to transcend the influences of society itself? Perhaps psychological or mythological approaches offer a greater payoff. Comparative mythologist Joseph Campbell suggested as much, stating that the "commonality of themes in world myths point[ed] to a constant requirement in the human psyche." In stories of travel and knowledge, Campbell saw the features of a monomyth: a structure basic to all hero stories across cultures. Into this basic template, we can fit travelers, real and fictitious, across the ages: Gilgamesh, Odysseus, Columbus, Humboldt, and Darwin. They leave home, suffer trials, gain insight, and transform the world in the process. Despite their great differences, each figure traces the same arc along Campbell's mythological chart.[5]

Yet even if we accept that the relationship between science and exploration touches upon something *a priori* within the human psyche, evidence suggests that it has been shaped by culture in meaningful ways. Ideas do not exist in the ether, nor within some impregnable fortress of the mind. They are subject to the influences of people, places, and things. It's not difficult to see exploration's role in changing the content of knowledge. The exchange of new species among the four continents of the Atlantic in the 1500s challenged European systems for organizing nature. Yet the greatest shifts in knowledge occurred outside the philosopher's study, as natives and commoners tried to make sense of the wonders of other worlds. Voyages of exploration set in motion a long cascade of discovery that reached beyond the explorer's visible horizon: West Africans' first encounters with cassava, Amerindians' first sightings of the horse, Europeans' first taste of the potato.[6]

Exploration changed the concepts and methods of science, too. By the 1600s, European scholars looked to exploration for more than marvels. It had become a symbol for the process of science itself. In his treatise, *Novum Organum*, Francis Bacon heralded exploration as a metaphor for the new science, arguing that the discovery of scientific methods was akin to the discovery of new lands. Within this metaphor, men of science operated as explorers of nature's laws. René Descartes was not an armchair philosopher but a voyager, a man praised for a genius "displayed in seeking out a new, albeit mistaken, route in the darkest night." Isaac Newton grew pale from long hours at his desk in Cambridge, but for William Wordsworth, his was "a Mind for ever voyaging through strange seas of Thought alone." Travel offered—through materials as well as metaphors—new ways of thinking about natural knowledge. [7]

The Age of Discovery

Influence traveled in both directions. As voyages of discovery gave conceptual tools to the scientific enterprise of the 1600s, so too did science offer ways of explaining exploration. In particular it offered a means of conceptualizing different periods of discovery. At first glance, the "Age of Discovery" doesn't need much conceptualizing. That Iberian exploration of the Atlantic represented something new seems self-evident: a state-sponsored, technologically sophisticated series of missions to open up Africa, expand trade, and find trade routes East. Yet science did play an important role in interpreting these events, particularly in the late 1600s when natural philosophers sought to define their methods as qualitatively different from those of their medieval predecessors. These natural philosophers began to categorize voyages of discovery in scientific terms: as the triumph of empirical knowledge over classical authority, as the death knell of a stuffy medieval scholasticism. According to this view, the intricate clockwork of medieval beliefs could not accommodate reports of new continents, species, races, and natural wonders. The mechanism failed and, in the process, a new method of inquiry was born. In short, the "Age of Discovery" became a geographical manifesto of the "Scientific Revolution."[8]

The real story was more complicated. It is true that Columbus and other early modern explorers were eager to claim geographical discoveries. Moreover, they were quick to boast about how their voyages had challenged widely held ideas of the medieval canon (e.g., that the equatorial zone was too hot to be inhabitable). Yet more often than not, their discoveries confirmed preexisting ideas current in Europe. After all, discovery is not just an event but a state of mind. Explorers must be prepared, and invested, in the action of discovery, in seeing people, places, and objects as new.[9] Columbus did not see his value in discovering new worlds but of finding better routes to old ones. For the rest of his life, he remained committed to seeing America as the outer edges of Asia. The marvels of the American continent, therefore, were ones that Columbus had already associated with the wonders and marvels of Asia: spices, Amazons, man-eating tribes, all of which had been reported by travelers before him.[10]

Even after it became clear in the 1500s that the West Indies were part of a "New World" and not the edges of an old one, travelers did not immediately identify or embrace the novelty of their experiences. For example, seventeenth- and eighteenth-century French colonists tended to identify New World species as close variants of European ones they already knew. Not only did this help settlers make sense of how to use new species but it also confirmed a widely held belief: New World organisms were similar to Old World ones but had degenerated through neglect. This also helped justify European colonization as a means of improving the wild garden of the New World and bringing it back into cultivation. Reports from the New World were read with interest back in Europe, but they only affected worldviews slowly.[11]

Other factors also make it difficult to assess the role of exploration in transforming European worldviews. Intellectual life in Europe had become turbulent long before Iberian mariners sailed into the Atlantic in the 1400s. The rediscovery and translation of classical texts in the twelfth century had broadened European horizons. It also prompted Desiderius Erasmus, Lorenzo Valla, and other classical humanists to search for the original meaning of biblical texts by retranslating them. In their discoveries of error, they raised doubts about the methods of medieval inquiry: how did one know that texts spoke truth? While exploration challenged ideas at the edges of medieval knowledge—on issues of geography, climate, religion—reformers like Martin Luther and John Calvin attacked that knowledge at its ecclesiastical heart, turning the belief systems of Europeans upside down.[12]

The Second Age of Discovery

The role of science within European culture changed in the 1700s. With it came changes in the practice of exploration. Natural philosophy, still an esoteric pursuit, gradually entered the world of public culture. As it did, it became a symbol of the power of human reason. Mathematicians, once figures isolated in the university, became celebrities of the salon. That mathematics and physics had practical applications, especially in navigation and surveying, only increased their cultural cachet. It was no longer enough to estimate one's course across the lines of the globe. Europe's monarchies, which had developed professional bureaucracies and sophisticated mercantile economies, demanded more precise information about the routes and the spaces of empire. Nothing illustrates this better than the magisterial national mapping survey of France, a process that took over a century and three generations of Cassini's to accomplish.[13]

Not surprisingly, this spirit of mathematics infused the expeditions of the age, which set out to measure the earth and the spaces beyond. Jacques Cassini's work had raised questions about whether the earth was truly spherical. He argued that it was slightly flattened at the equator (like a lemon). By contrast, British philosopher Isaac Newton predicted that the earth would be flatter at the poles (like a jelly donut). To resolve the dispute, Louis XV and the French Académie des Sciences sent two expeditions in the 1730s to measure an arc of latitude at different points on the earth's surface (see Figure 1.1). Pierre-Louis Moreau de Maupertuis set off to Lapland to measure a degree of arc at high latitude. Charles-Marie de La Condamine sailed for Peru to do the same in the equatorial regions of South America. The expeditions, which confirmed that Newton was right, created a new model of exploration that would be used by other European powers. Like the French geodetic expeditions, the Pacific expeditions of Englishman James Cook also took on questions of colossal scale, such as determining the distance of earth to the sun through observations of the transit of Venus. The maritime expeditions of the age, led by Louis-Antoine de Bougainville (France), Jean François de Galaup, comte de La Pérouse (France), Alessandro Malaspina (Spain), and in the 1800s, Charles Wilkes (United States), followed similar practices, mixing geographical discovery

Figure 1.1 Sailor using a sextant

with geodetic surveying, ethnographic observation, and vast amounts of collecting.[14]

So removed did these activities seem from the conquering, pillaging, and missionizing of the sixteenth century that historian Fernand Braudel detached them from the earlier Age of Discovery:

> The great maritime conquests, those of the end of the fifteenth century and sixteenth century, had ended with the conquest of the planet's *useful* ocean routes. Two centuries later the situation changed completely: The voyages around the world had no other goal than to obtain new information about geography, the natural world, and the mores of different peoples.[15]

In 1986, historian William Goetzmann expanded upon Braudel's earlier observations, titling this new era the "Second Age of Exploration." For Goetzmann, the Second Age represented more than an increase of science and a decrease of barbarism; it signaled new ideas about discovery itself. In the voyages of Condamine and others, men of science gathered data about the phenomena of the world in hopes of uncovering the systems that lay beneath. The confidence that human reason and observation could reveal the clock mechanism of the universe demonstrates a bit of Enlightenment swagger. If the all-knowing Newton was really an explorer "for ever voyaging through strange seas of Thought," then, maybe the inverse was also true: the explorer was a potential Newton whose measurements would reveal God's blueprint of creation.[16]

The Second Age produced a spectacular trove of information for Western audiences to sift through, not all of which added to the triumph of Western science and civilization. Social critics such as Michel de Montaigne, Denis Diderot, and Jean-Jacques Rousseau took away other meanings from expeditionary reports, particularly ethnographic observations of native life. In the view of these philosophers, native peoples lived close to nature, avoiding the artifice and corruption of civilized life. Enlightenment writers conjured the image of the Noble Savage—who took the brutish cannibal and transformed him into the sage of Nature—using it as a weapon to challenge the legitimacy of the Ancien Regime. If Pacific islanders exhibited such ingenuity and moral decency without the benefit of Europe's hereditary orders, what was the point in preserving Old World systems of government? In this way, exploration narratives provided ammunition for the political revolutions of the Atlantic World from 1776 to 1830.[17]

It is ironic that these expeditions, inspired by a faith in reason, became texts for those who felt reason had been carried too far. As historian J. C. Beaglehole observed, Tahiti did not merely offer the British explorer "a convenient port of call" but "a foundation stone of the Romantic Movement." In accounts of exploration, Romantics found confirmation of their basic beliefs: that nature was powerful, that its forces were complex and opaque, and that truth arrived through subjective experience as much as through philosophical instruments.[18]

This Romantic embrace of the opaque, the sublime, and the irrational may seem anti-scientific, yet in practice Romanticism inspired new methods of scientific exploration. If one accepts that nature operates in ways both complex and invisible, it is unlikely that science advances merely by recording new species and coastlines. Rather, the scientific explorer seeks truth from understanding the hidden forces that lie beneath the phenomena, requiring observations both systematic and comparative in nature. No one exemplified this approach better than Alexander von Humboldt, who explored South and Central America with his colleague Aimé Bonpland from 1799 to 1804. That Humboldt arrived on the continent three hundred years after Columbus was of little consequence to his audiences in

Europe and the United States: his expedition reports offered a comparative understanding of the Americas—geologically, botanically, and ethnographically—a feat that, to revolutionary leader Simon Bolivar, established him as "the true discoverer of America."[19]

"Humboldtian science," a term coined by Susan Cannon to refer to an approach to field work that was precise, systematic, and comparative, influenced exploration throughout the nineteenth century. Charles Darwin, who carried Humboldt's *Personal Narrative* with him in South America, discovered new connections in nature: "I am at present fit only to read Humboldt; he like another Sun illumines everything I behold." Darwin, like Humboldt, proved exceptional at integrating observations across disciplines, using geology, botany, and comparative anatomy to consider "the species question."[20]

There were other questions, too, that required a Humboldtian touch. Newton had explained the ocean tides as a phenomenon of universal gravitation, a deformation of the earth caused by the gravitational pull of the sun and moon. Yet Newton's general principle could not predict actual tides; it would not keep ships from grounding in the Thames. The great variability of tides, in timing and magnitude, required better knowledge of topography and hydrodynamics. Toward this end, William Whewell's "great tide experiment" of 1835 employed thousands of people in nine countries to make tidal readings simultaneously, an effort extended by the British Admiralty to the farthest edges of the Empire.[21]

While exploration made use of comparative and collaborative science in the nineteenth century, it was applied unevenly. Surveys of Atlantic coastlines and river systems, massive inventories of the Russian East and the American West, frontier meteorological stations linked by telegraph, all expressed the grand, holistic spirit of Humboldtian exploration. Yet other efforts, particularly the exploration of Africa and the polar regions, remained largely ad hoc activities, undertaken with narrow goals and few efforts at coordination.

The International Polar Year (IPY), which established a ring of international outposts in the high Arctic in the 1880s for the purpose of coordinated research, was the exception that proved the rule. While the IPY succeeded in envisioning the Arctic as a place of scientific investigation (rather than merely a field for achieving "Farthest North"), it did not fundamentally change the nature of Arctic exploration. In fact, the "Race to the Pole" heated up after the conclusion of the International Polar Year while the impressive body of data collected by IPY scientist-explorers gathered dust. In short, the explorers of the Second Age of Discovery may have exhibited a greater, more holistic, interest in science, but the impulse was not universal. Many explorers found meaning enough in planting flags, giving lectures, and receiving geographical medals of honor.[22]

The Third Age of Discovery

And what of the last century? In his work on nineteenth century exploration, Goetzmann suggests the appearance of a new framework for scientific exploration, one that embraces modernism, relativism, and pluralism:

> We are possibly experiencing a Third Great Age of Discovery delineated by the discovery of the relativity of times and spaces, streams of consciousness, a pluralistic universe and hence multiple perspectives, cultural relativism in anthropology, and the resurgence of systems thinking and equilibrium in geology and ecology.[23]

Goetzmann's suggestion, while vague, offers a provocative starting point: modern exploration takes place in a world that questions the existence of a holistic system of nature as well as the power of Western explorers and scientists to find it. While Goetzmann describes the Third Age in abstract terms—the view from the mountaintop as it were—historian Stephen Pyne considers it from the ground up, focusing on expeditionary activities that have typified the twentieth century: exploration of the deep ocean, Antarctica, and space. While these types of exploration seem different from one another, they all occur in realms without human societies. Pyne sees modern exploration as the investigation of the uninhabited. "These geographies remain, for all practical purposes, abiotic worlds." As such, he observes, they avoid "the coruscating ethical dilemmas of so much earlier exploring and empire building." Yet as much as explorers' encounters with native peoples resulted in tragedy, these encounters also gave exploration its narrative punch. Exploring the ocean floor and the vastness of space are exciting only insofar as they are dangerous. Framed within Campbell's monomyth, the hero leaves home to battle boredom, confinement, and equipment malfunction; there is no Medusa or Charybdis in the abiotic world of space. Modern exploration emerges as a self-referential, almost solipsistic, enterprise, "a technological equivalent to extreme sports," writes Pyne, "like white-water kayaking in Borneo or NASCAR's Daytona 500."[24]

Yet Pyne's theory of a Third Age, creative as it is, relies on a faulty premise. While the Moon, the South Pole, and the ocean floor may be iconic sites of exploration, they are not representative of twentieth century exploration work as a whole, nor of late twentieth century exploration in particular. The exploration of these "abiotic" spaces occurred in fits and starts over the course of the century. While Antarctic expeditions proliferated during the turn of the century, they fell off steeply after World War I and remained sporadic until the International Geophysical Year of 1959.[25] Space exploration and deep sea exploration took off quite late, in the 1960s, facilitated by new technologies and the imperatives of the Cold War. Yet even the iconic status of these expeditions remained uneven. Some expeditions, such as the Mercury and Apollo missions, generated popular interest, but most have been forgotten. Few can identify astronauts in the space shuttle program, deep sea missions, or Antarctic surveys. Even the popularity of the Apollo missions has been cast into doubt; historian Roger Launius uses public polling to show that support for human spaceflight, even at the height of Cold War activity in the1960s, remained tepid.[26]

Beyond these narrow fields of exploration identified by Pyne, most twentieth century explorers were not abandoning human environments but embracing them. The period identified by Goetzmann and Pyne as the decline of the Second Age of Exploration witnessed an explosion of archeological and anthropological activity. Archeologists made spectacular discoveries of lost civilizations at Great Zimbabwe (1867), Troy (1871), Angkor (1863), Machu Picchu (1911), and the Valley of the Kings (1922). Meanwhile, anthropologists discovered the hominid remains of Java Man (1891), Peking Man (1923), Zinjanthropus (1959), and Lucy (1972). It is telling that, by the 1920s, some Antarctic explorers decided to recast themselves as anthropologists. Sven Hedin, inspired by polar explorer Adolf Erik Nordenskiöld, set off to understand the human geography of Central Asia and became one of the most famous European explorers of his time. Johan Gunnar Andersson, who served in the Swedish Antarctic Expedition of 1901–1903, left the polar regions to pursue Chinese archeology. Thomas Griffith Taylor, who served with Robert Scott in Antarctica, returned to his native Australia to pursue the study of aboriginal peoples.[27]

This interest in human races, civilizations, and histories extended beyond explorers. From the 1870s through the 1930s, public interest in lost races and civilizations exploded, yielding thousands of books, essays, and newspaper articles. Works of "lost world" fiction became so popular that they spawned their own literary genre. As for iconic explorers of the twentieth century, a small cadre of cosmonauts, astronauts, and aquanauts such as Yuri Gagarin, Neil Armstrong, and Jacques Cousteau captured public attention, but so did a much larger group of anthropological explorers including Franz Boaz, Claude Lévi-Strauss, Margaret Mead, Lewis Leakey, Clifford

Geertz, and Jane Goodall. In short, only by ignoring a great deal of expeditionary activity in the past century can it be seen as the dawn of an abiotic Third Age. [28]

Reframing Exploration as a Global Activity

The main shortcoming of the idea of "ages of discovery," however, is not that they fall short of conceptualizing exploration across time but across cultures. Science and exploration are Western concepts that were forged at a particular cultural moments to describe a specific set of Western activities. As such, one might reasonably argue that they shouldn't be applied as frameworks for understanding non-Western cultures because they would impose an artificially Western structure upon them. Yet defining science and exploration as Western cultural practices limits the other kinds of expeditionary activity and knowledge gathering to a small segment of humanity. If the story of travel and knowledge are ubiquitous to all eras and cultures, the historiography of exploration does the reverse: defining historical traditions so narrowly that they guarantee science and exploration is a story exclusive to the West.

For example, by defining the Third Age as an era of exploration of abiotic, extreme environments, Pyne effectively limits exploration to the activities of the United States, the Soviet Union, and Western Europe since only they have, for the last fifty years, possessed the scientific and financial resources to travel into space, Antarctica, and the deep sea. [29] Meanwhile "biotic" exploration, a far more global and inclusive activity, has been omitted from the Third Age category despite its importance and abundance. Anthropological, archeological, and zoological expeditions have generated compelling science, involved international networks of people, and produced a pantheon of iconic explorers. The astronaut's view of earth rising over the moon may offer an unparalleled vision of the globe, but it offers a poor vantage from which to understand scientific exploration. Terrestrial scientists exploring in the field cannot be seen from space, but their work has had greater impact on human society than their orbiting peers.[30]

Faced with categories that privilege Euro-American exploration, some historians have tried to solve the problem by casting Eastern expeditions into a Western mold. For example, Joseph Needham describes the fifteenth century voyages of Chinese admiral Zheng He in similar terms to Portuguese exploration of the same period. Both were imperial missions that sailed for a variety of motives, principally being geographical discovery. In Zheng He's case,

Needham writes, the object was "an increase in knowledge of the coasts and islands of the Chinese culture area . . . and the routes to the Far West."[31] Having established Zheng He's voyages as similar to Western expeditions, Needham then uses them as a point of comparison with the West. While the admiral's expeditions offered an "urbane but systematic tour of inspection of the known world," Vasco da Gama's expeditions to the same region fifty years later opened a new chapter of European dominance and brutality. Yet, as historian Robert Finlay persuasively argues, the comparison is based upon a false reading of Zheng He:

> Zheng He did not, as Needham suggests, inspire the Ming voyages, and there is no significant sense in which he can be regarded as an explorer. He commanded the maritime expeditions as a military agent of the Yongle emperor, a ruler who had no interest in voyages of discovery.[32]

While Needham's approach expands the story of exploration, it does so by building false points of comparison. Not surprisingly, Needham's work has become the starting point for historians in understanding why the imperial activities of East and West turned out so differently. As Fernand Braudel observed, the story of Zheng He promised a way to "cut the Gordian knot" of world history, that is, "Why didn't the East dominate the West?" Yet this question has its own Western tilt. After all, counter-factual questions only make sense insofar as they reflect upon events as they occurred. In this case, the question reflects upon the West's domination of the East. Trying to escape this framework only brings us around full circle. Ironically, developing a global framework for exploration means acknowledging the asymmetries of science and exploration as Western cultural practices.[33]

Frontiers, Contact Zones, and Extreme Environments

Even if the history of exploration remains culturally asymmetrical, scholarship on the role of non-Western peoples within exploration remains vibrant, challenging basic assumptions about the work of discovery. Nineteenth- and early twentieth-century accounts of exploration tended to view native peoples as the objects of, rather than participants in, scientific study. Indeed, even the terms used to describe exploration—terra incognita, frontier, discovery—privileged the viewpoint of explorers rather than native peoples. Critiques of European exploration gained force in the 1960s as colonies in Asia, Africa, and the Americas gained their independence from Europe.

Empire, once a proud term in the vernacular of exploration, took on pejorative meanings in the 1970s. Marxist scholarship revealed the exploitative functions of imperial science while post-colonial critiques such as Edward Said's *Orientalism* exposed the exotic image of the East as an elaborate fantasy of the West. By the late 1980s, books and articles critical of the role of expeditionary science blossomed in the scholarly press.[34]

Within scholarly works, the meaning of expeditionary science was changing from an ennobling to a despotic practice of empire. Yet the power dynamics of the process remained unchanged. Specifically, exploration and empire remained practices that the West had imposed upon the passive "rest." In 1987, anthropologist Bruno Latour published a center-periphery model of scientific knowledge that seemed to corroborate this view. In Latour's model, knowledge of the world starts and ends in the metropole—the centers of calculation—where scientists provide the questions and instruments needed to understand nature at the edges of empire.[35]

By the 1990s, however, scholars started to question the Latourian model. While it worked well in describing many aspects of state-sponsored expeditions, particularly the scientific expeditions of the "Second Age," it failed to explain other types of knowledge networks. Current scholarship on exploration, while acknowledging the asymmetries of exploration as a practice, has emphasized the importance of local peoples—sailors, surgeon-barbers, Creole collectors, diasporic Arabs and Africans—at every level of expeditionary science: from field activities such as reconnaissance, observation, collection, to the production of scientific knowledge by means such as writing, illustration, and distribution. If London, Paris, and Madrid operated as hubs of scientific calculation, they were centers shaped by the spokes of the world around them.[36]

The terminology of exploration has changed to reflect new views of scientific exploration as a collaborative and reciprocal process between cultures, specifically between explorers and local inhabitants. Explorer-scientists may view new worlds as "frontiers," a word made famous by historian Frederick Jackson Turner, but the term ignores the local guides, scholars, and assistants who called such places home. In her 1992 book *Imperial Eyes*, Mary Louise Pratt drew upon linguistics, specifically to the idea of a "contact language" that is improvised between two foreign peoples, in developing the idea of a "contact zone."

> It treats the relations among colonizers and colonized, or travelers and "travelees," not in terms of separateness or apartheid, but in terms of copresence, interaction, interlocking understandings and practices, often within radically asymmetrical relations of power.[37]

Changes of exploration terminology are not limited to academics within the university. Frontier remains a popular word within the corridors of NASA: astronauts have not yet encountered any local inhabitants who would make space a "contact zone."[38] Yet even in NASA, subtle shifts in terminology reflect new visions of space. In her study of NASA culture, anthropologist Valerie Olson points out that the concept of a frontier—a place of struggle, renewal, and destiny—still remains central to NASA's vision of spaceflight. Yet when Olson asked engineers what they do in the course of an average day, talk of frontiers gave way to discussion of "environments." Keeping humans alive in extreme environments represents much of the work of the human spaceflight program. Reports one engineer, "Our thought process is . . . environment, environment, environment, everything interacts with everything." Environment is not merely a matter for life support engineers, it is also central to NASA's broader social relevance. In the creation of self-sufficient habitats in space lies the promise of sustainable technology spin-offs on earth.[39]

Ultimately, this increasingly interactive, reciprocal vision of exploration may be useful in reconnecting the history of exploration with global, rather than merely Western, histories. Taking the long view, historian Felipe Fernández-Armesto frames exploration as one component in a vast narrative of divergence and reconnection between the peoples of the earth. Modern humans remained in Africa until 60,000 years ago. At that time, a small group migrated over the Red Sea and began settling other parts of the world. This great divergence would continue until 1000 CE when cultures began to reconnect with each other through imperial conquest and trade. While scientific exploration may seem part of a grand history of Western conquest, seen in this vastly larger 60,000 year perspective, it is merely one component of the "Great Convergence," a process that "put sundered peoples back in touch with each other after their long history of divergence and enabled them to exchange objects, ideas, and personnel." Ultimately, Fernandez-Armesto's model of exploration, a 60,000 year process, offers a rebuttal to Pyne's vision of modern exploration: the role of the discovery is not abiotic or solipsistic but deeply humanistic: a way of rediscovering each other.[40]

NOTES

1. On metaphors of fever in exploration, see Michael Robinson, *The Coldest Crucible: Arctic Exploration and American Culture* (Chicago: University of Chicago Press, 2006), 159–164.
2. "Two Amateur Explorers," *Nature* 13: 264 (Feb. 3, 1876)

3. The term "explore" appeared in the 1500s as a synonym for "investigate." When "explorer" gains use in the 1600s, it shares a similar connotation: someone who investigates or examines. Both terms only take on the meaning of geographical investigation in the early 1800s about the same time that "scientist" comes into use. (*Oxford English Dictionary*, 2d ed., 1989)

4. Pliny the Elder; H. Rackman, *Natural History* (Cambridge, 1938–1963); John Mandeville; C. W. R. D. Moseley, *The Travels of Sir John Mandeville* (London: Penguin, 2005); Marco Polo; William Marsden; Manuel Komroff, *The Travels of Marco Polo* (New York: Modern Library, 1953). Edward B. Cowell; F. Max Müller; Junjiro Takakusu, *Buddhist Mahâyâna texts* (New York: Dover, 1969). Plato; Elizabeth Watson Scharffenberger; Benjamin Jowett, *The Republic* (New York: Barnes and Nobles Classics, 2004), 224–231; Linda Bird Francke, *On the Road with Francis of Assisi* (New York: Random House, 2006).

5. Joseph Campbell, *The Power of Myth* (New York: Doubleday, 1988), xvi.

6. Alfred Crosby, *The Columbian Exchange: Biological and Cultural Consequences of 1492* (Westport, Conn.: Praeger, 2003).

7. Mary Terrall, "Heroic Narratives of Quest and Discovery," *Configurations* 6.2 (1998) 223–242, including D'Alembert's quotation, 233; Wordsworth is quoted by Richard Holmes, *The Age of Wonder: How the Romantic Generation Discovered the Beauty and the Terror of Science* (New York: Pantheon Books, 2008), xvii.

8. Terrall, "Heroic Narratives," 223–225.

9. Barbara Stafford, *Voyage into Substance: Art, Science, Nature and the Illustrated Travel Account, 1760–1840* (Cambridge, Mass.: MIT Press, 1984).

10. On Columbus's preconceptions see Nicolas Wey Gomez, *The Tropics of Empire: Why Columbus Sailed South to the Indies* (Cambridge, Mass.: MIT Press, 2008).

11. Christopher Parsons, "Plants and Peoples: French and Indigenous Botanical Knowledge in colonial North America, 1600–1760" (PhD Thesis, University of Toronto, 2011). By contrast, other groups have seen objects as new even when they weren't. For example, twentieth century anthropologists—focused on scientific discovery—tended to identify hominid fossils as new species even when they were closely related variants. See Roger Lewis, *Bones of Contention: Controversies in the Search for Human Origins* (Chicago: University of Chicago Press, 1997).

12. Anthony Grafton, *New Worlds, Ancient Texts: The Power of Tradition and the Shock of Discovery* (Cambridge, Mass.: Belknap, 1992), 28–35.

13. Mary Terrall, *The Man Who Flattened the Earth: Maupertuis and the Science of the Enlightenment* (Chicago: University of Chicago Press, 2002) 4–6, 138; Anne Marie Claire Godlewska, *Geography Unbound: French Geographic Science from Cassini to Humboldt* (Chicago: University of Chicago Press, 1999).

14. John Dunmore, *Visions & Realities: France in the Pacific, 1695–1995* (Waikanae, New Zealand: Heritage, 1997); John Kendrick, *Alejandro Malaspina: Portrait of a Visionary* (Quebec: McGill-Queen's University Press,

1999); Herman J. Viola; Carolyn Margolis, *Magnificent Voyagers: the U.S. Exploring Expedition, 1838–1842* (Washington, D.C.: Smithsonian Institution Press, 1985).

15. Braudel quoted in William Goetzmann, *New Lands, New Men: America and the Second Great Age of Discovery* (New York: Viking, 1986), 1. Italics original.

16. Ibid.

17. Rousseau did not, however, coin the term noble savage, a term first used by John Dryden in 1672. Michel de Montaigne; Donald Murdoch Frame, *Selected Essays* (New York, 1943); Jean-Jacques Rousseau; Maurice Cranston, *A Discourse on Inequality* (New York: Penguin Books, 1984); Denis Diderot, *Supplement to the Voyages of Bougainville* (Paris, 1772).

18. J. C. Beaglehole, *The Journals of Captain Cook on His Voyages of Discovery* (Cambridge: Hakluyt Society, 1955–1974) quoted in Goetzmann, *New Lands*, 3; Eric Wilson, *A Spiritual History of Ice: Romanticism, Science, and the Imagination* (Basingstoke: Palgrave Macmillan, 2009); Holmes, *Age of Wonder*.

19. Aaron Sachs, *The Humboldt Current: Nineteenth Century Exploration and the Roots of American Environmentalism* (New York: Viking, 2006); Laura Walls, *Passage to Cosmos: Alexander von Humboldt and the Shaping of America*; Michael Robinson, "Why We Need a New History of Exploration," *Common-Place* 10 (1) (Oct 2009) http://www.common-place.org/vol-10/no-01/robinson/

20. Susan Faye Cannon, *Science in Culture: The Early Victorian Period* (New York: Science History Publications, 1978); Darwin quoted in Beagle Diary, ed. Kees Rookmaaker, (Genesis Publications, 1979), 115 (available at Darwin Online http://darwin-online.org.uk/).

21. Michael Reidy, *The Tides of History: Ocean Science and Her Majesty's Navy* (Chicago: University of Chicago Press, 2008), 8–9.

22. On science and the IPY, see William Barr, *The Expeditions of the First International Polar Year, 1882–83* (Calgary: Arctic Institute of North America, University of Calgary, 1985); Robinson, *Coldest Crucible*, 83–106.

23. Goetzmann, *New Lands, New Men*, 4.

24. Stephen J. Pyne, "Seeking Newer Worlds: An Historical Context for Space Exploration," in *Critical Issues in the History of Spaceflight* eds. Steven J. Dick; Roger D. Launius, (Washington, D.C.: NASA History Division, 2006), 29, 30; Stephen J. Pyne, *Voyager: Exploration, Space, and the Third Great Age of Discovery* (New York: Viking, 2010).

25. Peder Roberts, "A Frozen Field of Dreams: Science, Strategy, and the Antarctic in Norway, Sweden and the British Empire, 1912–1952," PhD Thesis (Stanford, Calif.: Stanford University 2010).

26. James Spiller, "Constructing America at the Peripheries: The Cultural Politics of U.S. Science and Exploration in Outer Space and Antarctica, 1950s–1990s," PhD Thesis (Madison: University of Wisconsin-Madison, 1999); Roger Launius, "Exploding the Myth of Popular Support for Project Apollo" http://launiusr.wordpress.com/2010/08/16/exploding-the-myth-of-popular-support-forproject- apollo/

SCIENCE AND EXPLORATION   37

27. On Antarctic explorers who transition to anthropology, see Roberts, "Field of Dreams"; on the popularity of late twentieth century anthropologists, see Lewis, *Bones of Contention*.

28. Allienne Becker, *The Lost World Romance: From Dawn Till Dusk* (Westport, Conn.: Greenwood, 1992).

29. While China, Japan, and India have developed nascent space programs, their work does not, as yet, fit the Pynian model of the Third Age.

30. Non-Western peoples have often been crucial to the success of Western exploration. The number of autonomous expeditions in developing countries is growing (along with expeditions in collaboration with Western explorers). See for example, Sonya Atalay, "Decolonizing Archaeology" *American Indian Quarterly* 30(3&4): 269–279; George Nicholas and Thomas Andrews, "Indigenous Archaeology in a Post-Modern World," in *At a Crossroads: Archaeology and First Peoples in Canada*, ed. George Nicholas; Thomas Andrews (Burnaby: SFU Archaeology Press, 1997), 1–18.

31. Needham quoted in Robert Finlay, "China, the West, and World History in Joseph Needham's 'Science and Civilisation in China'" *Journal of World History*, 11(2) (Fall, 2000): 293.

32. Ibid., 295.

33. Braudel quoted in Finlay, "China, the West," 299.

34. Edward Said, *Orientalism* (New York: Vintage, 1979); Donna Haraway, *Primate Visions: Gender, Race, and Nature in the World of Modern Science* (New York and London: Routledge, 1989); Lisa Bloom, *Gender on Ice: American Ideologies of Polar Expeditions* (Minneapolis: University of Minnesota Press, 1993).

35. Bruno Latour, *Science in Action: How to Follow Scientists and Engineers through Society* (Cambridge, Mass.: Harvard University Press, 1988).

36. Felix Driver, *Geography Militant: Cultures of Exploration and Empire* (Oxford and Malden, Mass.: Blackwell, 2001); James Delbourgo; Nicholas Dew, (eds.) *Science and Empire in the Atlantic World* (New York: Routledge, 2008).

37. Mary Louise Pratt, *Imperial Eyes: Travel Writing and Transculturation* (New York: Routledge, 1992), p.7.

38. On NASA's use of the term "frontier," see Roger Launius, "Compelling Rationales for Spaceflight? History and the Search for Relevance," in *Critical Issues in the History of Spaceflight* eds. Steven J. Dick; Roger D. Launius, (Washington, D.C.: NASA History Division, 2006), 37–70.

39. Valerie Olson, personal communication, Jan. 2011; Quotation from Olson, "American Extreme: An Ethnography of Astronautical Visions and Ecologies," PhD Thesis (Rice University, 2010), 5.

40. Felipe Fernández-Armesto, *Pathfinders: a Global History of Exploration* (New York: W.W. Norton, 2006), 350.

2

A HALF CENTURY OF SHIFTING NARRATIVE
PERSPECTIVES ON ENCOUNTERS

HARRY LIEBERSOHN

When we hear a travel story, whose version are we listening to? Most of us are familiar with this issue from vacations: after returning home, each family member has his or her account, and they may differ greatly, sometimes painfully so. The parents' unforgettable tour of Italian museums may be the children's blur of boring old buildings; one person's treasure hunt in Delhi markets is another's travail for trinkets; one member of a tour group remembers the monuments, while another thinks of the meals. Listeners back home may wonder whether they are hearing about the same trip. They may also wonder, as they hear about the push to the front of the Coliseum line or the restaurant waiting list, what the vacationers' hosts thought of their foreign guests and what stories *they* would have to tell. The simplest description of going from one society to another invites retelling from different participants. The same multiplicity of narrative points of view that we know from personal experience applies to travels from the past: the overseas explorer, the merchant abroad, the missionary in the field, the student, scholar, or sailor who settles in a new place—each has a story of his journey that could be retold with different accents by others. When scholars develop their own versions of earlier travels, in particular the kind of travel we call exploration, they have to make choices about which narrative perspective to adopt and which to subordinate or ignore.

At any moment in time, scholarly fashion prefers certain kinds of stories to others. At one instant it may expand on the heroic stories that great men like to tell about themselves, leaving out the stories of women and ordinary people; at another moment it may be ordinary people whose accounts matter, while socially privileged heroes' tales are suspect. During the past half century, scholars have experimented with a great many different points of view and have also tried to shape them into a larger narrative that can encompass more than one perspective. There have been so many attempts to rethink and retell the history of exploration, many of them vivid and valuable, that we can think of the era beginning in 1960 with the publication of Bernard Smith's *European Vision and the South Pacific* as one of extraordinary innovation.

This chapter attempts a brief survey of the changes that have taken place in the history of exploration, occasionally straying into the history of travel in order to include as much as possible of this widening range of perspectives. While "exploration" suggests expensive, well-organized, often state-run expeditions aiming at practical and scientific discovery—or to put it slightly more provocatively, mastery of terra incognita—"travel" encompasses a wider, possibly more inward-turning list of ends including education, religious quest, and personal amusement. Some examples of cultural encounter from the history of travel can deepen our understanding of similar encounters in the history of exploration. In any case, these are overlapping categories that should not be imposed too rigidly on trips that could have blurry motives and multiple goals: to mention just one important group, missionaries around the world aimed at saving souls, but also became early and intrepid explorers of unknown lands. "Exploration" does not come ready-made as an autonomous human activity, but overlaps with other kinds of ventures.

For the sake of clarity this overview focuses mainly on the aftereffects of two of the most important events in the history of exploration over the past five hundred years. One is the voyages of Columbus, whose cross-cultural encounters initiated the formation of an Atlantic world. The second is the voyages of Captain Cook, which brought Atlantic and Pacific societies together as never before. The scholarly literatures on Atlantic and Pacific exploration dramatically illustrate the multiplication of narrative points of view in recent decades. They also show how many disciplines in addition to history—notably art history, literature, the history of science, and anthropology—have contributed to this dislodging of any one kind of historical actor's claims on the past. The entrepreneurial energy of the history of exploration may suggest a historiography of rapid advances, with each new generation of researchers surpassing the one that came before. But the historical record also suggests a more cautionary tale, in which successive attempts to write the history of travel and exploration have had their different strengths.To recapitulate this history is also to take possession of the postwar era's full inventory of different styles, subjects, and research methods.

In the beginning were the heroes. Take Columbus: a deeply researched book that enjoyed both scholarly success and a wide readership was Samuel Eliot Morison's biography, *Admiral of the Ocean Sea* (1942). Morison notes in his preface that North Americans did not pay much attention to Columbus in the colonial era, but by the end of the nineteenth century were celebrating his discovery of the New World. The growing interest of the nineteenth century, according to Morison, was a response to American independence and European awareness of the importance of their former colonies. Morison himself turns back to Columbus as the hero of an earlier age of European despair. "At the end of the year 1492," he writes, "most men in Western Europe felt exceedingly gloomy about the future. Christian civilization appeared to be shrinking in area and dividing into hostile units as its sphere contracted"—an obvious if unstated parallel to the dark wartime mood of his own day.[1] Morison can be critical of Columbus's behavior.When it comes to Columbus's treatment of native peoples, he leaves no illusions about his disastrous treatment of them from the start. Columbus told King Ferdinand and Queen Isabella about the "gentleness and generosity" of the islanders. "Unfortunately," comments Morison, "this guilelessness and generosity of the simple savage aroused the worst traits of cupidity and brutality in the average European. Even the Admiral's humanity seems to have been merely political, as a means to eventual enslavement and exploitation. But to the intellectuals of Europe it seemed that Columbus had stepped back several millennia, and encountered people living in the Golden Age, that bright morning of humanity which existed only in the imagination of poets."[2] Columbus's atrocities toward the peoples of the Caribbean are incidental to the main line of Morison's story, which has mainly to do with establishing Columbus's route and the technical details of how he sailed across the ocean. His account remains eminently readable for its self-proclaimed goals, although few today would accept his writing off the decimation of New World peoples as collateral damage on the way to restoring European self-confidence.

Morison's biography was in its own sober way a corrective to the heroic interpretation of Columbus going back to Washington Irving's nineteenth-century biography. More recent biographers have moved from heroism (or anti-heroism) to the reconstruction of Columbus's personality within the institutional and intellectual contexts of his time. One of the most deeply researched biographies to emerge from the Quincentennial of Columbus's first voyage is William D. and Carla Rahn Phillips' *The Worlds of Christopher Columbus* (1992). The Phillipses permit us to view Columbus as a Genoese who benefited from the mercantile, entrepreneurial drive of his native city and a social climber who moved from a family of weavers to a life as a sailor and navigator. Columbus sailed in 1492 with the idea of trading with wealthy cities, as Marco Polo had done; failing to find them, he quickly adjusted his thinking to plan colonial settlements. In the Phillipses' interpretation, Columbus was highly motivated by the need to sell his island discoveries to his patrons and was embedded in the business practices of his time, relying on the standard contract forms of Castile for his written agreement with the monarchy. It is fascinating, and at times jarring, to be reminded of our nearness to and distance from a man who sometimes had the brisk practical language of the modern entrepreneur, at other times the nutty beliefs of an apocalyptic visionary. In another of the Quincentennial offerings, Valerie Flint evokes the tensions in Columbus's motivations between the adventurer's search for gold and a late medieval unease about the acquisition of wealth. Seen in the context of all the documentary evidence, Columbus was many things at once: greedy, ambitious, visionary, devout. Other writers hold Columbus responsible for social and ecological catastrophe. While the charges contain a great deal of truth, they are partial truisms trimmed to today's political rhetoric, not a satisfactory account of the historical record, unless they are grounded in the very different European world of half a millennium ago. The Phillipses and Flint have gone beyond romantic myths and political polemics alike to portray a far stranger, more complex adventurer.[3]

The biographies of Captain Cook, whose three world voyages in the late eighteenth century gave firm scientific outline to a large Pacific portion of the earth, follow a similar path from heroism to deep contextualization. J. R. Beaglehole's biography of Captain Cook was the outcome of a great scholarly enterprise, his edition of Cook's journals. The published journals were supposed to prepare the way for the biography, but in the end they have had the greater impact; the two are best considered together as part of a single enterprise. The rich notes and extra materials in the journals, as well as Cook's journal entries themselves, are still an indispensable initiation into the late eighteenth-century world, Pacific and Atlantic, of global voyaging.[4] A New Zealander, Beaglehole was intimately knowledgeable about the geography and peoples of the Pacific as well as Georgian England. More recently, Cook has had several remarkable biographers who have opened up perspectives different from the purely heroic. Compact and incisive, John Gascoigne's 2007 biography calls him a "voyager between two worlds" and makes each of those worlds newly perceptible through an intensely local sense of place, whether the Yorkshire of Cook's early years or his stops in Polynesia. Other new topics also come to the fore, such as Cook's association with Quakers, which opened up important personal and scientific networks to him. Yet another important topic is enlightened Europeans' confrontation with Polynesian sexuality, which was so different from their own mores that it challenged them to adopt a new cosmopolitanism. Cook emerges less as a hero of Western exploration than as a shaper of one world, Pacific and Atlantic united. Within this grand theme, Anne Salmond has added deep knowledge of Polynesian cultures to her portrayal of Cook, conveying Polynesians' motives and appreciation of how fully they were autonomous actors in their encounters with Cook. Glyn Williams has reviewed the transformation of Cook into a hero and returned to full size the punitive and arrogant sides of his personality that contributed to his death in a melee with Hawaiian islanders in 1779. With the help of these new biographies one can understand afresh how English conceptions of class merged with Polynesian social hierarchies, how the Enlightenment confronted the sophisticated men of knowledge of Tahiti, and how Protestantism limited Europeans' understanding of native religions. More than one would have imagined even a few decades ago, European and non-European cultures merged in Cook's voyages and in the person of Cook himself.[5]

The new round of Cook biographies suggests that the genre of biography itself as the story of an autonomous life has partly dissolved in recent years. To be sure, biographies have often presented a broader picture, signaled by the subtitle "Life and Times." In the case of explorers, the "life" merges with extra-European environments. But the "times" are a challenge to previous assumptions, when one is writing about explorers who must confront radically new places in the Americas and the Pacific. How much change takes place? To what extent are Europeans themselves made and unmade by the places they visit? This is an old topic of the history of exploration, which comes up, for example, in the recurring discussion of whether, in early encounters, non-Europeans regarded Europeans as gods. In the famous case of Captain Cook, Marshall Sahlins has in recent years deepened the argument that Cook met his death by accidentally walking into the role of the Hawaiian god Lono. This interpretation dates back to the explanations by Cook's shipmates. So does the counter-interpretation, recently taken up by Gananath Obeyesekere, that the Hawaiians killed Cook because he behaved like an overbearing conqueror. The contention of culturalists and pragmatists has subsequently taken an ironic turn. Obeyesekere wanted his readers to believe that Hawaiians were just as pragmatic as Europeans; recent biography suggests that Cook was just as intoxicated with his own greatness as were the *ali'i* (the Hawaiian elite). To state the more general implications of the controversy: The debate changes the biographer's method when we ask not just what indigenous people thought, but how the explorer's persona is altered.[6]

Once one begins thinking about how individuals underwent transformation in strange new worlds, questions about mutual influence begin to multiply. Some of the most original and important books in the history of travel take up this question of the impact of faraway places on Europeans and Europe itself. This puts them at a far remove from the older type of explorer narratives, with their implicit *veni, vidi, vici* stories of the Caesar-like men who go to new places, see them, and conquer them. Instead of conquering, the Europeans of these narratives engage in exchanges that never leave them quite the same again.

Bernard Smith's *European Vision and the South Pacific* (1960) raised these questions of reverse impact—that is, how exploration changed the explorers—decades before doing so became fashionable. Writing from Australia with erudition and the discerning eye of an art historian, Smith asks how the artists on the Cook and other expeditions of the late eighteenth and early nineteenth centuries developed fresh painterly approaches to the landscapes of Pacific islands. To give form to these novel places and the people who inhabited them required a process of accommodation; the artists' neoclassical model and familiar techniques for rendering landscapes had to change in order to record a previously unknown part of the world. Smith shows in detail how impressions from the Pacific ultimately fed the art and literature of Romanticism. A bold claim in its time, not calculated to please historians of art or exploration, it anticipated later generations of studies claiming colonial influence on the metropolis. Smith also writes with another quality scarce among his successors, a sense of irony. His book ends in a chapter on the triumph of scientific representation of the Pacific—but that triumph was a hollow one, for the scientific art and geography of the nineteenth century was an ideology of conquest, not a faithful rendering of its subjects. Smith's work inspired numerous younger scholars of art, anthropology and scientific discourse to investigate Antipodean challenges to European cultural assumptions.[7]

Like Smith for the South Pacific, J. H. Elliott in a series of lectures published in 1970, *The Old World and the New, 1492–1650*, opened up fruitful questions about the influence of the American periphery on the European metropolis. Elliott shares Smith's interest in questions of knowledge across geographies and cultures: when and how Europeans registered the newness of the new world that they had discovered. Despite an early European fascination with Columbus, the intellectual impact of his and subsequent voyages was "uncertain" and "the process of assimilation" was slow, extending over centuries. As a historian deeply read in the social history of the Atlantic, Elliott also tries to assess the impact of American bullion and Atlantic trade, and cautions against underestimating the gaps in scholarly research and overrating their effects. Elliott's lectures were fruitful both for opening up a wide range of questions about peripheral influence on the metropolis and for setting an example of critical scholarly scrutiny.[8]

Noisier productions followed, proclaiming a radical opposition between European self and exotic other. Unlike Smith and Elliott, who traced slow, uncertain, but appreciable advances in Europeans' comprehension of non-European cultures, a new wave of works proclaimed the radical inability of Europeans (and, more broadly, "Westerners") to understand the cultures of the overseas places they subjugated. The book that did the most to set off this new wave of scholarship was Edward Said's *Orientalism* (1978). In Said's interpretation the "Orient" in question was a creation of European and American scholarship and literature, which created a fantastic realm of the exotic as a place for imagining power, sex, and sensuous splendor at an exotic remove; the imperial imagination of nineteenth-century Europeans invented an Orient that was proffered as scientific fact and literary artifice. Recent scholarship has questioned Said's critique of Western scholarship of the Middle East and instead revealed a complex landscape of sympathy, prejudice, accuracy, and error.[9] Said's book focuses primarily on the nineteenth century, the moment when an expansion of technology and state power gave Europeans greater hegemony over non-Europeans than they have ever had before or since. His thesis seemed portable to other times and places, however, and became the best-known example of a larger current of radical critique, across the humanities, of Western conceptions of non-Western cultures. Tzvetan Todorov carries an analogous structure of self and other into the world of the conquistadors in *The Conquest of America: The Question of the Other* (1982). However, Todorov is more interested than Said in questions of mediation between cultures—that is, how they *do* communicate and learn about each other—and argues that Cortés was able to conquer Mexico because of the Spaniards' superior skills at understanding their enemy. "Language," writes Todorov, quoting the Spanish grammarian Antonion de Nebrija, "has always been the companion of Empire."[10] Nonetheless, language in his interpretation remains a medium that reaches across cultural divides.

Stuart Schwartz attacks the radical gesture of Said and his followers and speaks for a more subtle interpretation of cultural encounters in the early modern era in the introduction to *Implicit Understandings* (1994). Non-Europeans, he observes, were not always in a relationship to Europeans of "unequal power and subordination," certainly not in places like early modern China, Japan, and Southeast Asia; he is skeptical about the equation of linguistic representation of foreign cultures with power over them; and he points out that "otherness" came in gradations, not absolutes.[11] Rolena Adorno gives an example of this kind of subtle gradation in her essay on Amerindian ethnographers from the mid-sixteenth to the mid-seventeenth centuries who, she points out, were a mixed group without much in common by their own reckoning. Their writings on native religion and Christian evangelization "do not lend themselves to the simple or dichotomous characterizations of European versus Amerindian society and culture and . . . reveal instead the richer, more ambiguous strategies that characterize the roles of cultural mediation they inevitably played."[12] Adorno's careful scholarship suggests that the opposition of self and other is a misleading model; her work demonstrates that while sources for early encounters are limited and the work of historical reconstruction is painstaking, one can in fact recover a far more differentiated world of colonial societies.

Scholars of Oceania, too, have discovered a greater give and take between islanders and visitors than the opposition of self and other can contain. Nicholas Thomas, in works such as *Entangled Objects* (1991), *Colonialism's Culture* (1994), and *Oceanic Art* (1995), maintains the project of a critical history of colonialism, but is skeptical of ideological simplifications and urges a turn to localized, historicized studies, which his own research has exemplified especially well in the case of visual and material artifacts.[13] Anne Salmond's two-volume history of early contacts between Maoris and Europeans lays out the complexity of the encounters especially clearly, envisioning the mental world of each side as it came into contact with the others. Today we readily accept the notion of their equal humanity, but they, too, were sensitive to it. If they started out as "two worlds," by the early 1770s they were on their way to merged cultures and regularized exchanges. Salmond is particularly effective at explaining Maori principles like *utu* or balance, *tapu* or power of the gods, and *ora* or well-being, and how Europeans either collided or found points of agreement with them.[14] Salmond highlights Europeans' stumbles through their early encounters with Maoris and their conceptions of honor, gods, ancestors, and earthly well-being, alongside the human capacity on both sides for working toward stable relationships. The writings of Greg Dening bring the drama of Oceanic encounters to life with special flair. They ground our understanding of these events by spatializing them: the ship appears in his writings as a microcosmic British realm, while the beach is the main scene for dramatic action between explorers and islanders in places like Tahiti and Hawaii.The zone between land and water could be a place of peaceful exchange of tapa (native cloth) and pigs for mirrors and hatchets, or a place of conflict like the one that took Cook's life. *Mr. Bligh's Bad Language* (1992) expands from the beach to a global theater of Britain, Pacific islands, and ships in between; with the metaphors and passion of theater it alternates between general reflection and dense ethnography, enriching readers' understanding of its historical actors.[15]

Karen Kupperman's study of Indians and English in North America of the sixteenth century also takes up two sides of a historical encounter, doing so with fresh insight as she casts aside our retrospective knowledge and asks us to reimagine the worlds of the participants: "Both are foreign to us," she writes of the English and the eastern Algonquians, in the course of urging a deep knowledge of the English history of the period in order to understand the written accounts of their relationship. To make things more difficult, those who stayed at home might easily tout the superiority of Europeans, but those who went abroad learned a humility about their own culture and a respect for that of their Indian counterparts.[16] Each side tried to incorporate the other: native leaders did so by turning the English into dependent clients, while the English worked to civilize Indians according to their own standards; each side was suspicious of the other (were the English from the underworld and therefore not susceptible to epidemic disease? were Indians cannibals?), and sometimes hostile to each other, but economic interests yoked them together.[17] Co-scripting makes the story: Kupperman understands that Indians and English were no longer separate but had become actors in a shared situation encompassing both groups. Within that situation, many of their ethnographies were collaborations by Indians eager to explain their world and English eager to understand it. Difficulties stood in the way on both sides: as Roger Williams grew increasingly interested in Narragansett culture, John Winthrop accused him in 1638 of transmitting lies (to which he indignantly replied, "I am not yet turned Indian"); on the Indian side too, consorting with the English led to accusations of divided loyalties. Fears, tricks, and expectations of treachery from either side could lead to warfare. Mutual dependence and insight was not always enough to prevent an unraveling of civilities.[18]

A complicated and at times dangerous exchange took place between cultures in both the Atlantic and Pacific, with a wide spectrum of collaborations and conflicts. But how did communication take place? Who did the talking and how could they understand each other? It is not unusual for specially qualified mediators to do the work of weaving between cultures. At this point the logic of the inquiry changes, and so does the number of voices: we may no longer imagine just two worlds, but instead face multiple points of encounter between the extremes of European learned societies and the American West, London, and Tahiti, or more generally metropolis and periphery. At different stations along the way, talented or well-placed individuals may play the part of tour guide, leading travelers into cultures they could never otherwise understand. In order to capture the complexity of explorers' journeys, historians may move from two-sided histories of encounter to multiple narratives.

Captivity and marriage account for the cultural translating skills of many mediators in North American history. Pauline T. Strong has surveyed some of the kidnappings back and forth on the seventeenth- and early eighteenth-century frontier, which include historic figures later turned into American myths like Squanto and Pocahontas. Another nostalgized figure is Sacagawea, the Shoshone woman who, married to a trader of French descent named Toussaint Charbonneau, served as a guide to Lewis and Clark; James Ronda has commented on her helpful but not (as sometimes imagined) all-encompassing role in their expedition's trek to the Pacific.[19] Alexis de Tocqueville still found a network of such mediators in place when he visited the United States in the early 1830s, the descendants of trapping and trading collaborations between European and Indian communities. French settlers had been especially successful in developing these trade networks through partial assimilation, or rather, as Richard White has explained, through the creation of a "middle ground" that was neither exclusively French nor Indian any more, but rather something new. Tocqueville had a romantic hankering for experiencing life in the "wilderness" and made a special side trip to Detroit and from there to Flint, Michigan. At one point he and his travel companion, Gustave de Beaumont, needed help from an Indian boatman in order to cross a river; to Tocqueville's astonishment, the boatman sang songs that he recognized from his Norman childhood. French (and Anglophone) traders often married into Indian families, and the children of these families, possibly including his boatman, could serve as interpreters to both sides. A more important figure for Tocqueville was John Tanner, who as a boy in Kentucky was kidnapped by Shawnees and raised by an Ottawa woman who moved with him to Ojibwa territory; Tocqueville was fascinated by his passion for hunting, which was reminiscent, thought Tocqueville, of his aristocratic ancestors.[20]

Mediators were no less important in the Pacific. Vanessa Smith has drawn attention to the importance of beachcombers, the assorted deserters, stranded sailors, and other Europeans who began to dot Polynesian islands in the late eighteenth century. At times they assimilated into local cultures, marrying, owning land, and advising local paramounts, as did William Mariner, survivor of an attack on a ship anchored in Tonga. Beachcombers like Mariner got to know native societies in a way that was hard for officers and naturalists to do, for they spent months or years immersed in them without the benefit of the cannons that protected but also isolated explorer expeditions. His memoirs belong to a literary genre at the intersection of oral and written cultures, with a more educated amanuensis easing the transition from storytelling to print.[21] What emerges from Smith's account of Pacific beachcombers is not just the new (and particularly colorful) narrative voice of the beachcomber but a new attention to the different strands of literacy and orality that enter into travel texts.

Tony Ballantyne too addresses questions of orality and literacy in *Orientalism and Race: Aryanism in the British Empire* (2002). Ballantyne examines the ways in which ideas within the British Empire could pulsate from local centers of knowledge in places like India and New Zealand as well as London, and how they could undergo transformation by Hindus and Maoris as well as British colonial administrators and metropolitan intellectuals. Instead of defining his study around metropolis and periphery, Ballantyne imagines manifold "webs of empire." "Calcutta, for example," notes Ballantyne, "might be seen as being in a subaltern position in relation to London, but it in turn might be a sub-imperial centre where important lines of patronage, accumulation and communication flow out into the South Asian hinterland and beyond to South-East Asia or even the Pacific."[22] Travelers and explorers intersected with these networks of knowledge, in the British Empire and elsewhere, at various points on their routes to and from Europe, and they extended them to home on lines at least partly of their own preference and design.

Intellectual historians and historians of science have in recent years investigated just these routes at various stops on the way to and from their place of departure. Since Bruno Latour's influential discussion of "Centers of Calculation" in *Science in Action* (1987), historians of science have amplified (and criticized) his vision of metropolitan scientists expanding outward to non-European areas and accumulating knowledge capital analogous to the accumulation of material wealth.[23] Contributions in *Visions of Empire* (1996), edited by David P. Miller and Peter H. Reill, reveal how scientific collectors gathered artifacts and natural objects and returned them to Europe; E. C. Spary in *Utopia's Garden* (2000) recounts the European and global making of the Jardin du Roi (the royal botanical garden) in Paris; Richard Drayton in *Nature's Government*

(2000) surveys the decades of scientific travel that led to the creation of Kew Gardens as a center of botanical research.[24] These books tend to work from Europe outward, with non-Europeans largely outside their ken. A book with actors from multiple locations is Richard Grove's *Green Imperialism* (1995), which tries to show how, from the seventeenth to the nineteenth century, naturalists not only traveled to places like India, Indonesia, Mauritius, and the Caribbean, but also developed ideas of environmental management from the challenges of colonizing these places and from their conversations with local intellectuals. One can add still more actors to the passages back and forth, with patrons at home and missionaries abroad as significant parts of the mix, along with travelers and their patrons.[25]

Why is it that histories of travel and exploration have rapidly added new narrative voices since the publication of Smith's *European Vision* in 1960? It is not unreasonable to suppose that the dismantling of European empires since World War II has led to a historicization of explorers; Columbus, Cook, and the rest no longer seem to stride across the earth like heroes among ordinary mortals. Their relationships to their European and indigenous contemporaries have become multi-dimensional, and so have they. A second source of innovation seems to have been the stagnation and collapse of Marxism as a political ideology. Future intellectual historians can investigate whether Western intellectuals, disenchanted with Stalinism in the Soviet Union and disappointed by the failure of revolution in the 1960s, looked to non-European peoples for sympathetic historical actors, a shift that led to radical disenchantment with European overseas exploration and solidarity with the peoples whose societies they had damaged or destroyed. A third influential tendency is transnationalism: an increasing number of scholars are themselves neither "Western" nor "non-Western," but have been brought up in multiple cultures, are at home in several languages, have been educated on different continents, or jet back and forth between places like India and the United States or Britain and the Caribbean. As Tzvetan Todorov noted decades ago, the mediators between cultures of the past, who once looked like the exception to "normal" monocultures, now look like the forerunners of the polyglot cultures of our own time.[26] Once upon a time one might have said that the history of travel and exploration was a repository for colonial myths from Europe and its settler nations. Today, few fields of history lend themselves more naturally to a study of the complex relations between Europeans and non-Europeans through the centuries.[27]

NOTES

1. Samuel Eliot Morison, *Admiral of the Ocean Sea: A Life of Christopher Columbus*, 2 vols. (Boston: Little, Brown and Company, 1942), 13.

2. Ibid., 303. See also Morison's unsparing account of the Spanish forced labor system for gold in vol. 2, 173–176.

3. Valerie I. J. Flint, *The Imaginative Landscape of Christopher Columbus* (Princeton, N.J.: Princeton University Press, 1992). For the contemporary polemic, see Kirkpatrick Sale, *The Conquest of Paradise: Christopher Columbus and the Columbian Legacy* (New York: Penguin, 1991). The best recent introduction to Columbus is Geoffrey Symcox and Blair Sullivan, eds., *Christopher Columbus and the Enterprise of the Indies: A Brief History with Documents* (Boston: Bedford/St. Martin's, 2005).

4. James Cook, *The Journals of Captain James Cook on his Voyages of Discovery*, ed. J. R. Beaglehole, Hakluyt Society extra series 34–37 (Cambridge: Cambridge University Press, 1955–1974).

5. John Gascoigne, *Captain Cook: Voyager Between Worlds* (London: Continuum, 2007); Anne Salmond, *The Trial of the Cannibal Dog: The Remarkable Story of Captain Cook's Encounters in the South Seas* (New Haven, Conn.: Yale University Press, 2003); Glyn Williams, *The Death of Captain Cook: A Hero Made and Unmade* (Cambridge, Mass.: Harvard University Press, 2008). See also Nicholas Thomas, *Cook: The Extraordinary Voyages of Captain James Cook* (New York: Walker, 2003).

6. Marshall Sahlins, "Captain James Cook; or, The Dying God," in *Islands of History* (Chicago: University of Chicago Press, 1985), 104–135; Gananath Obeyesekere, *The Apotheosis of Captain Cook: European Myth making in the Pacific* (Princeton, N.J.: Princeton University Press, 1992); Marshall Sahlins, *How "Natives" Think: About Captain Cook, for Example* (Chicago: University of Chicago Press, 1995). On Oceania's challenges to the European self, see also Jonathan Lamb, *Preserving the Self in the South Seas, 1680–1840* (Chicago: University of Chicago Press, 2001). There is a separate debate—which should not be conflated with the debate over Cook, far removed in time, place and cultures—over whether indigenous Mexicans regarded Cortés and the other conquistadors as gods. For a critical viewof this claim, see Camilla Townsend, "Burying the White Gods: New Perspectives on the Conquest of Mexico,"*American Historical Review* vol. 108, no. 3 (June 2003): 659–687.

7. Bernard Smith, *European Vision and the South Pacific*, 2d ed. (New Haven, Conn.: Yale University Press, 1985); originally published as *European Vision and the South Pacific, 1768–1850* (Oxford: Clarendon Press, 1960). Cf. the "Antipodean inflection" (Preface) in Iain McCalman, general ed., *An Oxford Companion to the Romantic Age: British Culture, 1776–1832* (Oxford: Oxford University Press, 1999). For a sampling of subsequent work in the spirit of *European Vision*, see Nicholas Thomas and Diane Losche, eds., *Double Vision: Art Histories and Colonial Histories in the Pacific* (Cambridge: Cambridge University Press, 1999).

8. J. H. Elliott, *The Old World and the New, 1492–1650* (Cambridge: Cambridge University Press, 1970). For samples of subsequent works that take up issues raised by Elliott, see Anthony Pagden, *The Fall of Natural Man: The American Indian and the Origins of Comparative Ethnology* (Cambridge and New York: Cambridge University Press, 1982); and Fernando Cervantes, *The Devil in the New World: The Impact of Diabolism in New Spain* (New Haven: Yale University Press, 1994).

9. Edward W. Said, *Orientalism* (1978; New York: Vintage, 1979). Cf. the critique of Said in Robert Irwin, "Lured in the East," *Times Literary Supplement, Issue 5484* (May 9, 2008): 3–5; and the thorough going refutation in Suzanne L. Marchand, *German Orientalism in the Age of Empire: Religion, Race, and Scholarship* (Cambridge: Cambridge University Press, 2009).

10. Tzvetan Todorov, *The Conquest of America: The Question of the Other*, trans. Richard Howard (French original, 1982; New York: Harper & Row, 1984, 1987), 97, quote from 123. Mary Louise Pratt, *Imperial Eyes: Travel Writing and Transculturation* (London: Routledge, 1992) is, like *Orientalism*, a politically critical account of travelers' narratives of the non-European world; the nineteenth century is at the center of her story too, though it ranges from the 1750 to 1980. However, she develops a different kind of approach that works through the production and circulation of knowledge, emphasizing how non-Europeans made selective use of invaders' cultures and were in turn able to shape in part the images taken back to Europe (see esp. Pratt, *Imperial Eyes*, 5–9).

11. Editor's introduction in *Implicit Understandings: Observing, Reporting, and Reflecting on the Encounters Between Europeans and Other Peoples in the Early Modern Era*, ed. Stuart B. Schwartz (Cambridge: Cambridge University Press, 1994), 1–8, quote from 6.

12. Rolena Adorno, "The Indigenous Ethnographer: The 'Indio Ladino' as Historian and Cultural Mediation," in ibid., 383. See also Adorno, *Guzman Puma: Writing and Resistance in Colonial Peru* (1988; Austin: University of Texas Press, Institute of Latin American Studies, 2000).

13. For a succinct critique of the literature of self and other, see Nicholas Thomas, *Colonialism's Culture: Anthropology, Travel and Government* (Princeton, N.J.: Princeton University Press, 1994), 3. Cf. Thomas, *Entangled Objects: Exchange, Material Culture, and Colonialism in the Pacific* (Cambridge, Mass.: Harvard University Press, 1991); and Thomas, *Oceanic Art* (London: Thames and Hudson, 1995).

14. Anne Salmond, *Two Worlds: First Meetings Between Maori and European, 1642–1772* (New York: Viking, 1991); Anne Salmond, *Between Worlds: Early Exchanges Between Maori and Europeans, 1773–1815* (Honolulu: University of Hawai'i Press, 1997), quote from *Between Worlds*, 14, Maori terms from *Between Worlds*, 33.

15. On the ship, see Greg Dening, *Mr. Bligh's Bad Language. Passion, Power and Theatre on the Bounty* (Cambridge: Cambridge University Press, 1992); on the

beach see Dening, *Islands and Beaches: Discourse on a Silent Land—Marquesas 1774–1880* (Honolulu: University of Hawai'i Press, 1980).

16. Karen Ordahl Kupperman, *Indians and English: Facing Off in Early America* (Ithaca, N.Y., and London: Cornell University Press, 2000), x, 11. See also Kupperman, *Settling with the Indians: the Meeting of English and Indian Cultures in America, 1580–1640* (Totowa, N.J.: Rowman and Littlefield, 1980).

17. Kupperman, *Indians and English*, 174, 213–214.

18. Ibid., 204, 218–219, quote from 211.

19. Pauline Turner Strong, "Captivity in White and Red: Convergent Practice and Colonial Representation on the British-Amerindian Frontier, 1606–1736," in Daniel Segal, ed., *Crossing Cultures: Essays in the Displacement of Western Civilization* (Tucson: University of Arizona Press, 1992), 33–104; James P. Ronda, *Lewis and Clark Among the Indians* (Lincoln: University of Nebraska Press, 1984), 256–259.

20. Richard White, *The Middle Ground: Indians, Empires, and Republics in the Great Lakes Region, 1650–1815* (Cambridge: Cambridge University Press, 1991). On Tocqueville and Tanner, see Harry Liebersohn, *Aristocratic Encounters: European Travelers and North American Indians* (Cambridge: Cambridge University Press, 1998), 100.

21. Vanessa Smith, *Literary Culture and the Pacific: Nineteenth-century Textual Encounters* (Cambridge: Cambridge University Press, 1998), 18–52; and Smith's commentaries on beachcomber texts in Jonathan Lamb, Vanessa Smith, and Nicholas Thomas, eds., *Exploration and Exchange: A South Seas Anthology, 1680–1900* (Chicago: University of Chicago, 2000).

22. Tony Ballantyne, *Orientalism and Race: Aryanism in the British Empire* (Houndsmills, Basingstoke, Hampshire: Palgrave, 2002), 13–15, quote from 15.

23. Bruno Latour, *Science in Action: How to Follow Scientists and Engineers Through Society* (Cambridge, Mass.: Harvard University Press, 1987), chap. 6.

24. David P. Miller and Peter Hanns Reill, eds., *Visions of Empire: Voyages, Botany, and Representations of Nature* (Cambridge: Cambridge University Press, 1996); E. C. Spary, *Utopia's Garden: French Natural History from Old Regime to Revolution* (Chicago: University of Chicago Press, 2000); Richard Drayton, *Nature's Government: Science, Imperial Britain, and the 'Improvement' of the World* (New Haven, Conn.: Yale University Press, 2000).

25. Richard H. Grove, *Green Imperialism: Colonial Expansion, Tropical Island Edens and the Origins of Environmentalism, 1680–1860* (Cambridge: Cambridge University Press, 1995). For a systematic attempt to follow travelers from their dealings with patrons at home to their collaborations abroad and their philosophical reception after their return, see Harry Liebersohn, *The Travelers' World: Europe to the Pacific* (Cambridge, Mass.: Harvard University Press, 2006).

26. Todorov, *The Conquest of America*, 101.

27. Underdeveloped areas of study, such as environmental history, the history of sexuality, and the history of religion may continue to surprise us by opening

up new chapters in the history of cultural contact. On environmental history, see Grove, *Green Imperialism*; on the history of sexuality, see Lee Wallace, *Sexual Encounters: Pacific Texts, Modern Sexualities* (Ithaca, N.Y.: Cornell University Press, 2002) and Anne Salmond, *Aphrodite's Island: The European Discovery of Tahiti* (Berkeley: University of California Press, 2010); on religion a suggestive starting-point for further work is C. A. Bayly, *The Birth of the Modern World, 1780– 1914* (Oxford: Blackwell, 2004), chap. 9.

3

EXPLORATION AND ENLIGHTENMENT

PHILIP J. STERN

It is possible that nothing more embodied eighteenth-century Europeans'
concerns with the creation, collation, and the codification of knowledge
than contemporary efforts to explore and map peoples and places across the
globe. Their relationship was intimate and inextricable: The expectations
and pursuits of Enlightenment helped determine the motivation, means, and
ends of eighteenth-century exploration while "the new theatre of exploration and exchange in previously unknown worlds," as historian Dorinda
Outram has noted, "was a place where the Enlightenment was to work
out its own meaning."[1] Both were ostensibly moved to action by concerns
with empirical and rational inquiry, systematization, and discovery; both
primarily sought to give order to chaos. What constituted rational or trust-
worthy knowledge, however, was hardly self-evident. The coherence and
appeal of both enterprises rested not in discovering knowledge but rather in
constructing it.

As such, Enlightenment and exploration offered one another a bevy of
techniques and tools of persuasion, which may have spoken in the language
of reason but which inevitably also encompassed appeals to the emotions,
passions, preconceptions, and proclivities of its practitioners and audiences
alike: that is, in the terms of classical rhetoric, *logos*, *pathos*, and *ethos* in
equal proportions. Both were, at their most fundamental levels, forms of
culture and ways of knowing: ideologies, discourses, and epistemologies
embedded in and reinforced by a range of social, political, commercial,
technological, and textual practices.[2] Exploration and Enlightenment were
thus cut from the same cloth, amplifying, intensifying, and transforming
one another while exposing their mutual complexities, challenges, and
contradictions.

The Logics of Enlightenment and Exploration

While Europeans had had contact with the wider world for millennia and had been exploring it actively on sea and land for centuries, during the "long" eighteenth century, European expansion came to have a relatively unprecedented reach, vision, and ambition. In conjunction with commercial, martial, and imperial expansion, the period witnessed continental expeditions across North and South America as well as Eurasia, the systematic surveying and mapping of South Asia, the stirrings of exploration in the interior of Africa and the Arctic, and maritime circumnavigations, which reached their apotheosis in the race to chart the Pacific, its islands, and its littorals.

These encounters with new people, places, and things provided a good deal of the fuel for the "curiosity" that lay at the heart of Enlightenment self-image and definition.[3] Indeed, there were few Enlightenment enterprises that were left untouched by exploration and global expansion. Overseas exploration and navigation became critical subjects for European states, literati, and learned societies, including the British Royal Society and French Academy of Sciences.[4] As historian Roy Porter put it, "globalization set the terms for natural history," the interest in "useful" knowledge and "improvement" impacting enterprises ranging from astronomy to zoology, with botany, ethnography, geodesy, geology, hydrography, linguistics, oceanography, pharmacology, meteorology, mineralogy, thermometry, and many other subjects firmly in between. The growing interrelationship between exploration and natural philosophy was also reflected by the changing constitutions of voyages themselves, which increasingly included natural philosophers of varying sorts.[5] Itinerant painters and draftsmen, becoming increasingly commonplace particularly on maritime expeditions, imported back into Europe not only comprehensible and sometimes unsettling images of the globe but also new ideas about the practice, theory, and subjects of eighteenth-century European art.[6] A similar if perhaps less direct impact of travel appeared in theater and music as well.[7] Explorers also brought back many, many things: plants, animals, specimens, goods, and so-called "curiosities" that became critical objects of inquiry, shaping people's opinions about the world both at home and abroad. Of course, they brought back people as well—perhaps most famously the Tahitian Mai (or Omai), who returned with James Cook's second Pacific voyage—who were often subjected to similar treatment and scrutiny as the objects that accompanied them.[8]

This connection between explorers' encounters and Enlightenment inquiry was reinforced by the fact that geography was itself a critical subject for Enlightenment thinkers, standing as it did at the center of debates over education, empirical and theoretical science, theology, history, and moral philosophy. Increasingly distinguished from cosmography, geography in the Enlightenment encompassed an ecumenical set of terrestrial concerns, which included both the world's physical characteristics as well as its "moral" ones, such as manners, behaviors, politics, and history.[9] Embodying Enlightenment objectives, such enterprises also translated into its dialect, which historian of science Michael Bravo has aptly called a "vocabulary of precision": a shared language of instrumentation, measurement, and mathematical accuracy through which difference, diversity, and the chaos of the world could be standardized, measured, and even mastered in a way that rendered it comparable, universal, and thus comprehensible.[10] Articulated as such, geography compressed space and place, enabling, for example, someone like the British explorer, botanist, and gentleman scientist Joseph Banks or the Swedish botanist Carl von Linné (better known as Linneaus) to see the plant and animal world as something that could be categorized, taxonomized, collected, and transported; the idea behind the botanical gardens, so popular in Enlightenment Europe, that enabled this enterprise was precisely that they literally aspired to transplant one part of the globe to another.[11]

This impulse was no more vividly expressed than in the transformation experienced by eighteenth-century cartography. The objects of exploration changed the subjects of maps; amid a frenzy of global maritime exploration, for example, it was no coincidence that globes themselves, as geographer Denis Cosgrove has put it, took on an "oceanic character."[12] Enlightenment also ushered in a radical new cartographic methodology and ethic. Leading eighteenth-century geographers such as J. B. B. D'Anville in France and James Rennell in Britain self-consciously began to eschew the busy, populated interiors of their early modern predecessors—who had in their "Afric maps," Jonathan Swift famously lampooned, "place[d] elephants for want of towns"—for a more spartan aesthetic. Monsters disappeared from land and sea, as did many other common early modern flourishes, such as ships, not to mention any number of the imaginary political, topographical, and other markings common in earlier maps of the extra-European world.[13] Meanwhile, the decorations and illustrations that remained were often expelled quite literally to the margins and especially ornate cartouches. These new blanks, which the geographer and theorist J. B. Harley incisively referred to as "silences," were no less speculative or argumentative than their forbears. They embodied the Enlightenment emphasis on empiricism, verifiability, and disdain for ignorance and conjecture.[14] In turn, what remained—neat graticules, clearly marked routes, textual explanations—stressed the importance of classification and systematization, made claims to accurate knowledge based upon believable sources, and, as historian Matthew Edney argues, "served to establish and legitimate Enlightenment's ideological self-image as an inquisitive, rational, knowing, and hence empowered state."[15] Such maps also served as powerful justifications for their own enterprise, making the implicit demand that explorers and cartographers who had banished the elephants ultimately replace them with something else.[16]

"Just as geography was a subject of Enlightenment inquiry," historical geographer Charles Withers has observed, "so the world itself in the Enlightenment was an object for geographical inquiry."[17] Travel became a crucial metaphor and impetus for scientific discovery. The mapping of the physical globe made a strong argument for mapping what Francis Bacon called the "intellectual globe," challenging orthodoxies and opening spaces for new approaches not only to natural history but to even more "abstract" sciences, like mathematics.[18] Unsurprisingly, in return, exploration served as a popular genre for Enlightenment philosophical writing, particularly utopian and dystopian literature. Montesquieu's Persian travelers, Defoe's Crusoe, Swift's Gulliver, Johnson's Rasselas, Voltaire's Candide, and any number of far less famous terraqueous, aeronautic, extraterrestrial, and time travelers expressed a range of social, political, or cultural commentary and critique. Such texts not only imitated narratives of exploration but often responded to them: Horace Walpole's *Accounts of Giants Lately Discovered* (1766), for example, lampooned the speculation on the existence of Patagonian giants, encouraged by John Byron's recent circumnavigation on the *Dolphin*, while along the way registering blistering critiques of British politics, empire, and the East India Company's expansion in Bengal.[19]

Beyond its use as model and metaphor, contact with the extra-European world confronted Enlightenment thinkers with unprecedented diversity, against which they were compelled to define themselves and their place in that world.[20] On the one hand, difference in climate, society, politics, and culture argued for distinctions between and among the "west" and the "rest"; on the other, anything that seemed to remain consistent amid such vast differences, from gravity to human nature, provided powerful arguments for the sorts of universal truths and laws at the core of much Enlightenment political, epistemological, and metaphysical theory.[21] The German philosophers Johann Gottfried von Herder and Immanuel Kant were widely read in travel and exploration accounts.[22] Isaac Newton argued his way toward a universal theory of attraction (i.e., gravity) with examples culled less from falling apples than from travel accounts in French Guiana, West Africa, and the Caribbean; the influence was so pronounced that Voltaire once quipped that "never would Newton have made his discoveries" without the late seventeenth-century French Atlantic expeditions sponsored by Louis XIV and the Académie Royale des Sciences.[23] John Locke too was an avid consumer of travel literature, collecting almost two hundred travelogues or related compendia, plus a range of maps and surveys. These affected almost every aspect of his thought, underscoring some of his most influential theories on religious toleration, property, epistemology, and especially the concept of a state of nature, which stood at the heart of his political theory. As he put it, in words that have now become famous, "in the beginning all the World was America."[24]

In this sense, exploration not only offered "armchair" *philosophes* the opportunity to travel through space but also through time. Travel, especially in North Africa and the Western Levant, encouraged and was informed by great interest in the Enlightenment in antiquarianism, archeology, and biblical scholarship.[25] It was perhaps even more influential on the development of stadial or conjectural history, particularly popular in Scotland, which called upon examples from across the globe to illustrate its central principle that history was primarily the progress of civilization through various stages of development;[26] with overseas expansion, the Scottish historian James Mackintosh noted, "many dark periods of history have been explored."[27] Edmund Burke captured the correlation when he described William Robertson's *History of America* (1777) as having unfurled the "great map of mankind": "We no longer need to go to history to have it in all its periods and stages," Burke observed; "there is no state or gradation of barbarism, and no mode of refinement, which we have not, at the same instant under our view." Philosophy was critical to understanding travel, but contact with the globe, he wrote Robertson, had also provided unparalleled "new resources for philosophy."[28] For his part, Robertson explicitly credited the inspiration for his 1791 *Historical Disquisition Concerning the Knowledge Which the Ancients Had of India* to his reading of James Rennell's 1788 *Memoir of a Map of Hindoostan*.[29] The feeling, as Rennell replied to Robertson, was mutual: "for after all, whence does the Geographer derive his Materials, but from the labours of the Historian?"[30]

Exploration and Enlightenment met even more explicitly in texts that took the form of histories of the extra-European world and direct reflections on European expansion itself. Denis Diderot, for example, worked out his ideas about universal humanity in his own manuscript reflections on Bougainville's voyages. The Abbé Raynal's encyclopedic *Philosophical and Political History of European Trade and Settlements in the Two Indies* (1770) drew heavily, either directly or through its many contributors (including Diderot), on accounts of travel in the Americas, Asia, and the Pacific and, in the process, engaged with many of the critical themes of Enlightenment discourse, such as political economy, civilization and barbarity, colonialism, slavery, and human nature.[31] Indeed, any number of Enlightenment writings on human nature argued about whether Native American or Pacific societies were barbarous or idyllic, and whether their cultures or religions were enviable or odious. Even supposedly sympathetic accounts could oscillate between views of indigenous peoples as "noble savages" or as part of a universal and commensurable humanity, ranging, as historian Anthony Pagden has put it, from Rousseau's "feckless Carib" to Diderot's "wise *veillard.*"[32]

The Passions of Enlightenment and Exploration

Enlightenment geography may have made explicit and implicit claims to universality, but it clearly did not produce any universal answers or understanding of the world. Indeed, the manifold forms of knowledge it produced were very much affected by where, when, and how such knowledge was produced, communicated, and transplanted across time and place.[33] Conversely, exploration, along with colonial and overseas settlement, also broadened and complicated where, when, and among whom one might find "Enlightenment." If, for example, Ottoman, Mughal, and Qing empires had roughly contemporary "ages" of exploration, comparable technologies of geographical surveying, and parallel techniques of conceptualizing and representing the world cartographically, did they—despite the arguments of many eighteenth-century Europeans—also have an Enlightenment?[34] Certainly, for some in the late eighteenth century, exploration was a prime opportunity to export a European Enlightenment; the naturalist Georg Forster, for example, praised James Cook for advancing "his century in knowledge and Enlightenment," both for transforming what was known in Europe and, in turn, establishing the sinews along which Enlightenment itself could spread to the Pacific.[35]

As Europe expanded, then, so too did the content, culture, and geography of Enlightenment. Across the colonial world one found what historian Maya Jasanoff has called "archetypical" Enlightenment-style collectors and connoisseurs, whether Thomas Jefferson in Virginia or Claude Martin, who had been a surveyor in Bengal before retiring in genteel style in eighteenth-century Lucknow.[36] Unsurprisingly, then, exploratory enterprises increasingly found their origins and inspiration not only in London, Paris, and Madrid but also in European colonial centers and peripheries in the Atlantic and Asia. Expeditions in Spanish America, for example, were inseparable from their colonial context;[37] likewise, the English East India Company's eighteenth-century territorial and maritime expansion fueled a range of influential scholarly and geographical enterprises, such as George Bogle's expedition in Tibet, Alexander Dalrymple's hydrographical work, and, of course, Rennell's mapping of Bengal and then all of "Hindoostan."[38]

Empire and colonization were thus crucial in brokering the relationship between Enlightenment and exploration. Historian John Gascoigne has likened the "Enlightened" languages of disinterested and rational discovery in which expeditions were articulated as comparable to the ubiquity of spiritual mission amongst conquistadores in earlier centuries: neither disingenuous nor the whole story, eliding as they do the intertwined economic and national interests at their core.[39] Both on land and sea, mapmakers— like Rennell in India, Flinders in Australia, or the Napoleonic survey of Egypt—served to codify and capture nebulous imperial spaces, for colonial officials and domestic audiences alike.[40] The expansion of natural, geodetic, and cartographic knowledge buttressed new and expanding polities, like the eighteenth-century British or the post-Revolutionary French empires, and even allowed others without global imperial aspirations, like Sweden and Denmark, to compete in the European international theater.[41] The race for the Pacific—most famously between Cook and Bougainville, but including Vancouver, Flinders, Lapérouse, and others—was driven by global Anglo-French military and commercial competition in the eighteenth century. That rivalry in turn drew Russian and Spanish responses, perhaps most notably the Spanish expedition of the Italian navigator Alejandro Malaspina, who, like his competitors, sailed in the service of his patrons but drew upon his experiences to expound upon reformist political theory, natural history, and ethnography.[42]

If exploration was a way for Britain and France to gain new empires, for Spain it was intended to revitalize an older one, supplying, as historian Daniella Bleichmar has argued, "a new wave of an old phenomenon: the rediscovery and reconquest of the Americas."[43] Aside from its Pacific ambitions, the Spanish Crown sponsored over fifty expeditions to the Americas in the second half of the eighteenth century, close to one-fifth of which were predominantly botanical in their orientation. Meanwhile, defenses of Spanish imperial policy employed histories and accounts of travel in the Americas, particularly those from Italian Jesuits of the Catholic Enlightenment, to counter the accusations and aspersions—especially the so-called black legend of Spanish cruelty—popularized by other travel-driven *philosophes* like Raynal. Malaspina sailed with both Italian and Spanish copies of one such text, the Chilean Jesuit Juan Ignacio Molina's geographical, natural, and civil history of Chile.[44] When Raynal himself was translated into Spanish, the text contained significant editorial interventions that dramatically changed its meanings and implications.[45]

As Enlightenment exploration served empire, the ambitions of expanding European states offered material, political, and institutional support for exploration. Cook's voyages marked a dramatic increase in the role of the British Admiralty and other state agencies in expeditions, while expanding territorial states like the United States and Russia underwrote transcontinental ventures across both North America and Eurasia, respectively.[46] European botanical entrepots, like Joseph Banks's Royal Botanical Gardens at Kew, were possible only because of the expanding sinews of empire; the contacts and clients someone like Banks found in colonial and consular stations, from North Africa to India, served his own intellectual and political "empire" equally and in return.[47] Empire also made possible the exportation of the people, institutions, and infrastructure critical to exploration's project; by the early nineteenth centuries, there were such gardens at Kew and Calcutta, Madrid and Mexico City, and many points in between.[48]

Yet, as much as Enlightenment exploration served national ambitions, it also cut across national boundaries. Maps, texts, specimens, and explorers themselves circulated widely through the networks of European science and society.[49] Dutch maps, charts, and texts proliferated in Europe, even as the United Provinces retreated from an earlier nationally and imperially driven geographical project to one more oriented toward profit in a transnational European market.[50] German universities, particularly Göttingen, became centers of work on natural history and anthropology without even mounting expeditions, let alone imperial ventures, relying instead on others, especially the British. Joseph Banks and Johann Blumenbach at Göttingen had a particularly close relationship, Banks and his network providing Blumenbach with a wide range of materials for his collection, including satisfying his seemingly insatiable demand for human skulls. In return, Blumenbach trained students in languages, ethnography, instrumentation, and other necessary skills, ultimately employed on "British" expeditions abroad. Some of Göttingen's more famous alumni included Georg and Reinhold Forster, naturalists on Cook's second voyage, and Friedrich Hornemann and the

Swiss Johann Burckhardt, both of whom traveled on behalf of the African Association, with which Banks was heavily involved.[51] The Forsters and the ethnologist August Schlözer also cut their teeth traveling within the Russian Empire as well as on Russian Pacific expeditions.[52] Italian navigators, like Malaspina, sailed as they had for centuries in the service of other imperial and national ventures, while the American Revolution hardly stopped Banks from supporting the New Englander John Ledyard in his (failed) attempt to walk across Russia or his (fatal) service with the African Association. Even the most seemingly intractable national rivalries could be crosscut by those networks; in the brief window afforded by the Peace of Amiens, the British African Association even gifted a copy of the German Hornemann's published journal to the French Napoleon, in gratitude for the protection he had offered the explorer when in Egypt.[53]

Exploration reflected quite starkly the ambivalence between a national Enlightenment in an age of global imperial competition and war and a cosmopolitan Enlightenment, a "republic of letters," rooted in a sense of a shared European civilization and community; it thus provided the foundation for modern empire and the sine qua non of the Enlightenment critique of colonization, expansion, and slavery.[54] In fact, the intersections between exploration and Enlightenment highlighted any number of debates, tensions, and complexities in each. The limits of Enlightenment claims to empirical objectivity and universality were exemplified by the ways in which the knowledge generated by explorers and other authors was deeply embedded in its local contexts, the "itineraries" it traveled, and the wide range of European, indigenous, creole, and enslaved interlocutors, intermediaries, and "go-betweens" upon which it relied.[55] Subjects as seemingly straightforward as charting the Gulf Stream, for example, could easily be constructed differently depending upon where, how, and in what media they were represented.[56] Ostensibly rational and purposive, Enlightenment voyages were "more often itineraries of contingency than precision," inevitably defined as much by design as by chance, serendipity, and even failure; even as transformative a figure as Alexander von Humboldt engaged in his famous travels in America only after he found himself unable to join Napoleon's Egyptian expedition.[57]

Thus, the seemingly dispassionate rhetoric of Enlightenment exploratory pursuits was crosscut by a variety of institutional and individual circumstances, as often driven by rational inquiry as it was by accident, accommodation, and emotion. Of course, this too was an important facet of Enlightenment thought. For *philosophes* like the Earl of Shaftesbury, Jean-Jacques Rousseau, Adam Smith, and many others, emotions, sympathy, and sentimentalism played as crucial a role as reason in fashioning a sense of knowing and behaving.[58] Certainly, part of the appeal of exploration narratives was that they aimed to tame a world that was incomprehensibly vast and extremely difficult to master, yet they also titillated the imagination with their accounts of the exotic and the sublime. Travel accounts were as likely to prompt the "flights of fancies" of "sedentary philosophers" as sober reflection on the rational construction of the world.[59] Despite their banishment from the map, tales of monstrosities and marvels continued to excite fascination, even in the pages of the Royal Society's *Philosophical Transactions*.[60] Yet, one did not have to pay heed to such accounts to feel, as Humboldt put it, a "longing for the Tropics."[61] Steeped in both Goethe and the Encyclopedists, awed by laboratory and landscape alike, Humboldt offers the perfect example of how "Enlightenment" and "Romanticism" could easily blur, and just how closely tied the culture of instrumentation and inquiry could be to the contemporary culture of sensibility and sentimentality; "feeling and measuring," historian Michael Dettlebach has suggested, "were closely identified, even continuous activities."[62] Even the most seemingly pragmatic instruments of rule, like the British mapping of India, produced both written and visual texts that, in resonating emotionally with their domestic audiences, helped to mobilize support for the East India Company's imperial expansion.[63]

Such appeals to sentiment were perhaps partly intuitive, but they were also reinforced by social and cultural convention. In short, exploration became fashionable. The texts, products, and even people brought back to Europe from the extra-European world fit snugly alongside the vogue for conspicuous consumption, collecting, and curiosity that defined genteel élites in the Enlightenment.[64] Often, exploration was articulated, especially in England, within the context of gentlemanly travel, reflecting—or at least as some wanted to believe—the same impulses as the European Grand Tour, with its emphasis on itinerancy, antiquity, and learned collection; Joseph Banks supposedly quipped indignantly that "every blockhead" went to Europe, but that his "Grand Tour shall be one round the whole world." Botanical gardens may have been imperial laboratories but they also resembled the pleasure gardens and promenades of polite eighteenth-century society.[65] Part of the appeal of exploration and natural history, observes historian Janet Browne, was that many eighteenth-century landowners and literati were simply "*fond* of plants."[66]

"Polite" society fused explorers' knowledge to the world of collecting, sociability, confraternity, and clubbability that underscored the very essence of Enlightenment culture.[67] Thus, while Enlightenment and exploration may

have met influentially in the palaces, legislatures, and learned societies of
Europe, they also comingled equally productively in the eighteenth-century
salon, club, sermon, apothecary, cabinet, drawing room, and dining hall.
Exploration thus fed what historian Lorraine Daston has called the "great
echo chamber" of the Enlightenment, a culture and "collective personality"
characterized by the dedicated pursuit of "useful knowledge," but shaped by
a world of sociability, print, and letters.[68] It is worth observing that exploration also quite literally fed the Enlightenment: the African Association
grew out a gentleman's dining club, while the early nineteenth-century
Raleigh Club actually institutionalized eating exotic animals returned by its
travelers. Both clubs, among others, became the foundation for the Royal
Geographical Society in 1830.[69] Yet, in any number of ways beyond the
gastronomic, Enlightenment rendered exploration as something to be consumed. "Knowledge" in the Enlightenment was itself a form of desire, its
patrons and proponents possessing, as one scholar has described Locke, an
"unquenched appetite for travel literature."[70] Travel narratives, cartography,
and other geographical texts mingled easily among the "genres of polite literature and learning."[71] Accounts of Cook and Bougainville's voyages flew
off the shelves; Mungo Park's *Travels in the Interior Districts of Africa*,
published in 1799, sold its first print run of 1,500 within a month, followed
by more editions in London, Philadelphia, and New York, as well as translations into French, Dutch, German, and Italian.[72]

Exploration only flourished because of a sustained passion for the enterprise that was deeply embedded in Enlightenment culture and thought.
Joseph Banks so desired to disembark to collect specimens at Rio de Janeiro
on his voyage with Cook that he likened himself to "Tantalus in hell" or a
"French man laying swaddled in linen between two of his Mistresses both
naked using Every possible means to excite desire" when local colonial officials refused to allow him to do so.[73] Such a fusion of sexual and intellectual
desire was hardly anomalous, least of all for Banks. Much of the natural
historical interest of Enlightenment exploration, and especially botany, cen-
tered on questions of biology, reproduction, and genetics, which easily lent
themselves to sexualized representations.[74] (Banks, for one, evidently found
breadfruit remarkably erotic.) Popular literature like the *Arabian Nights*,
first translated into French and then other European languages in the eighteenth century, and accounts of mysterious sancta like the harem represented
a tradition of armchair travel that drew readers into the extra-European
world by appealing not to reason but imagination, magic, fantasy, and, of
course, sex.[75] As such, travel and cartography appeared as common tropes
in eighteenth-century erotica, often serving as tools by which one could

explore and master the (female) body.[76] It was thus hardly surprising that for explorers and their narratives, erotic desire merged easily with intellectual desire; the pleasure of the library mixed inseparably with the pleasure of the libido, perhaps no more famously than in the South Seas.[77]

The Authority of Enlightenment and Exploration

Of course, the passion that impelled exploration was also precisely what imperiled it. Some found—or claimed to find—the supposedly "natural" sexuality of an eroticized Tahiti repulsive; Banks's tales of sexual exploits in Tahiti and his horticultural obsessions certainly became fodder for his enemies and critics, who lampooned him as a foppish butterfly catcher and a "botanical libertine."[78] More broadly, Enlightenment thought was deeply conflicted on the nature of exploration. *Philosophes* like Diderot and Condorcet drew prolifically on travel accounts but remained deeply suspicious of them, precisely because of their popularity and appeal to wonder and the exceptional; Shaftesbury compared travel accounts to books of chivalry, while David Hume insisted they undermined "common sense."[79] By its very nature as an overseas and mobile enterprise, performed well outside the supervision of the institutional and cultural strictures of European science, exploration also brought to the fore a core dilemma between two quintessentially Enlightenment values: empiricism on the one hand, and authority and trustworthiness on the other. Some travelers, like Humboldt, Banks, and James Bruce, were wealthy, well-connected, and embedded in the structures of genteel Enlightenment society. Most were not. Even those who came from the scholarly or professional disciplines of Enlightenment science, like the surgeons George Bass in Australia and Mungo Park in Africa, nonetheless lacked independent income, social status, and, on their own, access to power.[80] Making matters worse, explorers by their very nature traveled beyond the confines of European civilization, confusing the boundary between artist and artisan, scientist and laborer. Hence the dilemma: direct, empirical observation was required to achieve the status of useful and reliable knowledge but not everyone's senses were created equally. Ironically, then, if the Enlightenment generated a hospitable environment for exploration, it also made for, as literary critic Jonathan Lamb has put it, a "climate of distrust." The explorer, whose job it was to observe, in the end did not always make a reliable "eyewitness."[81]

One way in which Enlightenment exploration confronted this challenge was to argue that it had indeed bred a new form of *savant*. Explorers, military and naval officials, colonial servants, and other itinerants, who cut their teeth in expeditionary ventures, now could, under the right circumstances and often once at home, achieve status as a certain kind of *philosophe*. James Rennell began his adult life as a midshipman on a Royal Navy vessel and ended it as the leading geographical authority in Britain. His home, like that of Joseph Banks, became a mandatory stop for explorers, his opinion highly valued by state officials, and his name on the rolls of several European learned societies, perhaps most crucially Banks's "circle of curiosi."[82] Antoine Simon Le Page du Pratz, a former soldier and tobacco plantation owner, converted his experiences into a three-volume history of Louisiana (1753), which engaged with themes very similar to those of Raynal and seemed to be read by philosopher and explorer alike: Thomas Jefferson owned a copy, and Lewis and Clark carried one on their cross-continental travels.[83]

Figures like Rennell and Le Page parlayed experience abroad into intellectual and cultural capital once home, but expeditions themselves also increasingly participated directly in the Enlightenment enterprise. This was particularly the case for maritime exploration. Especially after Cook, ships became sorts of floating laboratories, places both for scientific inquiry about the world as well as for experimentation on some of the most pressing problems of the day, from how to determine longitude at sea to how to cure scurvy.[84] The "philosophical traveler" also became a new ideal type of explorer, a *philosophe* on the move who—unlike the common soldier, sailor, or merchant—did not just report but could also interpret the world for the purposes of natural history, philosophy, and history alike. Such an identity was critical to many explorers' self-fashioning, like the aspiring American circumambulator and later short-lived African explorer John Ledyard, who envisioned (and represented) his work as a form of "philosophic geography," consciously distinguished from the mere travels of his predecessors and competitors.[85]

To achieve such a status, however, travelers and their narratives had to be filtered through individuals, institutions, and languages that could resolve the dilemmas implicit in their enterprise. Here patronage was key, critical to the financial and political support for overseas ventures but also to their prestige and authority. Patrons very much affected what explorers were looking for, how they went about finding it, and the ways they communicated what they found.[86] Thomas Jefferson, for example, insured his "corps of explorers" would attend to issues of particular interest to him: climate, meteorology, physical geography, and the like. His most famous acolytes, Meriwether Lewis and William Clark, "adhered obediently" to their instructions and the resulting travel account, ethnographic charts, and maps hewed to contemporary geographical conventions, which in turn helped both visualize and justify American westward expansion.[87]

Such authorial strategies were central to assuaging the epistemological crisis of Enlightenment travel. Charles-Marie de La Condamine's Amazonian expedition in the 1730s, historian of science Neil Safier has shown, was given meaning only once inscribed and interpreted by "armchair" academicians and cartographers in Europe, not to mention La Condamine's own self-censorship and self-fashioning of his narrative.[88] Indeed, exploration rarely if ever came to readers unmediated, arriving often in the form of translations, redactions, and compilations, like Hawkesworth's accounts of South Seas voyages or Charles de Brosses's 1756 *Histoire des navigations aux terres australes*—a form consonant with the broader "encyclopedic impulse" of the Enlightenment.[89] Indeed, everything about a text, from its illustrations to its dedications, affected its authority and the nature of the knowledge it communicated. Even fictive accounts played upon such tropes. The utopian *Travels of Hildebrand Bowman*, for example, opened with the not uncommon dedicatory epistle to two very real figures: Joseph Banks and his librarian and compatriot on the Cook voyage, the Linnaean acolyte Daniel Solander.[90]

It was thus the very institutions and instruments of the Enlightenment—print culture, coffee houses, museums, gardens, zoos, societies, clubs, and so on—that made it possible in the end for travel to, in a sense, return home.[91] As Enlightenment offered authority to exploration, however, exploration offered purpose to Enlightenment, helping to reinscribe its intellectual and cultural currency. Yet, those strategies were complicated and revealed that the nature of Enlightenment knowledge was hardly as clear as its own rhetoric insisted. As Lamb has argued, Hawkesworth's compilation of South Sea voyages aimed at being both useful and interesting; in offering scientific knowledge and moral instruction, it mixed generic techniques and narrative strategies drawn from experimental philosophy, the novel, and periodical writing alike.[92] Paul Carter has observed that both "the knight of romance and the empirical scientist" shared in common an emphasis on surprise, struggle, and determination, notions that were fairly common in explorers' accounts of their successes and failures abroad.[93] Mungo Park's African *Travels* self-consciously balanced its empirical foundations with the form of a "Quixotic" heroic quest tale: Park even supposedly confessed over drinks to the luminaries Sir Walter Scott, Dugald Stewart, and Adam Ferguson that his published journal deliberately left out "many real incidents and adventures" precisely because they might "shake the probability of his narrative in the public estimation." Like many others, "Park's" journal was hardly entirely his own; it was heavily edited by Bryan Edwards, the Jamaican planter and African Association secretary, and was packaged with maps and a lengthy interpretive geographical "memoir" by James Rennell, which deeply affected the way the journal would be read—not to mention its credibility.[94]

The ad hominem authority and imprimatur of interlocutors like Rennell were key to the reliability and integrity of an account of exploration, but so too were their methods. Here too the languages of reason, modernity, and empiricism were complicated by a range of scholarly techniques, all of which resonated with Enlightenment audiences' expectations of what ultimately established authority and trust. Humboldt's travels reflected a range of influences beyond mere observation, including encounters with contemporary and antiquarian European scholarship, colonial records, *salons*, correspondents, and, of course, the "intellectual milieu" and natural historical thought of the America (and those Americans) he encountered.[95] Indeed, the nature and appeal of a great deal of eighteenth-century exploration rested not necessarily in new "modern" objectives but in quite well-established and familiar concerns. The search for both a Northwest Passage and a large southern continent, which animated Enlightenment Pacific exploration, dated back centuries.[96] The notion of an American El Dorado, which had sent Sir Walter Raleigh to Guiana centuries earlier, continued to animate and fascinate the ostensibly rational European Enlightenment imagination.[97] J. B. B. D'Anville, the leading Enlightenment geographer in France, engaged in a lifelong obsession with the geography of ancient Egypt, while Rennell's magnum opus and great pride was his two-volume exposition of the geographical system of Herodotus. Indeed, Rennell's maps and writings on Africa—particularly his contributions both to Park's journal and that of Park's successor Friedrich Hornemann—filtered (and even sometimes discounted) explorers' empirical findings not only through other contemporary authorities but also ancient Greek and Roman scholarship, medieval Arab geography, and his own geographical theories and principles.[98]

Enlightenment knowledge as evidenced in exploration was thus a curious and complicated combination of empirical evidence, deductive theory, scholarship, emotional attachment, storytelling, and personal authority; in turn, exploration was crucial in shaping the ways in which all of those factors defined "Enlightenment." This meant that the self-conscious pioneering spirit that was at the heart of both exploration and the Enlightenment could ironically possess a fundamentally conservative, recalcitrant, even at times tautological character. For example, Rennell's commitment to route surveys and his early experiences with maritime surveying likely contrib-uted to his influential objections to the new trigonometric surveying in early nineteenth-century India; meanwhile, his enduring and intractable belief that the Niger terminated inland not only successfully marginalized early contrary (some correct) arguments but also contributed to his invention of a large (non-existent) mountain range in West Africa, which only disap-peared from maps and atlases in the 1890s.[99] It is hard not to see a personal, emotional, and political character to many of the disputes over global geog-raphy in the eighteenth century. The conflicts and debates between the natu-ral philosopher Joseph Banks and the astronomer royal Nevill Maskelyne, reminiscent of those between Newton and Leibniz over the invention of cal-culus, arose as much from disputes over method as from differences in per-sonal preferences, social connections, authority, and prestige. Even more vicious was the feud between the hydrographer Alexander Dalrymple and John Hawkesworth, which arose when Dalrymple simply refused the impli-cations of Hawkesworth's compilation: namely, that recent Pacific expedi-tions had cast serious doubt on the existence of a *Terra Australis*. In trading gibes, the two men may have in fact offered as apt a summary as possible of the odd admixture of reason and emotion, authority and empiricism, induction and deduction, desire and faith that made for exploration in the Enlightenment and Enlightenment in exploration. "I most sincerely wish," Hawkesworth taunted Dalrymple, "that a southern continent may be found, as I am confident nothing else can make him happy and good-humoured." Dalrymple, in turn, dismissed Hawkesworth's work as a "Canterbury Tale," insisting his own "inferences" were simply "from the facts reported"—after all, no one had definitively proven that a southern continent did not exist. So, while "my happiness or good humour does not depend on the existence or non-existence of a Southern Continent," he protested, "I *still believe* there *is one*."[100]

NOTES

1. Dorinda Outram, *Panorama of the Enlightenment* (Los Angeles: J. Paul Getty Museum, 2006), 130.

2. On "cultures of exploration," see Felix Driver, *Geography Militant: Cultures of Exploration and Empire* (Oxford: Blackwell, 2001), esp. 8–9; on the culture of the Enlightenment, see, amongst many others, László Kontler, "Introduction: What is the (Historians') Enlightenment Today?," *European Review of History* 13, 3 (2006): 357–371.

3. Susan Scott Parrish, *American Curiosity: Cultures of Natural History in the Colonial British Atlantic World* (Chapel Hill: Omohundro Institute and University of North Carolina Press, 2006).

4. See, for example, John Gascoigne, "The Royal Society, natural history and the peoples of the 'New World(s)', 1660–1800," *British Journal of the History of Science* 42, 4 (2009): 539–562; Jordan Kellman, "Discovery and Enlightenment at Sea: Maritime Exploration and Observation in the Eighteenth-Century French Scientific Community" (PhD Diss, Princeton University Press, 1998). For a sense of the limits of the Royal Society's power to make the prestige of an explorer, see Andrew S. Cook, "James Cook and the Royal Society," in Glyndwr Williams, ed., *Captain Cook: Explorations and Reassessments* (Woodbridge: Boydell Press, 2004), 37–55.

5. Roy Porter, "The terraqueous globe," in G. S. Rousseau and Roy Porter, eds., *The Ferment of Knowledge: Studies in the Historiography of Eighteenth-Century Science* (Cambridge: Cambridge University Press, 1980), 312. See, among others, Richard Drayton, *Nature's Government; Science, Imperial Britain, and the 'Improvement' of the World* (New Haven: Yale, 2000); Richard Grove, *Green Imperialism: Colonial Expansion, Tropical Island Edens, and the Origins of Environmentalism 1600–1860* (Cambridge: Cambridge University Press, 1996); Londa Schiebinger, *Plants and Empire: Colonial Bioprospecting in the Atlantic World* (Cambridge, MA: Harvard University Press, 2004); John Gascoigne, *Joseph Banks and the English Enlightenment: Useful Knowledge and Polite Culture* (Cambridge: Cambridge University Press, 1994); Dorinda Outram, "Cross-Cultural Encounters in the Enlightenment," in Martin Fitzpatrick, et al., eds., *The Enlightenment World* (New York: Routledge, 2004), 552–553; see also Outram, *The Enlightenment* (Cambridge: Cambridge University Press, 1995), chap. 4.

6. Harriet Guest, *Empire, Barbarism, and Civilization: Captain Cook, William Hodges, and the Return to the Pacific* (Cambridge: Cambridge University Press, 2007); Bernard Smith, *European Vision and the South Pacific* (New Haven: Yale University Press, 1985); Mary D. Sheriff, ed., *Cultural Contact and the Making of European Art since the Age of Exploration* (Chapel Hill: University of North Carolina Press, 2010); Luciana Martins, "The Art of Tropical Travel, 1768–1830," in Miles Ogborn and Charles W. J. Withers, eds., *Georgian Geographies: Essays on Space, Place, and Landscape in the Eighteenth Century* (Manchester: Manchester University Press, 2004), 72–91; Claudio Greppi, "'On the Spot': Traveling Artists and the Iconographic Inventory of the World, 1769–1859," in Felix Driver and Luciana Martins, eds., *Tropical Visions in an Age of Empire* (Chicago: University of Chicago Press, 2005), 23–42.

7. Vanessa Agnew, "Listening to Others: Eighteenth-Century Encounters in Polynesia and their Reception in German Musical Thought," *Eighteenth-Century Studies* 41, 2 (2008): 165–188; Felicity Nussbaum, "The Theatre of Empire: Racial Counterfeit, Racial Realism," in Kathleen Wilson, ed., *The New Imperial*

History: Culture, Identity, and Modernity in Britain and the Empire 1660–1840 (Cambridge: Cambridge University Press, 2004), 71–90.

8. Guest, *Empire, Barbarism, and Civilization,* chap 3; Guest, "Ornament and Use: Mai and Cook in London," in Wilson, ed., *New Imperial History,* 317–344.

9. David N. Livingstone, *The Geographical Tradition: Episodes in the History of a Contested Enterprise* (Oxford: Blackwell, 1992), chap 4. Robert Mayhew, *Enlightenment Geography: The Political Languages of British Geography, 1650–1850* (London: Palgrave Macmillan, 2000); Paul Elliott and Stephen Daniels, " 'No Study So Agreeable to the Youthful Mind': Geographical Education in the Georgian Grammar School," *History of Education* 39, 1 (2010), 15–33.

10. Michael T. Bravo, "Precision and Curiosity in Scientific Travel: James Rennell and the Orientalist Geography of the New Imperial Age," in Jaś Elsner and Joan-Pau Rubiés, eds., *Voyages and Visions: Towards a Cultural History of Travel* (London: Reaktion Books, 1999), 163; Marie-Noëlle Bourguet, Christian Licoppe, and H. Otto Sibum, eds., *Instruments, Travel and Science: Itineraries of Precision from the Seventeenth to the Twentieth Century* (London and New York: Routledge, 2002); Felix Driver and Luciana Martins, "Views and Visions of the Tropical World," in Driver and Martins, eds., *Tropical Visions,* 11.

11. Paul Carter, *The Road to Botany Bay: An Essay in Spatial History* (London: Faber and Faber, 1987), 21.

12. Denis Cosgrove, *Apollo's Eye: A Cartographic Genealogy of the Earth in the Western Imagination* (Baltimore: Johns Hopkins, 2001), 176–192, quote on 188; David Buisseret, "Charles Boucher of Jamaica and the Establishment of Greenwich Longitude," *Imago Mundi* 62, 2 (2010): 239–247.

13. Richard W. Unger, *Ships on Maps: Pictures of Power in Renaissance Europe* (Basingstoke: Palgrave Macmillan, 2010), 177.

14. Amidst other essays, see J. B. Harley, "Silences and Secrecy: The Hidden Agenda of Cartography in Early Modern Europe," repr. in J. B. Harley, *The New Nature of Maps: Essays in the History of Cartography* (Baltimore, Md.: The Johns Hopkins University Press, 2001), 83–108.

15. Matthew Edney, "Reconsidering Enlightenment Geography and Map Making: Reconnaissance, Mapping, Archive," in David N. Livingstone and Charles W. J. Withers, eds., *Geography and Enlightenment* (Chicago: University of Chicago Press, 1999), 173.

16. John Gascoigne, "Motives for European Exploration of the Pacific in the age of the Enlightenment," (2000), repr. Gascoigne, *Science, Philosophy and Religion in the Age of the Enlightenment* (Farnham: Ashgate Variorum, 2010), VI.

17. Charles W. J. Withers, *Placing the Enlightenment: Thinking Geographically About the Age of Reason* (Chicago: University of Chicago Press, 2008), 15.

18. Amir R. Alexander, *Geometrical Landscapes: The Voyages of Discovery and the Transformation of Mathematical Practice* (Stanford, Calif.: Stanford University Press, 2002).

19. G. S. Rousseau and Roy Porter, "Introduction," in G. S. Rousseau and Roy Porter, eds., *Exoticism in the Enlightenment* (Manchester: Manchester University Press, 1990), 8; Guillaume Ansart, "Imaginary Encounters with the New World: Native American Utopias in 18th-Century French Novels," *Utopian Studies* 11, 2 (2000): 33–41; Gregory Claeys, ed., *Modern British Utopias* 8 vols. (London and Brookfield, Vt.: Pickering & Chatto, 1997), esp. vols. 1–4.

20. Anthony Pagden, *Encounters with the New World: From Renaissance to Romanticism* (New Haven: Yale University Press, 1993).

21. Nicholas Dew, "Vers la ligne: Circulating Measurements around the French Atlantic," in James Delbourgo and Nicholas Dew, eds., *Science and Empire in the Atlantic World* (New York and London: Routledge, 2008), 53–54.

22. John Gascoigne, "The German Enlightenment and the Pacific," (2007) repr. in Gascoigne, *Science, Philosophy and Religion*, IX: 169–170.

23. Dew, "Vers la ligne," 53, 55–57, 65; Margaret C. Jacob and Larry Stewart, *Practical Matter: Newton's Science in the Service of Industry and Empire, 1687–1851* (Cambridge, Mass.: Harvard University Press, 2004), 16–17.

24. P. J. Marshall and Glyndwr Williams, *The Great Map of Mankind: Perceptions of New Worlds in the Age of Enlightenment* (Cambridge: Harvard University Press, 1982), 191–192; Daniel Carey, *Locke, Shaftesbury, and Hutcheson: Contesting Diversity in the Enlightenment and Beyond* (Cambridge: Cambridge University Press, 2006), 25 and *passim*; Daniel Carey, "Travel, Geography, and the Problem of Belief: Locke as a Reader of Travel Literature," in Julia Rudolph, ed., *History and Nation* (Lewisburg, Pa.: Bucknell University Press, 2006), esp. 102; Ann Talbot, *"The Great Ocean of Knowledge": The Influence of Travel Literature on the Work of John Locke* (Leiden: Brill, 2010); Dew, "Vers la ligne," 54, 66n1.

25. Marshall and Williams, *Great Map*, 60; Rosemary Sweet, *Antiquaries: The Discovery of the Past in Eighteenth-Century Britain* (London: Palgrave Macmillan, 2004), esp. 149–150.

26. See Karen O'Brien, *Narratives of Enlightenment: Cosmopolitan History from Voltaire to Gibbon* (Cambridge: Cambridge University Press, 1997).

27. Quoted by Jorge Cañizares-Esguerra, *How To Write The History of the New World; Histories, Epistemologies, and Identities in the Eighteenth-Century Atlantic World* (Stanford, Calif.: Stanford University Press, 2001), 51.

28. Edmund Burke to William Robertson, June 10, 1777 in *The Works and Correspondence of Edmund Burke*, 8 vols. (London: Francis & John Rivington, 1852), I: 339; Marshall and Williams, *Great Map of Mankind*, 1.

29. Simon Schaffer, "'On Seeing Me Write': Inscription Devices in the South Seas," *Representations* 97, 1 (2007): 101.

30. Rennell to Robertson, July 2,1791, National Library of Scotland, MS 3944, f. 68; William Robertson, *An Historical Disquisition Concerning the Knowledge Which the Ancients Had of India; and the Progress of Trade With that Country Prior to the Discovery of the passage to it by the Cape of Good Hope* (London 1791), v; Simon Schaffer, "The Asiatic Enlightenments of British Astronomy," in Simon

Schaffer, et al., eds., *The Brokered World: Go-Betweens and Global Intelligence, 1770–1820* (Sagamore Beach, Mass.: Science History Publications, 2009), 66.

31. Peter Jumack and Jenny Mander, "Reuniting the World: The Pacific in Raynal's *Histoire des Deux Indes*," *Eighteenth-Century Studies* 41, 2 (2008): 189–202.

32. Pagden, *European Encounters*, 13–14; Glyndwr Williams, "Seamen and Philosophers in the South Seas in the Age of Captain Cook," (1979), in Tony Ballantyne, ed., *Science, Empire and the European Exploration of the Pacific* (Aldershot: Ashgate, 2004), 294; Sankar Muthu, *Enlightenment Against Empire* (Princeton, N.J.: Princeton University Press, 2003), 49–50; John Gascoigne. "German Enlightenment," 156–57; Gascoigne, "Pacific Exploration as Religious Critique," *Parergon* 27, 1 (2010): 143–162.

33. See Withers, *Placing the Enlightenment*.

34. Giancarlo Casale, *The Ottoman Age of Exploration* (New York: Oxford University Press, 2010); Laura Hostetler, *Qing Colonial Enterprise: Ethnography and Cartography in Early Modern China* (Chicago: University of Chicago Press, 2001); Kapil Raj, *Relocating Modern Science: Circulation and the Construction of Knowledge in South Asia and Europe, 1650–1900* (Basingstoke: Palgrave Macmillan, 2007), 65–72, 91.

35. Forster quoted by John Gascoigne. "German Enlightenment," 162–163.

36. Maya Jasanoff, *Edge of Empire: Lives, Culture, and Conquest in the East, 1750–1850* (New York: Alfred A. Knopf, 2005), 76.

37. Cañizares-Esguerra, *History of the New World*, esp. chap. 5.

38. Matthew Edney, *Mapping an Empire: The Geographical Construction of British India, 1765–1843* (Chicago: University of Chicago Press 1997); Gordon T. Stewart, *Journeys to Empire: Enlightenment, Imperialism, and the British Encounter with Tibet, 1774–1904* (Cambridge: Cambridge University Press, 2009); Kate Teltscher, *The High Road to China: George Bogle, the Panchen Lama, and the First British Expedition to Tibet* (New York: Farrar, Straus, and Giroux, 2006); Michael T. Bravo, "Precision and Curiosity," 172; Michael Mann, "Mapping the Country: European Geography and the Cartographical Construction of India, 1760–90," *Science, Technology and Society* 8, 25 (2003): 25–46.

39. Gascoigne, "Motives for European Exploration," 233.

40. John Gascoigne, "Joseph Banks, Mapping, and the Geographies of Natural Knowledge," repr. in Gascoigne, *Science, Philosophy and Religion*, VII: 160; Edney, *Mapping an Empire;* Anne Godlewska, "Map, Text and Image: The Mentality of Enlightened Conquerors: A New Look at the *Description de l'Egypte*," *Transactions of the Institute of British Geographers* 20, 1 (1995): 5–28 and Godlewska, *Geography Unbound: French Geographic Science from Cassini to Humbolt* (Chicago: University of Chicago Press 1999). On the relationship between maps and power more generally and theoretically, see, among others, James R. Akerman, ed., *The Imperial Map: Cartography and the Mastery of Empire* (Chicago: University of Chicago press 2009); J. B. Harley, "Maps, Knowledge, and Power," in J. B. Harley, *The New Nature of Maps: Essays in the History of*

Cartography (Baltimore, Md.: The Johns Hopkins University Press, 2001), 51–
82; Denis Wood with John Fels, *The Power of Maps* (New York: Guilford Press,
1992); Denis Wood with John Fels and John Krygier, *Rethinking the Power of Maps*
(New York: Guilford Press, 2010); David Buisseret, ed., *Monarchs, Ministers, and
Maps: The Emergence of Cartography as a Tool of Government in Early Modern
Europe* (Chicago: University of Chicago Press 1992); Mark Monmonier, *How to Lie
with Maps* (Chicago: University of Chicago Press 1991); Anne Godlewska and Neil
Smith, eds., *Geography and Empire* (Oxford: Blackwell, 1994).

    41. John Gascoigne, *Science in the Service of the Empire: Joseph Banks, the
British State and the Uses of Science in the Age of Revolution* (Cambridge: Cambridge
University Press, 1998); Drayton, *Nature's Government;* Carol E. Harrison,
"Projections of the Revolutionary Nation: French Expeditions in the Pacific, 1791–
1803," *Osiris* 24, 1 (2009): 33–52; Richard Wortman, "Russian Noble Officers and
the Ethos of Exploration," *Russian History* 35, 1&2 (2008): 181–197; Sverker Sörlin,
"Science, Empire and Enlightenment: Geographies of Northern Field Science,"
European Review of History 13, 3 (2006): 455–472; Karen Oslund, " 'Nature in
League with Man': Conceptualising and Transforming the Natural World in
Eighteenth-Century Scandinavia," *Environment and History* 10 (2004): 305–325.

    42. James K. Barnett, "Alaska and the North Pacific: A Crossroads of Empires,"
and Phyllis S. Herda, "Ethnology in the Enlightenment: The Voyage of Alejandro
Malaspina in the Pacific," in Kames K. Barnett, Stephen Haycox, and Caedmon
A. Liburd, eds., *Enlightenment and Exploration in the North Pacific 1741–1805*
(Seattle and London: University of Washington for the Cook Inlet Historical
Society, 1997), 11–12, 65–75; Manuel Lucena-Giraldo, "The Limits of Reform
in Spanish America," in Gabriel Pacquette, ed., *Enlightened Reform in Southern
Europe and its Atlantic Colonies, c. 1750–1830* (Farnham: Ashgate, 2009), 319–
320; Simon Werrett, "Russian responses to the voyages of Captain Cook," in
Williams, ed., *Captain Cook,* 179–197; Roger Lawrence Williams, *French Botany
in the Enlightenment: The Ill-Fated Voyages of La Pérouse and His Rescuers*
(Boston: Kluwer Academic Publishers, 2003).

    43. Daniela Bleichmar, "Visible Empire: Scientific Expeditions and Visual
Culture in the Hispanic Enlightenment," *Postcolonial Studies* 12 (2009): 448.

    44. Ibid., 442; Bleichmar, "Atlantic Competitions: Botany in the
Eighteenth-Century Spanish Empire," in Delbourgo and Dew, eds., *Science
and Empire,* esp. 225–227; Paula De Vos, "Natural History and the Pursuit
of Empire in Eighteenth-Century Spain," *Eighteenth-Century Studies* 40, 2
(2007), 209–239; Victor Peralta Ruiz, "The Spanish Monarchy and its Uses of
Jesuit Historiography in the 'Dispute of the New World,'" in Pacquette, ed.,
Enlightened Reform, 94–95.

    45. See, for example, Gabriel Pacquette, "Enlightened Narratives and Imperia
Rivalry in Bourbon Spain: The Case of Almodóvar's *Historia Política de los
Establecimientos Ultramarinos de las Naciones Europeas (1784–1790),*" *The
Eighteenth Century* 48, 1 (2007): 61–80.

46. William A. Koelsch, "Thomas Jefferson, American Geographers, and the Uses of Geography," *The Geographical Review* 98, 2 (2008), 275.

47. David Philip Miller, "Joseph Banks, empire, and 'centers of calculation' in late Hanoverian London," and David Mackay, "Agents of empire: the Banksian collectors and evaluations of new lands," in David Philip Miller and Peter Hans Reill, eds., *Visions of Empire: Voyages, Botany, and Representations of Nature* (Cambridge: Cambridge University Press, 1996), 21–57.

48. Bleichmar, "Visible Empire," 447.

49. Neil Chambers, "Letters from the President: The Correspondence of Sir Joseph Banks," *Notes and Records of the Royal Society of London* 53, 1 (1999); Charles W. J. Withers, "Writing in Geography's History: *Caledonia*, Networks of Correspondence and Geographical Knowledge in the Late Enlightenment," *Scottish Geographical Journal* 120, 1&2 (2004): 33–45.

50. Benjamin Schmidt, "Mapping an Exotic World: The Global Project of Dutch Geography, circa 1700," in Felicity Nussbaum, ed., *The Global Eighteenth Century* (Baltimore and London: The Johns Hopkins University Press, 2003), 37.

51. John Gascoigne, "Blumenbach, Banks, and the Beginnings of Anthropology at Göttingen," in Gascoigne, *Science, Philosophy and Religion*, 88–89; Gascoigne, "German Enlightenment," 142, 144–146, 167–168.

52. Gascoigne. "German Enlightenment," 144–146.

53. Philip J. Stern, " 'Rescuing the Age from a Charge of Ignorance': Gentility, Knowledge, and the British Exploration of Africa in the Later Eighteenth Century," in Wilson, ed., *New Imperial History*, 125.

54. O'Brien, *Narratives of Enlightenment*, 3; Robert Mahew, "Mapping science's imagined community: geography as a Republic of Letters, 1600–1800," *British Journal of the History of Science* 38, 1 (2005), 73–95; Muthu, *Enlightenment Against Empire*.

55. Neil Safier, "Global Knowledge on the Move: Itineraries, Amerindian Narratives, and Deep Histories of Science," *Isis* 101 (2010): 133–145; Simon Schaffer et al., eds., *The Brokered World:* Susan Scott Parrish, "Diasporic African Sources of Enlightenment Knowledge," in Delbourgo and Dew, eds., *Science and Empire*, 281–310; Michael T. Bravo, "Ethnographic Navigation and the Geographical Gift," in Livingstone and Withers, eds., *Geography and Enlightenment*, 199–235; Raj, *Relocating Modern Science*, 60–94; Louis De Vorsey, Jr., "The Importance of Native American Maps in the Discovery and Exploration of North America," *Terrae Incognitae* 42 (2010): 5–17; G. Malcolm Lewis, ed., *Cartographic Encounters: Perspectives on Native American Mapmaking and Map Use* (Chicago: University of Chicago Press, 1998); John Rennie Short, *Cartographic Encounters: Indigenous People and the Exploration of the New World* (London: Reaktion Books, 2009).

56. Charles W. J. Withers, "Science at Sea: Charting the Gulf Stream in the Late Enlightenment," *Interdisciplinary Science Reviews* 31, 1 (2006), 66; Joyce E. Chaplin, "Knowing the Ocean: Benjamin Franklin and the Circulation of Atlantic

Knowledge," in Delbourgo and Dew, eds., *Science and Empire,* 73–96. See also Chaplin, *The First Scientific American: Benjamin Franklin and the Pursuit of Genius* (New York: Basic Books, 2006), esp. 196–200.

57. James Delbourgo and Nicholas Dew, "Introduction: The Far Side of the Ocean," in Delbourgo and Dew, eds., *Science and Empire,* 4.

58. William Reddy, *The Navigation of Feeling: A Framework for the History of Emotions* (Cambridge: Cambridge University Press, 2001), chaps 5–6, esp. 143.

59. Neil Safier, " 'Every day that I travel . . . is a page that I turn': Reading and Observing in Eighteenth-Century Amazonia," *Huntington Library Quarterly* 70, 1 (2007): 103.

60. Jonathan Lamb, *Preserving the Self in the South Seas, 1680–1840* (Chicago: University of Chicago Press 2001, 87; Michael Hanger, "Enlightened Monsters," in William Clark, Jan Golinski, and Simon Schaffer, eds., *The Sciences in Enlightened Europe* (Chicago: University of Chicago Press, 1999),

61. Quoted by Michael Dettelbach, "The Stimulations of Travel: Humboldt's Physiological Construction of the Tropics," in Driver and Martins, eds., *Tropical Visions,* 52.

62. Dettelbach, "The Stimulations of Travel," 43–58, quote on 58; Dettelbach, "Alexander Von Humboldt Between Enlightenment and Romanticism," *Northeastern Naturalist* 1 (2001), 9–20. See also, Aaron Sachs, *Humboldt Current: Nineteenth-Century Exploration and the Roots of American Environmentalism* (New York: Penguin, 2006); Delbourgo and Dew, "Far Side of the Ocean," 4; Anne Marie Claire Godlewska, "From Enlightenment Vision to Modern Science? Humboldt's Visual Thinking," in Livingstone and Withers, eds., *Geography and Enlightenment,* 236–275; Godlewska, *Geography Unbound,* esp. 112, 119–127.

63. Ian J. Barrow, *Making History, Drawing Territory: British Mapping in India, c. 1756–1905* (New Delhi: Oxford University Press, 2003), 35–61.

64. Gillian Russell, "An 'entertainment of oddities': fashionable sociability and the Pacific in the 1770s," in Wilson, ed., *New Imperial History,* 48–70;

65. Paul Elliott, *Enlightenment, Modernity and Science: Geographies of Scientific Culture and Improvement in Georgian England* (London and New York: IB Tauris, 2010), 125.

66. Janet Browne, "Botany in the boudoir and garden: the Banksian context," in Miller and Reill, eds., *Visions of Empire,* 153.

67. Gascoigne, *Joseph Banks and the English Enlightenment,* 70.

68. Lorraine Daston, "Afterward: The Ethos of Enlightenment," in Clark, Golinski, and Schaffer, eds., *Sciences,* 495–504.

69. Livingstone, *Geographical Tradition,* chap 5.

70. Daniel Carey, "Travel, Geography, and the Problem of Belief: Locke as a Reader of Travel Literature," in Julia Rudolph, ed., *History and Nation* (Lewisburg, Pa.: Bucknell University Press, 2006), 98.

71. Richard B. Sher, *The Enlightenment & The Book: Scottish Authors & Their Publishers in Eighteenth-Century Britain, Ireland, & America* (Chicago: University of Chicago Press, 2006), 77.

72. Dorinda Outram, "Cross-Cultural Encounters in the Enlightenment," in Martin Fitzpatrick, et al., eds., *The Enlightenment World* (New York: Routledge, 2004), 561; Charles W. J. Withers, "Geography, Enlightenment, and the Book: Authorship and Audience in Mungo Park's African Texts," in Miles Ogborn and Charles W. J. Withers, eds., *Geographies of the Book* (Farnham: Ashgate, 2010), 199.

73. Joseph Banks to William Philp Perrin, Dec. 1, 1768 in Neil Chambers, ed., *The Indian and Pacific Correspondence of Sir Joseph Banks*, vol. I. (London: Pickering & Chatto, 2008), 35; Lamb, *Preserving the Self,* 105–106.

74. Patricia Fara, *Sex, Botany & Empire: The Story of Carl Linnaeus and Joseph Banks* (Cambridge: Icon, 2003).

75. See, among other essays in the volume, Sarree Makdisi and Felicity Nussbaum, "Introduction," in Sarree Makdisi and Felicity Nussbaum eds., *The Arabian Nights in Historical Context: Between East and West* (Oxford: Oxford University Press, 2008), esp. 4, 21; Suzanne Rodin Pucci, "The discrete charms of the exotic: fictions of the harem in eighteenth-century France," in Rousseau and Porter, eds., *Exoticism in the Enlightenment*, 145–174; Joanna de Groot, "Oriental Feminotopias? Montagu's and Montesquieu's 'Seraglios' Revisited," *Gender and History* 18, 1 (2006): 66–86.

76. Karen Harvey, "Spaces of Erotic Delight," in Miles Ogborn and Charles W. J. Withers, eds., *Georgian Geographies: Essays on Space, Place, and Landscape in the Eighteenth Century* (Manchester: Manchester University Press, 2004), 131–132.

77. Roy Porter, "The Exotic as Erotic: Captain Cook at Tahiti," in Rousseau and Porter, eds., *Exoticism in the Enlightenment,* 117–144; Kathleen Wilson, *The Island Race; Englishness, Empire and Gender in the Eighteenth Century* (London: Routledge, 2003), 200.

78. Alan Bewell, " 'On the Banks of the South Sea': botany and sexual controversy in the late eighteenth century," in Miller and Reill, eds., *Visions of Empire,* 181.

79. Cañizares-Esguerra, *History of the New World,* 14; Lamb, *Preserving the Self,* 83, 86–87; Neil Safier, *Measuring the New World: Enlightenment Science and South America* (Chicago: University of Chicago Press 2008), 10.

80. Miriam Estensen, *The Life of George Bass: Surgeon and Sailor of the Enlightenment* (London: National Maritime Museum, 2005); Withers, "Geography, Enlightenment, and the Book," 195.

81. Lamb, *Preserving the Self,* 81; Lamb, "Eye-Witnessing the South Seas," *The Eighteenth Century: Theory and Interpretation* 28 (1997), 201–228; Dorinda Outram, "On Being Perseus: New Knowledge, Dislocation, and Enlightenment Exploration," in Livingstone and Withers, eds., *Geography and Enlightenment*; Charles W. J. Withers, "Mapping the Niger, 1798–1832: Trust, Testimony, and 'Ocular Demonstration' in the Late Enlightenment," *Imago Mundi* 56, 2 (2004): 170–193; Wilson, *Island Race*, 172; Andrew Lewis, *A Democracy of Facts: Natural History in the Early Republic* (Philadelphia: University of Pennsylvania, 2011).

82. Michael T. Bravo, "Precision and Curiosity," 170.

83. Shannon Lee Dawdy, "Enlightenment from the Ground: Le Page du Pratz's *Histoire de la Louisiane*," *French Colonial History* 3 (2003): 19–21.

84. Richard Sorrenson, "The Ship as a Scientific Instrument in the Eighteenth Century," *Osiris* 11 (1996); Daniela Bleichmar, *Visible Empire: Colonial Botany and Visual Culture in the Eighteenth-Century Hispanic World* (Chicago: University of Chicago Press, 2012); Bleichmar, "Visible Empire," 441–466; Carol E. Harrison, "Projections," 43.

85. Muthu, *Enlightenment Against Empire*, 32; Safier, *Measuring the New World*, 11; Larry Wolff, "The Global Perspective of Enlightened Travelers: Philosophic Geography from Siberia to the Pacific Ocean," *European Review of History* 13, 3 (2006): 438–439; Schaffer, "On Seeing Me Write," 101–102.

86. Harry Liebersohn, "Patrons, Travelers, and Scientific World Voyages, 1750–1850." Paper presented at Seascapes, Littoral Cultures, and Trans-Oceanic Exchanges, Library of Congress, Washington, D.C., February 12–15, 2003. http://webdoc.sub.gwdg.de/ebook/p/2005/history_cooperative/www.historycooperative.org/proceedings/seascapes/liebersohn.html.

87. Koelsch, "Thomas Jefferson," 266; Martin Brückner, *The Geographic Revolution in Early America: Maps, Literacy, and National Identity* (Chapel Hill: Omohundro Institute and University of North Carolina Press, 2006), 215, 217–218.

88. Safier, *Measuring the New World,* esp. chaps 3–5.

89. Neil Safier, " ' . . . To Collect and Abridge . . . Without Changing Anything Essential': Rewriting Incan History at the Parisian Jardin du Roi," *Book History* 7 (2004): 65; Tom Ryan, " 'Le Président des Terres Australes,': Charles de Brosses and the French Enlightenment Beginnings of Oceanic Anthropology," *The Journal of Pacific History* 37, 2 (2002): 157–186; Cañizares-Esguerra, *History of the New World,* esp. 22–26.

90. *The Travels of Hildebrand Bowman, Esquire, Into Carnovirria, Taupiniera, Olfactaria, and Auditante, in New-Zealand, In the Island of Bonhommica, and in the Powerful Kingdom of Luxo-Volupto, on the Great Southern Continent* (London, 1778).

91. Withers, *Placing the Enlightenment,* 11; Carla Hesse, "Print Culture in the Enlightenment," in Martin Fitzpatrick, et al., eds., *The Enlightenment World* (New York: Routledge, 2004), 368.

92. Lamb, *Preserving the Self,* 101.

93. Carter, *Road to Botany Bay,* 73–74.

94. Park quoted by Withers, "Geography, Enlightenment, and the Book," 208–209; Stern, "Rescuing the Age," 128–132; Tim Fulford, Debbie Lee, and Peter J. Kitson, *Literature, Science, and Exploration in the Romantic Era: Bodies of Knowledge* (Cambridge: Cambridge University Press, 2004), chap. 4.

95. Jorge Cañizares-Esguerra, "How Derivative Was Humboldt? Microcosmic Nature Narratives in Early Modern Spanish America and the (Other) Origins of Humboldt's Ecological Sensibilities," in Londa Schiebinger and Claudia Swan,

eds., *Colonial Botany: Science, Commerce, and Politics in the Early Modern World* (Philadelphia: University of Pennsylvania, 2005), 149, 164.

96. Glyndwr Williams, *Voyages of Delusion: The Quest for the Northwest Passage* (New Haven, Conn.: Yale University Press, 2002).

97. D. Graham Burnett, *Masters of All They Surveyed: Exploration, Geography, and a British El Dorado* (Chicago: University of Chicago Press, 2000).

98. See, among others, Mahew, *Enlightenment Geography,* 204–206, and "Geography as the Eye of Enlightenment Historiography," *Modern Intellectual History* 7, 3 (2010): 611–627; David Arnold, *The Tropics and the Traveling Gaze: India, Landscape, and Science, 1800–1856* (Seattle: University of Washington Press, 2006), 116.

99. Edney, *Mapping an Empire,* 157, 229; Bravo, "Precision and Curiosity," 181–182; Thomas J. Bassett and Philip W. Porter, " 'From the Best Authorities': The Mountains of Kong in the Cartography of West Africa," *Journal of African History* 32 (1991): 367–413.

100. John Hawkesworth, *An Account of the Voyages Undertaken by the Order of His Present Majesty for Making Discoveries in the Southern Hemisphere*, 2d ed., 3 vols (London, 1773), preface to second edition. Partially quoted by Jonathan Lamb, *Preserving the Self in the South Seas, 1680–1840* (Chicago: University of Chicago Press, 2001), 90. For Dalrymple's accusations, see Alexander Dalrymple, *A Letter from Mr. Dalrymple to Dr. Hawkesworth, Occasioned By Some Groundless and Illiberal Imputations in his Account of the Late Voyages to the South* (London, 1773), l; Alexander Dalrymple, *Mr. Dalrymple's Observations on Dr. Hawkesworth's Preface to the Second Edition* (London, 1773), 2–3.

4

EXPLORATION IN PRINT: FROM THE MISCELLANY TO THE NEWSPAPER

CLARE PETTITT

Cutting and Pasting

Sometime in the late 1870s, Ellen Mary Lotham carefully cut out an image from an illustrated paper and glued it with flour-and-water paste onto the inside back cover of her Scrap Album[1] (see Figure 4.1). Next to it was a picture of the head of a large dog, and below it, a composite group of pictures of well-dressed children and babies stuck one on top of another. The facing page was decorated with an illustration from a magazine story, more children and babies, and a couple, a man and woman, "montaged" on the page from two different printed sources. Much of the rest of Ellen's album is peopled with trim ladies cut from the fashion plates and then carefully water-colored, and color-lithographed greetings cards marking Christmases, the turn of the year, and birthdays.

The image was an engraving from a studio photograph of Henry Morton Stanley, the celebrated explorer of Africa, and the African Kalulu, who was described in Madame Tussaud's London waxwork exhibition catalogue of 1879 as "[a] favourite African Attendant of Mr. H. M. Stanley."[2] Kalulu was a slave-boy whom Stanley bought and freed to be his personal servant on his first African expedition of 1871. That printed images of Stanley and Kalulu were chosen to be cut out and pasted into this album from the sheaf of old periodicals, *cartes de visites*, topographical views, and used greetings cards available to an unexceptional young scrap collector in the 1870s can perhaps reveal something important not only about the circulation of print and its relationship to celebrity in the latter half of the nineteenth century,

Figure 4.1 A page from Ellen Mary Lotham's scrap album

but also about the importance of new print culture forms to the representation of travel and exploration in this period.

This chapter focuses on two explorers who published prolifically and were famous in their lifetimes: Basil Hall and Henry Morton Stanley. While Basil Hall's travel writing was much excerpted in the monthly and weekly miscellanies of the early nineteenth century, at the end of the century Stanley's narratives of his African explorations were serialized in daily newspapers. This chapter brings recent work on book and media history to bear on the history of exploration and argues that close attention to the materiality of print reveals how closely the genres of narrative exploration were determined by the forms in which they were first published. Thinking more precisely about the development of forms of travel writing in this period means exploring changing forms of print more deeply. The term "print culture"could grow even more generous in its embrace of the many ways in which any printed matter was used, played with, commented on, passed around, written over, saved, glued into albums, pinned on the wall, or thrown out. By the late nineteenth century, print culture was already extending into the unexceptional medium it is today—a kind of print "eco-sphere" absent mindedly inhabited by a largely literate public—but it was also still new enough to be appropriated in intense and particular practices: print culture could still be something one *did*, too. That explorers were among the first to

be accorded a modern celebrity status has a great deal to do with the reportage of their travels in the press, and particularly in the illustrated press.
In the later part of the nineteenth century, their much-reproduced images
became accessible and identifiable from the bewildering mass of available material. A scrapbook is a haphazard form, but what it catches is not
entirely random. The visibility of exploration in the press made it a subject
for scrapbooking and for conversation in households across Britain. Ellen's
scrapbook gives us a glimpse of the kinds of participative readership invited
by exploration writing, models of readership that, as this chapter argues,
were increasingly to be encoded in emerging news rhythms and celebrity
culture as the nineteenth century progressed.

Exploration Narrative and Active Reading

Literary critic Ellen Gruber Garvey reminds us that "[t]he scrapbook was
often understood as a liminal form between book and newspaper, and making scrapbooks was described in nineteenth-century books and articles on
the subject as taking place on the border between reading and authoring."[3]
The "border between reading and authoring" was critical to the popularity of exploration narratives and therefore to the celebrity of travelers and
explorers in the nineteenth century in ways not yet fully grasped. Travel
historians Peter Hulme and Tim Youngs gesture toward this when they
point out that forgery and parody are always close to travel writing and
remind us that some of the greatest travel books are fictions: Mandeville's
Travels; Moore's *Utopia*; Swift's *Gulliver's Travels*; Verne's *Around the
World in Eighty Days*; Conrad's *Heart of Darkness*: they go so far as to
identify a "feedback loop" by which these fictionalized travels have influenced the forms of the narratives of actual explorers.[4] Historical geographer
Felix Driver's work has gone further in its attention to the unsettlement of
generic and disciplinary boundaries in texts generated by explorers: "[i]
t is not that boundaries do not exist between, say, scientific exploration
and adventurous travel, the sober and the sensational, or the analytical and
the aesthetic," he tells us: "It is just that these boundaries are always in
the process of construction."[5] This chapter considers this unsettlement of
boundaries both in the writing generated by explorers themselves and in the
ways in which the circulation of text and image worked further to undo the
specificities of analytical, empirical, and scientific accounts of exploration.
It argues that by that very undoing, the experience of distance, travel, and
discovery was opened up in ways that made the form of these exploration

accounts oddly porous and appropriable by their readers, who could participate alongside the narrator in a distinctly contemporary relation with the narrative. Margaret Cohen, in *The Novel and the Sea*, reads sea fiction as a subset of "adventure fiction," narratives she defines as offering their readers a "romance of practice," inviting the reader's armchair participation in the "performance of craft"and problem solving.[6] A similar case can be made for exploration narrative within the context of ephemeral print culture. In a time of burgeoning news media, explorers became "events" to be consumed and shared. If Stanley and Kalulu initially seem anomalous glued into a scrapbook next to a fashion model—if it seems at first that they inhabit an entirely different world—the scrapbook itself proves that they do not. They are in fashion too, co-opted into the mixed and cosmopolitan company of its pages, "date stamped" in media historian Margaret Beetham's phrase, and topical like the Christmas, birthday, and the new season's fashions that will soon be the last season's fashions.[7] The scrapbook works to fix the ephemeral, to solidify a moment of "news" into a memorialization or a souvenir, and to place it in dialogue with a miscellany of other competing events. These albums form a record of the consumption of time: both the time spent carefully cutting out, arranging, pasting, and water-coloring, and "news time": the insistently renewable ongoing present of the news and novelty glued down to make a conversation piece and to survive into posterity, in James Secord's words, as "a tangible memorial of wider networks of sociability."[8]

In her imaginative excavation of the Victorian parlor, Thad Logan includes the scrapbook and the album of "foreign views" as among "the objects likely to be found on a typical lamplit table at the center of the parlour, objects that often seem to speak of a longing to explore the world from the safety of home."[9] Print culture surely undid distance and opened up exploration from the parlor armchair, but the scrap albums are not quite as passive and quiet as Logan suggests. Ellen's scrapbook also contains pictures of St. Petersburg, Vienna, Moscow, and London, a print of a giraffe, and a pen-and-ink drawing of a cockatoo, possibly copied by Ellen herself; an elaborately detailed illustration of a well-stocked aquarium in a conservatory; and a picture, colored by Ellen, of the American celebrity preachers Ira Sankey and Dwight Moody who had visited Britain in 1875: her album does not express her "longing" to explore the world, but rather enacts her colorful exploration of it: the ever rising tide of print and news culture together washing the whole world into Ellen Lotham's possible present experience.The nineteenth-century scrapbook does not, like the polite book of picturesque engravings of the previous century, articulate an aesthetic

of distance, but rather a jostling and noisy hubbub of contemporaneous-
ness, a sense of a lot of things happening on the same page at the same
time. Looking through Ellen Lotham's scrapbook does not leave one with
an impression of her longing for distant places and scenes, but rather of her
confidence that those distant places and scenes were available all around
her, merely a scissor-snip away.

Child's Play and Print Culture

In a "literally true" passage of his autobiographical novel, *David Copperfield*,
Charles Dickens remembers his early life at Chatham and the:

> small collection of books in a little room upstairs . . . I had a greedy relish
> for a few volumes of Voyages and Travels—I forget what now—that were
> on those shelves; and for days and days I remember to have gone about my
> region of our house armed with the centrepiece of an old set of boot-trees—
> the perfect realisation of Captain Somebody, of the Royal British Navy, in
> danger of being beset by savages, and resolved to sell his life at a great price.[10]

Around the same time, at the Brontë parsonage in Haworth, Yorkshire, the
children of Patrick Brontë played with toy soldiers, using them to reenact
the voyages and explorations they read about in their father's copies of
Blackwood's Magazine. They wrote the stories of their "Young Men" into
the "Glass Town Saga". While Charlotte made her toy soldier the Duke
of Wellington, and "Branwell chose Bonaparte," Emily and Anne, after
some deliberation, chose to make their soldiers into Sir William Parry and
Sir John Ross, the famous Arctic explorers.[11] The children were following
the account of the polar adventures of Parry and Ross reported through a
series of letters in *Blackwood's*, which lent it an exciting "up to the minute"
quality:

> [s]ince the preceding intelligence was printed, intelligence has been received
> of the arrival of the Isabella and the Alexander, under the command of Captain
> Ross and Lieutenant Parry . . . . [t]hey discovered a savage tribe of Esquimaux
> Indians who regarded the ship, as an animal, and its crew as people who had
> descended from the moon. They were only about *five* feet high and seemed
> never to have seen any other people but themselves.[12]

Blackwood's was also reviewing and reprinting extracts from the posthumously published African adventures of Mungo Park in the late 1820s,
inspiring the children to make their ninepins into Africans and to enact

complicated narratives of imperial discovery and expansion on their nursery floor. These stories they then wrote up into narratives of their own and
"published" in a series of miniature journals, painstakingly sewn together
and "written in a tiny script designed to look as much like print as possible."[13]

The children of Haworth parsonage did not read passively, but re-created
and republished their reading in a "print medium" of their own. The Glass
Town stories are fantastical fictions, but they are held oddly in the frame of
"fact" by the format of their tiny "Young Men's Magazine" with its con-
tents page, front matter, and careful serial dating. In their sustained response
to *Blackwood's*, the Brontë children exploited the slipperiness between fact
and fiction in exploration narratives. And indeed the stories of "real" travelers were often confounded with fictional adventurers. "For weeks after
reading [*Robinson Crusoe*]," remembered the poet, Laetitia Landon:

> I lived as if in a dream, indeed I rarely dreamt of anything else at night, I went
> to sleep with the cave, its parrots and goats, floating before my closed eyes;
> I wakened in some rapid flight from the savages landing in their canoes. The
> elms in our own hedges were not more familiar than the prickly hedges which
> formed his palisade.[14]

Although by 1889, *Blackwood's* is bemoaning the demise of *Robinson
Crusoe* as every child's favorite travel book, and sighing "[n]owadays boy-
thought starts with Phileas Fogg for a trip 'Round the World in 80 Days',"
it is still clear that travel narratives, factual or fictional, continued to inspire
young readers.[15] Looking back to her childhood in the 1860s, Edith Fowler
used Stanley's famous description of Africa to remember, "the great dark
continent of the night nursery, with its tent for explorers made out of the
curtains of nurse's bed."[16]

Literary historian Leah Price has commented that "any simple opposition between productive writers and passive readers has given way to a
new consensus that readers make meaning."[17] Adults also seem to have participated in fictional and factual accounts of exploration in ways that seem
far from passive. At the end of the nineteenth century, coalminer Percy
Wall borrowed books from his Colliery Institute reading room in his Welsh
village, delighted by the experiences they opened up to him: "I could . . .
penetrate darkest Africa with Rider Haggard as my guide."[18] While adventure fiction and exploration narratives generally assumed a male reader, it
is clear from the examples above that they attracted as many female readers as male ones. Literary historian Kate Flint has shown that girl readers
preferred the adventure-heavy *Boy's Own Paper,* which serialized Stanley's
African explorations, to the anodyne *Girl's Own*.[19] The print culture of

travel and exploration in the nineteenth century, then, far from being consumed passively as objective reportage from hazily distant places, was more often appropriated, inhabited, and imaginatively reconstructed in peculiarly active and vivid ways by both adult and child readers. It was this level of active readerly participation that helped the emergence of the modern category of "celebrity" in the period, an emergence that has often been attributed to the growth of "the media" alone.[20] Celebrity is created not by mere media representation, but rather by a process of embedding by its viewers and readers into the rhythms of their own daily lives. Literary historian Leo Braudy noticed some time ago that, "[i]nstead of passively responding to its idols," the audience "takes an active role in defining them."[21] Travel and explorer narratives are particularly permeable to this appropriative style of reading due to their ambivalent status as witness reports: they waver between fact and fiction.

Fact and Fiction in Print

The sometimes uncomfortable proximity of fact and fiction, of lies and truth, and of exaggeration and reportage encountered in travel writing makes it a curiously porous form. Print culture, of course, provided a very practical help to explorers, enabling them to report, record, and authenticate their discoveries to much wider and more diverse audiences than had previously been possible, and thereby to profit from them, and to recruit others too. The Royal Geographical Society published *Hints to Travellers* in 1854, and "[t]hose travelling outside the British sphere were instructed to send out frequent dispatches, including tracings of maps, to preserve their work from accidents."[22] The process by which the manuscripts and sketches, water colors, scribbled notebooks and disorderly scraps of paper sent back by explorers were rendered into coherent printed accounts has been helpfully discussed elsewhere, for example by historian Leila Koivunen, whose work on illustrations in travel books in this period suggests that these "were neither exact documents of what travelers had witnessed, nor of what they had recorded by visual means" but instead "the result of a long construction process, which, in many respects, resembled the editing of texts for publication, but included an even greater variety of different stages and persons."[23]

Over the nineteenth century, the exploration narrative came to stand as a test case for the wider problems of authenticating facts in news journalism. The explorer's undoing of distance, his or her transparent mediation of "fact", drew attention to the way in which all travel writing performs *mediation* in a startlingly obvious way. Because the travel writer describes places generally remote and unknown to the reader, she or he is required to mediate this information in a peculiarly conspicuous way. The reader is forced to rely on the accurate transmission of information through the instrument of the traveler with no corroboration. Like all forms of mediation, this generated problematic issues of trust and authenticity. The explorer in print culture is an archetypally modern figure because she or he highlights the problem of representation, and the ultimate unverifiability of most facts for most readers. It is no coincidence that, by the end of the century, novelist Joseph Conrad was to make many of his most fascinatingly unreliable narrators explorers and travelers. As historians Barbara Shapiro, Steven Shapin, and Adrian Johns have each shown, from the early modern period onward, trust was becoming an unspoken foundation for factual knowledge.[24] Shapin suggests that the community of reliable witnesses for scientific experiment started as rather a closed one, confined to those with gentlemanly status. But the "facts" of natural history or ethnography were often reported by people who were not gentlemen-scientists and therefore they remained something of an epistemological problem. This held true for explorers too. Slavery abolitionist Horace Waller, for example, described Stanley, who was not considered a gentleman-explorer, as "utterly unworthy of credence."[25] As modern news culture developed, what sociologist Niklas Luhmann has called "second-order observation" came into being—the reading public, at a distance from events, had to rely on "experts" for their interpretation and the public had to learn to trust both its explorers and its journalists.[26] This awkward negotiation of trust was already underway in the Georgian period. One contemporary reader of the explorer Basil Hall's adventures in Loo Choo remarked, "I shrewdly suspect that the author gives his subject much extra-colouring, and no small quantity of ingenious exaggeration."[27]

News culture more generally was engaged in an energetic attempt to define itself as fact-driven. In fact, the early-modern trade of crying the news and touting broadsheets had not been entirely overtaken by newspaper trade even by the mid-nineteenth century, when journalist and social campaigner Henry Mayhew interviewed a hawker of broadsheets on the London streets who, "told me that in the last eight or ten years, he . . . had twice put the Duke of Wellington to death, once by a fall from his horse, and the other time a 'sudden and myst-*erious* [*sic*] death', without any condescension to particulars."[28] Then, as now, it was not a good idea to believe everything in print, and some kinds of publications were more credible than others. Then, as now, people thoroughly enjoyed novelties and striking facts, even if they were not convinced they were necessarily fully true. Part of the pleasure of reading travel writing is its marginal association with the realm of the known and epistemologically sound: it is always trembling on the border between wonder and knowledge.

Book History and Exploration in Print

While it is possible to chart the move of the exploration narrative in print from an eighteenth-century model of polite sociability into nineteenth-century mass news culture, it is also possible to suggest that older models of miscellaneity and sociability persisted even in the modern news media at the beginning of the twentieth century. Historian Rolf Engelsing's famous moralized narrative of a "fall" in the late eighteenth century from the intensive reading of a few texts to the skimming and skipping of a shallow ephemeral modern print culture has been extensively challenged by book historians who have argued that this merely dramatizes a conservative distaste for modern mass culture.[29] Niklas Luhmann has retorted that "[i]t is most assuredly incorrect to characterize modern society as an impersonal mass society," suggesting that it is important to seek to keep in view the ways in which individual and particular readers might have interacted with texts at particular times and in particular locations.[30]

While Felix Driver and others rightly see generic and disciplinary boundaries as under construction throughout the nineteenth century in a progressive narrative of institutionalization and professional formation, it might be more helpful for the purposes of this chapter to think of these boundaries as under tireless de-construction, constantly dissolved and eroded by the backwash of the ocean of expanding media. Over the last twenty-five years or so, what has become known as "book history" has exerted ever greater influence over humanities subjects. Literary scholars and historians have moved away from a simple model of the circulation of knowledge by a process of "trickle-down" from elite to so-called "popular" culture and have started to reconceptualize the movement of ideas in far more complex and sophisticated ways.[31] A focus on practice and on the materiality of text has brought into view the ways in which playing with, cutting or tearing out, puzzling over, collecting, or sharing printed matter might have altered and affected its meanings for different readership groups. Starting perhaps with the groundbreaking work of book historians Robert Darnton and Roger Chartier, it has become possible to understand the ways in which, as Darnton put it in 1984, "[c]ultural currents intermingled, moving up as well as down, while passing through different media and connecting groups as far apart as peasants and salon sophisticates."[32] While Darnton is concerned with the complexity of a multi-nodal cultural network, Roger Chartier's definition of "popular" stresses individual practice and the ways in which people make use of what is available to them—for Chartier "the popular qualifies a kind of relation, *a way of using* cultural products such as legitimate ideas and attitudes . . . [we need to look at] the specific ways in which such cultural sets are appropriated."[33] [emphasis added] A full account of exploration in print culture would therefore involve attention not only to the texts themselves but also to the uses to which they were put by different constituencies in conversation, in play, for display, and in other genres in which identity was written and performed. Such an account would require attention to resistant as well as appropriative reading.[34]

Material Form and Genre: Basil Hall and Henry Morton Stanley

In order to test some of these ideas, two well-known explorers at either end of the nineteenth century, Basil Hall and Henry Morton Stanley, provide contrasting case studies. When their print histories are compared, it becomes clear that changes in the material form and layout of text over a period of seventy years or so had a highly determinative effect upon the changing form of travel writing itself. Over this seventy-year period, too, a recognizably modern version of "celebrity" can be seen developing.[35] The well-known explorer and Naval Captain, Sir Basil Hall, published accounts of his journeys under titles such as *Fragments* and *Patchwork*, and they were frequently chopped up and reprinted in miscellanies, anthologies, and the monthly and weekly magazines in the 1820s and early 1830s. Yet Basil Hall never became a celebrity in the way in which Henry Morton Stanley was to be by the end of the nineteenth century. Why? The difference might be between the monthly and the daily rhythm, between the miscellany and the serial narrative, between topicality and news. An ever-expanding daily news media intensified the experience of personal connection with celebrity "events." Stanley's travel narratives both fed off and helped to sustain the serial logic of newspapers in the later period: particular forms of ephemeral print culture were critical to making media events out of discoveries, and, later, by transforming personalities into "events" too. Literary historian Mark Turner is right that, "[t]he periodical-ness of periodicals requires us to think not only about the material object more closely but also about the conceptual challenges offered by those objects."[36] The development from miscellany to popular newspaper has important implications for the developing form of travel writing. In the miscellany or weekly magazine of the 1820s or 1830s, extracts from Hall were detached both from the body of his work and from any clear chronology of travel, and were reprinted as self-contained "blazons," offering "useful" or "picturesque" information descriptive of some remote custom or country, invariably presented in the past tense. But in the daily newspaper, Stanley's narratives were just that: narratives, which placed himself and his own body at the center of an experience that unfolded in a carefully logged chronological time. Much of his narrative used the historic present tense as if it was directly reprinted from the log books and journals he kept on the journey. By the end of the century, a proliferating print culture predicated on a logic of seriality meant that the same personality-event could be repeatedly encountered, engendering a sense of familiarity through and across time. Victorian celebrity was thus created in print culture through networks of mediated sociability that simulated the structures of familiarity and recognition like those that usually underlay patterns of friendship. In order to do this, celebrity crucially depended upon the new structures of time generated by the media. Bibles, recipe books, scientific papers, reference works of all kinds, as well as fiction were serialized in this period. If the second half of the nineteenth century witnessed the serialization of everyday experience, this was both inculcated and reflected by a proliferating print culture of serialization.[37]

Basil Hall: Miscellaneous Adventures

On a walking tour in Wales in the 1830s, John Walker Ord found himself in want of something to read and so repaired to the local circulating library, which, he discovered, "contained what every library in the British Empire boasts of, viz. some of Sir Walter Scott's novels, also . . . the Arabian Nights Entertainments, with some of Basil Hall's entertaining voyages."[38] From the 1820s to the 1840s, it seems that it was difficult to avoid some acquaintance with the extensive writings of Basil Hall (1788–1844), naval officer and popular author, whose "manly, unaffected style—rough but racy"— enlivened his accounts of his many voyages.[39] These accounts, although they first appeared in volume form, were also variously excerpted, serialized, pirated, anthologized, and reprinted in both the high-end and the cheap periodical press.[40] Hall's books were passed around artisans' reading circles in pubs and taverns, and on the shelves of Mechanics' Institute libraries and provincial circulating libraries across the land.[41]

Hall's first published exploration narrative was his celebrated *Account of a Voyage of Discovery to the West Coast of Corea and the Great Loo-Choo Islands* (1818) which John Ord describes as "a strange anomoly, [*sic*] but exceedingly interesting."[42] Hall went on to publish accounts of his travels in Chile, Peru, and Mexico. Anomalous his travels may have seemed, but no less a figure than natural philosopher John Herschel cited Hall as an example of "impressive" scientific practice. Herschel admiringly describes Hall's reliance on astronomical observations alone for his navigation of an 8,000-mile voyage from the west coast of Mexico, around Cape Horn to Rio de Janeiro during which no land was sighted for three months.[43] At Rio de Janeiro and at the Galápagos, Hall had carried out a series of geophysical pendulum observations, the account of which was published in the *Philosophical Transactions of the Royal Society*.[44] In America, Ralph Waldo Emerson included him as an example of the new empiricism when he announced that: "Malthus and Basil Hall, Humboldt and Herschel have arrived," to sweep away a "sky full of cobwebs."[45] Yet Basil Hall was also described as a "distinguished ornament" of "the world of literature."[46] He seems to have occupied an awkward territory between naval officer, popular writer, explorer, scientist, and adventurer: between ornament and philosopher, as much read by ladies as by men, particularly by "the ladies who have learnt their Ologies . . . [and] who think Captain Basil Hall a greater man than Cook, Frobisher and Raleigh united."[47] Walter Scott wrote to his friend, Lady Abercorn, in 1824 that "I can easily conceive your Ladyship must have been amused with [reading] Basil Hall, and struck with the very direct and almost abrupt mode in which he always prosecutes the object of his inquiry."[48]

Hall's life enacts perfectly the symbiotic relationship between exploration and print in the Georgian period as he was a founder of both Lord Brougham's cheap-publishing venture, the Society for the Diffusion of Useful Knowledge (SDUK), and a member of its Committee formed in 1827, and then three years later he helped to found the Royal Geographical Society (RGS), serving on its first Council.[49] By 1830, the SDUK was far from alone in the field of "popular" publishing. According to the literary correspondent of the *Ladies' Museum* in October 1830, "the 'Libraries,' as they are called, are becoming . . . manifold and numberless." The "Libraries" were series of selected titles reissued by publishers in cheap editions, such as that which Dickens's father bought. The very first book published in the cheap *Constable's Miscellany* series was Hall's *Loo Choo*, in response to "the unlimited desire for knowledge that now pervades every class of society."[50] By 1845, excerpts from Hall's explorations had become a regular feature in children's reading primers in Britain and America.[51]

The long series of nine volumes of *Fragments* (three series of three volumes), which Hall published between 1831 and 1833, presented a "variety of miscellaneous incidents and adventures in the peninsula of India, Ceylon, and Borneo." The fragments were well named, as each episode was short and compact, as one reviewer remarked: "we suspect that its very diminutiveness will recommend it; for an idler, in a few hours reading, may acquire from Capt. Hall's sketch, a better notion of the various topics connected with India, than from works in which a greater breadth of discussion is given to them."[52] The *Spectator* described *Fragments* as "a kind of Autobiographical Miscellany," and Hall's miscellaneous style of authorship is further exemplified in his aptly named *Patchwork*, a series of brief sketches of France, Italy, and Switzerland.[53] "Fragments" and "patchworks" are non-diachronic frames that encompass selections from many different time registers. Similarly, "miscellanies" evoke an Enlightenment trans-historical model of description. They present not time-sensitive "events" arranged with reference to an historical or chronological index, but rather a collection of detached observations and static "facts." The anthologizing of the miscellany is also non-territorial: it selects and collects while evincing no desire to stay around in any particular place, or to settle in, or to inhabit any particular excerpt. Its borrowings from diverse sources preclude any clear editorial "position" or space.

Miscellaneity was traditionally both a feature of travel writing and a challenge to it. Shaftesbury had warned travelers against becoming too fixated on every detail of the places they explored and had warned readers against being too much captured by the romance and melodrama of "the monstrous birth, the horrid fact, or dire event" in faraway places.[54] The problem of how to create narrative shape from the wandering and often repetitive picaresque experience of travel was an old one. Michael McKeon's work on the origins of the novel focuses on the new scientific methods in natural history: "[t]he demand for quantitative completeness in narrative was, of course, entirely consistent with the Baconian method and the ideal 'natural history' which encouraged, as Michael Hunter points out, 'indiscriminate collecting of information relevant to no particular hypothesis.'"[55] From the very beginning, the explorer who sat down to write a narrative of his or her travels had been faced with dilemmas of selection and the impossibility of comprehensiveness.

The "minuteness" with which Basil Hall rendered each incident or detail lent itself well to extraction and reprinting in the miscellanies of the 1820s and 1830s.[56] The *Mirror*, for example, a two-penny illustrated weekly which launched in 1822, shamelessly "shared" extracts from the more expensive quarterlies.[57] Basil Hall's work frequently provided the weekly with short descriptions, such as that of "An American Stagecoach," "Franklin's Grave," or of an "Indian Palankeen" (a kind of sedan chair). Sometimes the extracts were lent topicality: in 1834, a *Mirror* article called "Recent Earthquake in Peru" resurrected Hall's descriptions of Peru from 1823. At other times the pieces were generalized, so that, for example, a story about the Chinese fishermen's practice of frightening fish with a loud gong to force them into nets, was reprinted on two separate occasions, the second time under the rather grand title "On the Effects of Music on Man and Animals." In the first half of the eighteenth century, historian Barbara Benedict has noticed that, "[m]iscellanies seem designed for an audience who are lured by the marvelous, the new, and the usefully religious," and Jon Klancher describes the *Mirror* as firmly in this tradition, as made up of "discontinuous shards with no visible principle of continuity."[58] But the *Mirror* is important in the history of print culture for its updating of the miscellany form.[59] As literary historian Andrew Piper rightly claims, the miscellanies also "played an important role in marking the transition from the cyclicality to the seriality of cultural production that would become a hallmark of both nineteenth-century literature and twentieth-century mass media more generally."[60] While it retains some of the antiquarian variety and promiscuity of content over its twelve-year run, the *Mirror* also strained increasingly toward topicality and editorial direction.

The SDUK's *Penny Magazine,* which launched in 1832, also used extracts from Hall, either as picturesque "word-pictures," as his "Sun-Rise on Mount Etna"; or episodes from his travels, which are reprinted and generalized so that his account of talking to a peasant in Tuscany about salt production reappears under the heading "The Salt-Trade of Foreign Countries," or an article on "The Locomotion of Animals" quotes Hall's close and precise descriptions of flying fish.[61] Historian Barbara Shapiro is right that "[t]he history of 'news' and 'facts' cannot be separated from the 'wonders' and 'marvels' of the age," but in the cheap popular press of the first half of the nineteenth century, it is possible to see the transition from wonder to fact and, thereby, towards news.[62]

For example, "wonders" such as flying fish had once been considered the stuff of fantastic lies and travelers' tales, but in 1845 the *Penny Magazine* supplied illustrative diagrams to establish the seriousness and veracity of its article on "The Locomotion of Animals." At around the same time, novelist Elizabeth Gaskell in *Mary Barton* (1848) playfully used the flying fish

as proof of the sailor Will Wilson's truthfulness and not his mendacious-
ness: "What's the use, Mary, if folk won't believe one," sighs Will. "There
are things I saw with my own eyes, that some people would pish . . . .
This did stagger Mary. She had heard of mermaids as signs of inns and
as sea-wonders, but never of flying fish."[63] Gaskell is here slyly reflecting
an important shift in the epistemology of natural history: from the eighteenth century onwards, the Royal Society had been working to relocate
truth in the authority of the observer rather than in the force of tradition.[64]
Alongside this shift, travel writing was being deliberately recast as factual,
and not fictional: Job Legh, the working-class naturalist in Gaskell's novel,
recognizes the truth of Will's account of the flying fish at once.

The nineteenth-century miscellanies such as the *Mirror* and the *Penny
Magazine* were innovative in their presentation not of wonders, "horrid
fact or dire event," but of factual tidbits about life in other places and cultures that sat alongside domestic stories. Oddly though, the effect of all this
information gathered together on one page is not of simultaneity. Rather it
seems that many different, miscellaneous times are represented in the same
space. The monthlies and weekly miscellanies could not achieve the same
level of "temporal embedding" in their readers' lives nor the same sense
of a global simultaneity on one specific day that the daily newspaper press
would achieve by the end of the century. And Basil Hall himself was never
represented as the embodied mediator of his travels in the way that later
explorers would come to be in the daily press.

Henry Morton Stanley and Eventfulness

"Thank goodness I have nearly finished [Stanley's] 'Darkest Africa'" wrote
Charles Darwin's wife, Emma, in November 1890, "it must be the most
tiresome book in the world, so confused and diffuse, with immense long
conversations that end in nothing."[65] Like many others, Emma Darwin was
plowing through Stanley's latest book on the Emin Pasha Relief Expedition
not for its style or content, but because in the winter of 1890 it was required
reading for anyone who prided themselves on being up to date with the latest fashions.

At the end of *In Darkest Africa, or the Quest, Rescue, and Retreat of Emin
Governor of Equatoria*, Henry Morton Stanley (1841–1904) boasts about
how he hastily dashed off the book in fifty days in a hotel room in Cairo,
which may of course account for some of Emma Darwin's discomfort with
the finished text.[66] By 1890, Stanley was already an international celebrity.

Indeed, he was even followed to Cairo by his publisher, Edward Marston, who subsequently published a book about the writing and publication of Stanley's book.[67] Since 1871, when he had found the missionary-explorer David Livingstone in Ujiji in a stunt sponsored by the *New York Herald*, the ex-journalist explorer had maintained a strong presence in the press. Historian John MacKenzie notes that "Leibig's Extract of Meat Company seized upon the...expedition...issuing posters and adverts of members of the relief party revived by its product."[68] The United Tea Company had already used Stanley and Emin in advertisements followed by Bovril and Pears' Soap. Stanley's image endorsed Victor Vaissier's Congo soap, Keble's pipes, and Edgington's tents.[69] It is true that Basil Hall's face was drawn in pencil and sculpted in marble, and his portrait was engraved, but his image never reverberated through the print media as did Stanley's.[70] This was due in part, of course, to the "New Journalism" of the late nine-teenth century, itself supported by developments in printing technology that now made it possible cheaply to produce illustrations set into text, and to produce machine-colored images too. Literary historian James Mussell describes how the "New Journalism" "drew upon techniques from the American dailies, such as cross heads, interviews, bold headlines, illustra-tion, indices and specials."[71] The typography supported a distinctly modern form of address.The "New Journalism" interpellated a newly literate mass market with a studied familiarity, coopting the individual into the member-ship of its readership as if into a club. *In Darkest Africa*, the account and self-exculpation of Stanley's ill-managed Emin Pasha Relief Expedition caused a sensation. Stanley's correspondence reveals a "feeding frenzy" among publishers all trying to persuade him to repackage the book in dif-ferent ways for what was by now a highly segmented market. "I'm sure a *shilling book* would be a great success," wrote one, "with men of the working class."[72] He went on: "[t]here is at the present time a huge craving after anything and everything relating to central Africa, and with the strong interest created by Mr. Stanley's thrilling adventures."[73]

A "huge craving" "at the present time": Stanley and Africa were in fashion in 1890 in a way that would have astonished Basil Hall, who had died in 1844.[74] Stanley claims that he wrote *In Darkest Africa* so fast in response to reader demand, but of course the speed of writing was really all about creating precisely that demand.[75] Stanley understood very well the value of news: and he understood, too, that to keep himself in the news he needed to provide events upon which the press could fix stories. He made the speed-writing and publication of his book into an event. Similarly, the mix of science and sensation in the Stanley and Africa exhibition made an event of its opening in March 1890 in the Victoria Gallery on Regent Street. But what exactly was a news event in 1890 and how did it make the media coverage of Stanley's explorations different from that of Basil Hall?

A century before the publication of *In Darkest Africa*, the Romantic poet William Wordsworth had already noted the growing interest in "the great national events which are daily taking place." He had pointed presciently to urbanization and the standardization of labor as creating "a craving for extraordinary incident, which the rapid communication of intelligence hourly gratifies."[76] By the end of the nineteenth century, the acceleration of communications had multiplied daily eventfulness many times over. At the most general level, both through and alongside the development of the media, time began in this period to be socially understood as serial and open-ended rather than cyclical and repetitive.[77] Philosopher Walter Benjamin recognized the emergence of a capitalist model of progress reliant on "the schema of progression within an empty and homogeneous time" in the nineteenth century, and Benedict Anderson later picked up this idea of open serial time in his work on nationalism.[78] While there is more to say than is possible here about changing temporalities and cosmologies across the nineteenth century, it is undeniable that readerships for the periodical press were growing fast in the second half of the century. More and more people began to see themselves as living in "a serial world punctuated by singular events."[79] The yearly almanac gave way to the daily newspaper with a more socially inclusive circulation, and news events became "singularities that are part of a common, collective, available, shareable public life. They are marked up not only on the calendar of 'public history' but also on the private calendars of people's lives."[80]

Literary historian Kevis Goodman has written about "the sense of the historical present that is fostered by a nascent news culture."[81] She argues that the sense of presentness created by the news is less cognitive than affective and sensory, and she calls this consciousness a "virtual historicity,...[which] includes the desire for—but also desire's counterpart, an anxiety about—historical participation."[82] People rushed to buy Stanley's book not just because it was so heavily advertised and trailed in the press (although it was) but because they wanted to participate in the experience of his experience. Similarly, they entered the Stanley and Africa Exhibition through "the gate of a village palisade ornamented with skulls" and emblazoned with the message "*EN ROUTE* FOR THE HEART OF SAVAGE AFRICA," and they were then directed through rooms filled with potted palms and ferns, into a virtual Africa that invited them to fantasize their own participation in the exploration narrative. In this sense, the Stanley phenomenon operated like fiction in opening itself to the appropriation and imaginative habitation by its readers. The book and the exhibition were both early examples of what media historian Daniel Boorstin has famously called "pseudo-events," meaning media constructions that masquerade as "real" events.[83] Toys and games capitalized on this desire to participate: "Stanley in Africa," for example, was a jigsaw puzzle that accompanied a "toy-book"; the "Stanley Souvenir" was a maze game for marbles in which players had to negotiate the route of the Emin Pasha expedition via Stanley's Pool, the Congo Forest, and Wambutti before reaching Kavalli. The children of the 1890s did not have to resort to making believe with boot trees or toy soldiers, but were supplied with ready-made apparatus for playing explorers. Stanley's "celebratization" can also be seen as the process of his fictionalization, as his "personality-event" entered the public imagination of the 1890s alongside, for example, those of Sherlock Holmes and Jack the Ripper.[84] Exploration narratives were structurally particularly open to active or participative reading. *In Darkest Africa* is written like a log-book or journal, in which the explorer, in literary scholar Stuart Sherman's words, "plots motion through remote space by a structure of incremental time."[85] Sherman is discussing the attraction of sea journals to eighteenth-century readers and he continues, "[b]y virtue of their structure, [sea journals] constantly collate the data of exotic space with that of familiar time—with dates that their first readers had simultaneously occupied at home, and could recall . . . the sea journals mediate a growing sense of 'simultaneity' between the sedentary reader and the outwandering narrative."[86] Of course this effect was much heightened by the late nineteenth century when the rapid growth of telegraph networks meant that Stanley was able to cable dispatches from points along his route and thereby provide the newspapers with an almost "real time" narrative of his progress. In 1872 when Stanley was searching for Livingstone, novelist H. G. Wells remembered that his school teacher, known to his class as "Old Tommy," would "get excited by his morning paper and then . . . we would follow the search for Livingstone by Stanley in Darkest Africa" on "a decaying yellow map . . . that hung on the wall."[87]

Stanley's newspaper reports from Africa produced a thrilling sense of simultaneity, as Stanley acted as the intermediary between the known (here) and the unknown (there), in contrast to the retrospective anthologization of Basil Hall's polite fragments in the miscellanies. Stanley's celebrity in 1890 is both part of and subject to what historian Peter Fritzsche has called, "a dramatic reorganization of modern time and space, so that contemporaries felt themselves as *contemporaries*, as occupants of a common time zone with mutually recognizable personalities, dramas and processes."[88] The daily newspaper was fundamental to this sense of social and temporal calibration, as its regular reports of the "external events of the world" are embodied in an "idea of continuity and recentness [which] implies the reader's involvement in that externality."[89] Stanley's daily insertion into readers' lives fed an appetite for more, an appetite that a proliferating print culture was by now fully able to meet. Once the daily newspaper press had established its inexorable time-rhythm, it was possible for other kinds of print media to grow up around it, counterpointing its rhythm with their own. On March 3, 1890, for example, the *Illustrated London News* produced a Special Number on Stanley and Emin, "with two supplements." On April 30, 1890 the *Graphic* trumped it with its lavishly illustrated *Stanley Number*: a whole issue of the popular illustrated weekly devoted to Stanley and offered as a kind of souvenir supplement. These are, in effect, Stanley extras: the idea of the supplement promising that there is more to be revealed than can be easily dealt with in the fast turnover of the daily news agenda, and that the *Graphic*'s weekly format can offer a more leisured and intimate in-depth account of its subject than the daily press. A similar "deep immersion" effect was given by Poole's Myriorama, which Molly Bloom remembers visiting in the last scene of James Joyce's *Ulysses*. The Poole brothers toured a show called "Stanley in Darkest Africa," which used cut-out figures moving across the scene, accompanied by music, lighting, and sound effects.But the Stanley supplements and the Stanley shows would have made no sense at all without the insistent and repetitive coverage of Stanley in the daily press.

There is evidence that Stanley in fact himself saw *In Darkest Africa* as a kind of supplement. In 1873, he had defended his earlier book *How I Found Livingstone* against criticisms that it was "too bulky" by saying: "[s]o are newspapers too large, and contain a great deal more reading matter than any one man cares to read. In a book of travels some readers prefer adventures, the incidents of the chase; others prefer what relates to the ethnography of a country; others, geography; others dip into it for matters concerning philology."[90] His view of his own books is odd and unexpected: rather than see "a book" as an integrated and organic narrative, he rather recommends it should be read selectively, and "dipped into" as if it were a newspaper. Stanley in fact never made the literary mistake of privileging the book form over the newspaper form, knowing as he did that it was the newspapers that sold his books and not the other way around. There is a sense that *In Darkest Africa* is "the book of the Stanley show" rather than the show itself.

Several further versions of the expedition by other members appeared in print soon after *In Darkest Africa*; most were highly critical of Stanley's abandonment of the rear guard and of his brutality towards Africans. These attracted some angry comment in the press:

> England, at least, must countenance such murderous raids no more,
> Nor honour sham explorers who, when they'd a land explore,
> Gather a venal, cut-throat gang, too vicious to control.
> And march through rapine, fire, and blood, to gain their useless goal![91]

Yet, despite the assaults on his integrity and the truth of his version of the story, the public continued to be fascinated by Stanley, and his popularity rather grew than suffered by the frequency with which printed images of his face appeared. If Stanley's was, on the Emin Pasha expedition, "a useless goal" (and very probably it was) this seemed to make little difference to most of his readers: the logic of imperial exploration was, in effect, a process of eventful forward progress, which was not necessarily goal-orientated.[92] Indeed, *In Darkest Africa* is repetitious, as Emma Darwin noticed. It seems a narrative without memory, which starts constantly afresh. A process of eventful forward progress also characterizes the logic of the serial news media. And indeed the irrational throwaway logic of consumption depends on a similar loss of memory and forward-directed appetite. In 1890, open-ended exploration narrative mapped particularly well onto a developing serial advertising and media culture.

The application of the techniques of the history of the book and of media history to the historiography of imperial and scientific exploration opens up new research questions. Attending closely to the publication histories of travel and exploration accounts can illuminate the moments of "knowledge transfer" when new meanings are created. The transition from manuscript to published book is only one model of publication history, and, as this chapter has shown, the mediation of the periodical and newspaper press creates new social formations of knowledge and celebrity, which alter again the value and reach of explorers' accounts of their travels. The insights of book and media history are perhaps most salutary in drawing attention to the way that explorers themselves are not in full control of their journeys or their narratives of those journeys. Ultimately, the explorer-writer is always an unreliable narrator.

As the French theorist Michel de Certeau reminds us, "[r]eaders are travelers, they move across lands belonging to someone else, like nomads poaching their way across fields they did not write, despoiling the wealth of Egypt to enjoy it for themselves."[93] Travel and exploration narratives have always offered a representation of repeated practice and movement, which readers could appropriate, inhabit and in which they could imaginatively participate. In this, these narratives operate like fiction, but with the added frisson of the empirically authentic. Throughout the long nineteenth century, the porosity of travel writing as a form increased exponentially due to the extraordinary developments in what might be called "print culture" but is perhaps better called the "practices of print." But there was something more about the form of exploration narratives in particular that rendered them so open to their readers. As Emma Darwin noticed, formally they depend upon repetition (of daily practices of note-taking in the log book or diary, and measurement-making, halts, packing and unpacking, camp-building, and dismantling, and so on) but this repetition is held in a constant tension with another narrative of the achievement of onward progress. On an expedition, it is through repeated daily practice that progress and even history is imagined as being made. Similarly, through the repetition of the reading of the daily newspaper, the nineteenth-century reader could imagine his or her own insertion into the onward eventful flow of progress and history.

NOTES

1. British scrapbook inscribed inside front cover, "Ellen Mary Lotham With Mother's Love April 20th 1877." In author's collection.

2. *Madame Tussaud & Sons' Exhibition Catalogue containing biographical & descriptive sketches of the distinguished characters which compose their exhibition and historical gallery.* (London: Ben George, 1879), 22.

3. Ellen Gruber Garvey. "Scissorizing and Scrapbooks: Nineteenth-Century Reading, Remaking, and Recirculating" in *New Media, 1740–1915*, ed. Lisa Gitelman and Geoffrey B. Pingree (Cambridge, Mass. and London: MIT Press, 2003), 207–227, both quotations 214.

4. Peter Hulme and Tim Youngs. "Introduction," *The Cambridge Companion to Travel Writing.* Cambridge University Press, 2002. Cambridge Collections Online.Cambridge University Press. September 28, 2010 <http://cco.cambridge.org/uid=17532/extract?id=ccol052178140x_CCOL052178140X_root>.

5. Felix Driver. "Distance and Disturbance: Travel, Exploration and Knowledge in the Nineteenth Century." *Transactions of the Royal Historical Society* (Sixth Series) (2004): 73–92, 75. Driver's book, *Geography Militant: Cultures of Exploration and Empire* (Oxford: Blackwell, 2001) charts the emergence of a modern culture of exploration.

6. Margaret Cohen, *The Novel and the Sea* (Princeton: Princeton University Press, 2010), 15.

7. Margaret Beetham, *A Magazine of her Own? Domesticity and Desire in the Woman's Magazine, 1800–1914* (London; Routledge, 1996), 9.

8. James A. Secord, "Scrapbook Science: Composite Caricatures in Late Georgian England," in *Figuring It Out: Science, Gender and Visual Culture* eds. Ann B. Shteir and Bernard V. Lightman (Hanover, N.H.: Dartmouth College Press, 2006),164–191, 176.

9. Thad Logan, *The Victorian Parlour* (Cambridge: Cambridge University Press, 2001), 124.

10. John Forster, *The Life of Charles Dickens*, "Household Edition" (London: Chapman and Hall, n.d.), 4. Dickens wrote this recollection of his own childhood some years before inserting it into *David Copperfield*, "the only change in the fiction being his omission of the name of a cheap series of novelists then in course of publication, by which his father had become happily the owner of so large a lump of literary treasure in his small collection of books." 4.

11. Charlotte Brontë, "The History of the Year" (March 12, 1829) reprinted in Christine Alexander, ed. *The Brontës, Tales of Glass Town, Angria, and Gondal: Selected Early Writings* (Oxford: Oxford University Press World's Classics, 2010), 3–4, 4. The children had also been lent "an old Geography . . . an hundred and twenty years old" by their father, 3.

12. "Analysis of Mr. Barrow's Chronological History of Voyages into the Arctic Regions,"*Blackwood's* (November 1818): 187–193, 193.

13. Mungo Park disappeared, presumed drowned in 1806, and his *Journal of a Mission to the Interior of Africa* appeared posthumously in 1815. For a detailed publishing history of Mungo Park, see Charles W. J. Withers, "Geography, Enlightenment and the Book: Authorship and Audience in Mungo Park's African Texts" in *Geographies of the Book*, ed. Miles Ogborn and Charles W. J. Withers (Farnham: Ashgate, 2010), 191–220. Heather Glen, "Configuring a World: Some Childhood Writings of Charlotte Brontë," in *Opening the Nursery Door: Reading, Writing, and Childhood 1600–1900*, eds. Mary Hilton, Morag Styles and Victor Watson (London: Routledge, 1997), 215–234, 218.

14. L. E. L. [Laetitia Landon], "The History of a Child," in *Traits and Trials of Early Life*, (London: Henry Colburn, 1836): 283–312, 294–295.

15. Axel Munthe, "Diary of an Idle Doctor," *Blackwood's*, 146: 889 (November 1889): 592–614, 602

16. Edith Henrietta Fowler, "Fragments of Child-life," *Longman's Magazine*, 24:140 (June 1894): 169–182, 169.

17. See Leah Price, "Reading: The State of the Discipline," *Book History*, Volume 7, (2004): 303–320, 311.

18. Quoted in Jonathan Rose, *The Intellectual Life of the British Working Classes* (New Haven: Yale University Press, 2001), 243.

19. Kate Flint, *The Woman Reader 1837–1914* (Oxford: Clarendon Press, 1993), 217.

20. Chris Rojek, *Celebrity* (London: Reaktion Press, 2001); P. David Marshall, *Celebrity and Power: Fame in Contemporary Culture* (Minneapolis: University of Minnesota Press, 1997).

21. Leo Braudy, *The Frenzy of Renown: Fame and Its History* (New York: Oxford University Press, 1986), 381.

22. Robert A. Stafford, "Scientific Exploration and Empire," in *The Oxford History of the British Empire: The Nineteenth Century*, ed. Andrew Porter (New York: Oxford University Press, 2001): 294–319, 302.

23. Leila Koivunen, *Visualizing Africa in Nineteenth-Century British Travel Accounts* (London: Routledge, 2009), 206. See also Dorothy O. Helly, *Livingstone's Legacy: Horace Waller and Victorian Myth-Making* (Athens: Ohio University Press, 1987); James R. Ryan, *Picturing Empire: Photography and the Visualization of the British Empire* (Chicago: University of Chicago Press, 1997); Annie E. Coombes, *Reinventing Africa: Museums, Material Culture and Popular Imagination in Late Victorian and Edwardian England* (New Haven, Conn.: Yale University Press, 1997).

24. Barbara J. Shapiro, *A Culture of Fact: England 1550–1720* (Ithaca, N.Y.: Cornell University Press, 2000); Steven Shapin, *A Social History of Truth: Civility and Science in Seventeenth Century England* (Chicago: University of Chicago Press, 1994); Adrian Johns, *The Nature of the Book: Print and Knowledge in the Making* (Chicago: University of Chicago Press, 1998), 58–186; Peter Howlett and Mary S. Morgan, eds., *How Well Do Facts Travel? The Dissemination of Reliable Knowledge* (Cambridge: Cambridge University Press, 2010).

25. Horace Waller to H. W. Bates, (October 9, 1872) [Fellows' Correspondence, RGS Archives], quoted in Felix Driver, *Geography Militant*, 129.

26. See Niklas Luhmann and Rhodes Barrett, *Risk: A Sociological Theory* (New York: Walter de Gruyter, 1993).

27. John Walker Ord, *Rural Sketches and Poems: Chiefly Relating to Cleveland* (London: Simpkin and Marshall, 1845), 261.

28. Henry Mayhew, *London Labour and the London Poor*, 4 vols. 2d ed. (London: Griffin, n.d. [1865]) vol. I, 244.

29. See Rolf Engelsing, "Die Perioden der Lesergeschichte in der Neuzeit," *Archiv für geschichte des Buchwesens*10 (1970): 945–1002. Reinhard Wittmann, "Was There a Reading Revolution at the End of the Eighteenth Century?" in *A History of Reading in the West*, ed. Guglielmo Cavallo and Roger Chartier (Amherst: University of Massachusetts Press, 1999), 284–312. Robert Darnton, "Readers Respond to Rousseau," in *The Great Cat Massacre and Other Episodes*

in French Cultural History (London: Allen Lane, 1984), 215–56. Cathy Davidson, *Revolution and the Word: The Rise of the Novel in America* (New York: Oxford University Press, 1986).

30. Niklas Luhmann, *Love as Passion* (London: Polity Press, 1986), 12.

31. See, for example, James Secord, "Knowledge in Transit," *Isis*, 95 (2004): 654–672.

32. Darnton, *The Great Cat Massacre*, 63. Darnton's work is focused on eighteenth-century France.

33. Roger Chartier, "Culture as Appropriation: Popular Cultural Uses in Early Modern France," in *Understanding Popular Culture: Europe from the Middle Ages to the Nineteenth Century* ed. Steven L. Kaplan (Berlin: Mouton Publishers, 1984), 229–253, 233. Emphasis added.

34. Space does not permit a full consideration of reader-response theories here. See the work of Wolfgang Iser, Hans Robert Jauss, and Hans-Georg Gadamer. Book historian Bill Bell has usefully considered models of individual and resistant readership in the nineteenth century.

35. See Edward Berenson, "Charisma and the Making of Imperial Heroes in Britain and France, 1880–1914," in *Constructing Charisma: Celebrity, Fame and Power in Nineteenth-Century Europe*, ed. Edward Berenson and Eva Giloi (New York: Berghahn Books, 2010), 21–40; Eric Eisner, *Nineteenth-Century Poetry and Literary Celebrity* (London: Palgrave Macmillan, 2009); John Plunkett, *Queen Victoria: First Media Monarch* (Oxford: Oxford University Press, 2003).

36. Mark Turner, "Time, Periodicals, and Literary Study," *Victorian Periodicals Review* 39/4 (2006): 309–316, 311.

37. The phrase "serialization of everyday experience" comes from Nick Hopwood, Simon Schaffer and Jim Secord, "Seriality and Scientific Objects in the Nineteenth Century," *History of Science*, 48 (2010): 251–285, 263. They go on to suggest that "[s]eriality, based in material arrangements rather than idealized abstractions, is a promising category for historical analysis," 279. See also Linda K. Hughes and Michael Lund, *The Victorian Serial* (Charlottesville and London: University Press of Virginia, 1991).

38. Ord, *Rural Sketches and Poems*, 260.

39. "Fragments of Voyages and Travels, including Anecdotes of a Naval Life; chiefly for the use of young persons," *Quarterly Review*, 45: 89 (April 1831): 145–167, 145.

40. Compare"Manners and Customs" in the *Mirror of Literature, Amusement, and Instruction* 27: 776 (May 14, 1836): 311, and 'Fragments of Voyages and Travels, including Anecdotes of a Naval Life; Chiefly for the Use of Young Persons," *Quarterly Review* (April 1831): 145–167.

41. William St. Clair in *The Reading Nation in the Romantic Period* (Cambridge: Cambridge University Press, 2004), 252–253, shows that the holdings of book clubs in the early nineteenth century generally included many travel narratives.

42. Ord, *Rural Sketches and Poems,* 261.

43. J. Herschel, *Preliminary Discourse on the Study of Natural Philosophy* (London: Longman, Rees, Orme, Brown and Green, 1830), 28–29. My attention was drawn to this by Felix Driver, *Geography Militant,* 54.

44. *Philosophical Transactions of the Royal Society* (1823), 211–88.

45. Ralph Waldo Emerson, "The Present Age," in *The Early Lectures of Ralph Waldo Emerson* (Oxford: Oxford University Press, 1972), vol. 3, 213. The lecture was first given in 1839.

46. "Naval and Military Intelligence," *Illustrated London News* (21 September 1844), 190.

47. "Spirit of the Public Journals," *Mirror of Literature, Amusement, and Instruction* 6:155 (13 August 1825): 123–125, 124.

48. Scott to Lady Abercorn, Abbotsford, August 1st 1824, in *Familiar Letters of Walter Scott,* vol. ii (Edinburgh David Douglas, 1894), 212.

49. In addition to his fellowship of the Royal Geographical Society, Hall was a fellow of the Royal Society, and of the Royal Astronomical and Geological Societies.

50. "Publisher's Preface," to Basil Hall, *Voyage to Loo-Choo, and Other Places in the Eastern Seas, in the Year 1816* (Edinburgh: Archibald Constable & Co. 1826), i (unpaginated).

51. Basil Hall, "A Visit to Rockall," in William Draper Swan, *The District School Reader: or, Exercises in Reading and Speaking; Designed for the Highest Class in Public and Private Schools* (Boston: Charles C. Little and James Brown, 1845), 110–117.

52. Review of third series of Hall's "Fragments," *The Asiatic Journal and Monthly Register for British and Foreign India, China, and Australasia* (vol xi, n.s., May–August 1833) (East India Company, London: Parbury Allen & Co., 1833), 154–157, both quotations 154.

53. The *Spectator,* quoted in an advertisement for "Captain Basil Hall's Works" inserted into the *Edinburgh Review* (March-June 1831), vol. 53, 3 of advertising booklet.

54. Anthony Ashley Cooper, 3d Earl of Shaftesbury, *Characteristics of Men, Manners, Opinions, Times* ed. Laurence Klein (Cambridge: Cambridge University Press, 1999), 156.

55. Michael McKeon, *The Origins of the English Novel, 1600–1740* (Baltimore: Johns Hopkins University Press, 2002), 106.

56. "Fragments of Voyages and Travels, including Anecdotes of a Naval Life; chiefly for the use of young persons," *Quarterly Review,* 45: 89 (April 1831): 145–167, 167 and 146.

57. Brian Maidment, *Into the 1830s; Some Origins of Victorian Illustrated journalism Cheap Octavo Magazines of the 1820s and their Influence* (Manchester: Manchester Polytechnic Library, 1992), 9. See also Maidment, *Reading Popular Prints 1790–1870* (Manchester: Manchester University Press, 2001); Jonathan R. Topham, "The Mirror of Literature, Amusement and Instruction

and Cheap Miscellanies in Nineteenth-century Britain," in *Science in the Nineteenth-Century Periodical: Reading the Magazine of Nature* eds. G. N. Cantor, Gowan Dawson, Graeme Gooday (Cambridge: Cambridge University Press, 2004), 37–66; Barbara Benedict, *Making the Modern Reader: Cultural Mediation in Early Modern Literary Anthologies* (Princeton, N.J.: Princeton University Press, 1996); Ina Ferris "Antiquarian Authorship: D'Israeli's Miscellany of Literary Curiosity and the Question of Secondary Genres," in *Studies in Romanticism*, 45 no. 4 (Winter 2006): 523–542.

58. Barbara M. Benedict, "Literary Miscellanies: The Cultural Mediation of Fragmented Feeling," *ELH*, vol. 57, No. 2 (Summer, 1990): 407–430, 409; Jon P. Klancher, *The Making of English Reading Audiences, 1790–1832* (Madison: The University of Wisconsin Press, 1987), 79. John Topham disagrees and sees the emergence of a "topicality" in the Mirror as evidence of its development from a miscellany into a newspaper.

59. Brian Maidment has described the *Mirror* as "a key periodical for understanding the transitions from polite to mass culture," Maidment, *Into the 1830s*, 5. He shows how the *Mirror* prefigures Charles Knight's *Penny Magazine of the Society for the Diffusion of Useful Knowledge*, a miscellany of "useful information" published for the SDUK, which launched ten years after the *Mirror* in 1832.

60. Andrew Piper, *Dreaming in Books: The Making of the Bibliographic Imagination in the Romantic Age* (Chicago: The University of Chicago Press, 2009), 123.

61. "Sun-Rise on Mount Etna.," *Penny Magazine*, 10: 612 (1841: Oct. 16) 408; "The Salt-Trade of Foreign Countries," *Penny Magazine*, 13: 763 (1844: Feb. 24): 66–68; "Locomotion of Animals -No. XVI," *Penny Magazine*, 14: 848 (1845: June 21): 236–240.

62. Barbara Shapiro, *A Culture of Fact: England 1550–1720* (Ithaca, N.Y.: Cornell University Press, 2000), 87.

63. Elizabeth Gaskell, "A Traveller's Tales," *Mary Barton: A Tale of Manchester Life* [1848], ed. Shirley Foster (Oxford: Oxford University Press, 2006), 149.

64. Michael McKeon has written that "the epistemology of the travel narrative" promoted by the Royal Society in the eighteenth century located truth in the authority of the observer rather than in the force of tradition. He reads the travelogue as a precursor of the novel as it participates in an epistemological shift away from scholasticism and romance and toward empiricism. Michael McKeon, *The Origins of the English Novel 1600–1740* (Baltimore: Johns Hopkins University Press, 1987), 101.

65. Emma Darwin, between November 1 and 31, 1890. Henrietta Litchfield, ed., *Emma Darwin: A Century of Family Letters, 1792–1896* (New York: D. Appleton and Co., 1915), vol. 2, 290.

66. Henry Morton Stanley, *In Darkest Africa or, The Quest, Rescue and Retreat of Emin, Governor of Equatoria* (London: Sampson Low, Marston, Searle & Rivington, 1890), 577.

67. "On January 25 of this year, not a line of it had been written. Then it was that Mr. Stanley sat down at the Villa Victoria in Cairo, with a firm determination that nothing earthly should stop him till he had finished it. In fifty days" Edward Marston, *How Stanley Wrote "In Darkest Africa: A Trip to Cairo and Back"* (London: S. Low, Marston, Searle & Rivington, 1890), 72.

68. John MacKenzie, *Propaganda and Empire: The Manipulation of British Public Opinion, 1880–1960* (Manchester: Manchester University Press, 1984), 26.

69. Richards, *The Commodity Culture of Victorian England* 136. See Thomas Richards, "Selling Darkest Africa," in *The Commodity Culture of Victorian England: Advertising and Spectacle 1851–1914* (Stanford, Calif.: Stanford University Press, 1990), 199–167. Tim Youngs, "Consuming Stanley," in Tim Youngs, *Travellers in Africa, British Travelogues, 1850–1900* (Manchester: Manchester University Press 1994), 151–181. Daniel Bivona, "Why Africa Needs Europe: from Livingstone to Stanley," in Daniel Bivona, *British Imperial Literature, 1870–1940: Writing and the Administration of Empire* (Cambridge: Cambridge University Press, 1998), 40–68. Felix Driver, *Geography Militant;* and Clare Pettitt, *"Dr. Livingstone, I Presume?" Missionaries, Journalists, Explorers and Empire* (Cambridge, Mass.: Harvard University Press, 2007).

70. The *Oxford Dictionary of National Biography* lists the following four likenesses of Basil Hall: F. Chantrey, pencil drawing, (National Portrait Gallery); S. Joseph, marble bust, Pollok House, Glasgow; J. Swaine, line engraving, British Museum; J. Swaine, stipple and line (pubd 1842; after Bonnor), National Portrait Gallery.

71. James Mussell, "New Journalism," in *Dictionary of Nineteenth-Century Journalism in Great Britain and Ireland* eds. Laurel Brake and Marysa Demoor (Gent: Academia Press, 2009), 443. See also Richard Salmon, "A Simulacrum of Power: Intimacy and Abstraction in the Rhetoric of New Journalism," *Victorian Periodicals Review* vol. 30, no.1 (Spring 1997): 41–52, and Kate Jackson, "The *Tit-Bits* Phenomenon: George Newness, New Journalism and the Periodical Texts" *Victorian Periodicals Review* vol. 30, no. 3 (Fall, 1997): 201–226.

72. J. Scott Keltie, ed., *The Story of Emin's Rescue as told in Stanley's Letters* (New York: Harper & Bros. 1890), 3. Quoted by Youngs, "Consuming Stanley," 173.

73. Ibid., 173.

74. Hall died insane, "constant literary exertion" apparently having "weakened his brain." "Biographical Preface" to *Voyages and Travels of Captain Basil Hall, R. N.,* (London, Edinburgh and New York: Thomas Nelson & Sons, 1895), 5–6, 6.

75. Before commencing the expedition, Stanley had required that his European co-explorers sign a contract undertaking not to publish anything on the expedition until six months after the publication of his own account. See James L. Newman, *Imperial Footprints: Henry Morton Stanley's African Journeys* (Washington, D.C.: Potomac Books, 2004), 227.

76. William Wordsworth, "Preface 1800/1802/1805 to *Lyrical Ballads*," in *William Wordsworth and Samuel Taylor Coleridge Lyrical Ballads 1798 and 1800* eds. R. L. Brett and A. R. Jones (London: Routledge, 1991), 241–272, 249.

77. See, for example, E. P. Thompson, "Time, Work-Discipline, and Industrial Capitalism." *Past and Present* 38 (December 1967): 56–97.

78. Walter Benjamin, "Paralipomena to 'On the Concept of History,'" in eds. Marcus Paul Bullock and Michael William Jennings, *Walter Benjamin: Selected Writings Volume 4 1938–1940* (Cambridge, Mass.: Harvard University Press, 2003), 401–424, 406. Benedict Anderson, *Imagined Communities: Reflections on the Origins and Spread of Nationalism* (London: Verso, 1983) 24. Anderson considers the logic of seriality more closely in *The Spectre of Comparisons: Nationalism, Southeast Asia and the World* (London: Verso, 1998). Anderson's influential work has provoked many responses. Particularly relevant to this chapter is the criticism of Anderson's use of Benjamin launched by Adam Barrows in his *The Cosmic Time of Empire: Modern Britain and World Literature* (Berkeley and Los Angeles: University of California Press, 2011).

79. Paddy Scannell, *Radio, Television, and Modern Life* (Oxford: Blackwell, 1996), 156.

80. Ibid., 91.

81. Kevis Goodman, "The Loophole in the Retreat: The Culture of News and the Early Life of Romantic Self-Consciousness," *The South Atlantic Quarterly* 102:1 (Winter 2003): 25–52, 44.

82. Ibid., 31.

83. See Daniel J. Boorstin, *The Image: A Guide to Pseudo-Events in America* (New York: Atheneum, 1973).

84. For a discussion of the muddling of fact and fiction in the public imagination of celebrity in the late nineteenth century, see Michael Saler, "'Clap if you Believe in Sherlock Holmes': Mass Culture and the Re-enchantment of Modernity, c.1890–1940," *Historical Journal* 46: 3 (September 2003): 599–622.

85. Stuart Sherman, *Telling Time: Clocks, Diaries and English Diurnal Form, 1669–1785* (Chicago and London: The University of Chicago Press, 1996), 162.

86. Ibid., 169.

87. Herbert George Wells, *Experiment in Autobiography: Discoveries and Conclusions of a Very Ordinary Brain (Since 1866)* (London: Victor Gollancz Ltd., 1934), vol. I, 91.

88. Peter Fritzsche, *Stranded in the Present: Modern Time and the Melancholy of History* (Cambridge, Mass.: Harvard University Press, 2004), 9–10.

89. Lennard J. Davis, *Factual Fictions: The Origins of the English Novel* (New York: Columbia University Press, 1983), 73 and 74.

90. H. M. Stanley, *My Kalulu* [1873], (New York: Charles Scribner's Sons, 1890), vi–vii. I am grateful to Brian Murray for drawing my attention to this quotation.

91. *Truth* (October 25, 1888). The poem was written shortly after reports of Major Bartellot's death in the rear column. Quoted in Tim Youngs, *Travellers in Africa*, 167.

92. For a full description of the reasons why the Emin Pasha Relief Expedition was unnecessary, see Iain R. Smith, *The Emin Pasha Relief Expedition 1886–1890* (Oxford: Clarendon Press, 1972).

93. Michel de Certeau, *The Practice of Everyday Life*, trans. Steven Rendall (Berkeley: University of California Press, 1984), 174.

5

THE MAKING OF BRITISH AND FRENCH
LEGENDS OF EXPLORATION, 1821–1914

BERNY SÈBE

Characterized by contemporaries as the standard-bearer of civilization in strange lands, the explorer embodied, more than anyone else, the encounter (in the physical as well as metaphorical sense) of the West with the "Rest." The explorer was also the producer of knowledge, upon whom rested the development and credibility of geography, a science in the making, in the nineteenth century. By making discoveries that placed his country ahead of rivals, the explorer could also become a national hero full of exemplary value.[1] This chapter looks at the socio-cultural and institutional processes that transformed the activities of explorers into national causes. The growing appeal of cultural history, and especially the history of the metropolitan public's attachment to the empire, has generated renewed interest in the *modus operandi* of expeditions, the political and cultural backdrops against which they developed, and the features that helped them attract public acclaim. The "legends of exploration" were one of the most distinctive and efficient means of fostering geographical awareness while highlighting the role of the geographical establishment in the education of the nation.

The domestic impact of British and French heroes of exploration was bound up with a complex set of social, political, and cultural agendas at play within these countries. The role played by geographical societies as agents of racial and imperial propaganda is inseparable from the race for a "place in the sun," also known as the New Imperialism. The legends that developed around explorers, who became household names in their home countries, resulted from the active support of propaganda networks aimed at increasing popular endorsement of the imperial idea. Explorers' activities were often linked to religious proselytism and military conquest, which was tied in turn to inter-European (and especially Anglo-French) competition. Finally, the key role of explorers as agents of propagation of knowledge about non-Western societies should not be overlooked.

For a long time, biographers of explorers wrote hagiographic works intended to justify the Empire and convey to the new generations the patriotic appeal of their exploits. In the era after decolonization, explorers were often appraised as the associates or lackeys of the Western project of exploitation of the world.[2] More recent interpretations of the explorer have tried to offer a more balanced appraisal, stressing his dependence on indigenous agents and the complexity of the interplay between exploration and imperialism. This has produced a better acknowledgement of the propaganda mechanisms that sustained nineteenth-century exploration, allowing historians to understand the role of the explorer in metropolitan culture. The first section of this chapter offers an overview of this historiography, while the second section closely inspects a few revealing case studies on each side of the Channel, with a view to distinguishing three main chronological phases.

Who is an explorer? The Oxford English Dictionary defines the explorer as someone who "search[es] into or examine[s] (a country, a place, etc.) by going through it . . . for the purpose of discovery." Rarely a full-time job, it was undertaken by a variety of individuals, such as missionaries and military officers. Military commanders often published lengthy reports that were appreciated in geographical circles, such as Fernand Foureau's eight-hundred-page account of his travels from Algiers to the Congo as the leader of the "Foureau-Lamy" mission.[3] Conversely, self-described "explorers" sometimes behaved like military commanders, as was the case for Henry Morton Stanley. Religious figures often became explorers, David Livingstone and Charles de Foucauld being obvious examples. Who the home society perceived to be an explorer matters more than any essentialist definition: the explorer was very much in the eyes of the European beholder. Viewed from this perspective, a wide range of individuals were considered explorers and enjoyed privileged links with the geographical establishment. The sociological function of the explorer in British and French societies over the period from 1821 to 1914 will be the defining criterion here.

* * *

Popular interest in explorers and the success of exploration accounts were not a nineteenth-century novelty *per se:* in the eighteenth century, attempts to circumnavigate the globe, very much inspired by the scientific ideals of the Enlightenment, had been followed closely in learned circles. The exploration of the Pacific by Louis-Antoine de Bougainville, James Cook, and Jean-François de Lapérouse had sparked sustained interest among elites, including the French king Louis XVI, who famously asked shortly before being beheaded, "have we had any news from M. de Lapérouse?" Narratives of exploration in Oceania by Bougainville and Lapérouse were much publicized in pre-revolutionary France. Not only did books such as *The Voyage of Bougainville* comfort nationalistic feelings, but they also "stimulated the popular imagination, much the way news of the moon shots would do two hundred years later."[4] Diderot's attack on Bougainville in the *Supplement to the Voyage of Bougainville* further demonstrated the influence of exploration in the late eighteenth century. In the following decades, Mungo Park's *Travels in the Interior Districts of Africa* and James Bruce's *Travels to Discover the Source of the Nile* succeeded in establishing narratives of exploration as an "influential literary genre."[5]

What changed in the nineteenth century were the means through which an explorer acquired a "heroic reputation,"[6] and the backdrop against which this process took place. The "structures of feeling" changed dramatically as the industrial revolution swept Britain and then France.[7] The ceaseless work of philanthropic and antislavery associations in the first half of the nineteenth century, and the New Imperialism later in the century, changed the ways unknown territories were perceived. How great power status was asserted shifted over time from informal control to formal annexation. These developments, combined with new cultural practices resulting from industrialization, had a decisive impact on the hero-making processes. Print culture was a key factor. Higher literacy rates and technological improvements in paper production, printing, and transport led to the blossoming of the popular press, and its role became more important with the extension of the franchise. Labor regulations gave workers more leisure time to read. Newspaper articles praising the achievements of explorers and calling for heroes' welcomes reached a growing number of readers. New strategies devised by publishers to expand their customer base, the so-called "New Journalism," ensured that biographical or hagiographical works found more customers. The press had the power to drum up the achievements of heroes of exploration with more speed and efficiency as the century went on.

The last three decades have seen increased research on the development of these "legends of exploration" in Europe. Edward Said's *Orientalism* (1978), Terence Ranger and Eric Hobsbawm's *The Invention of Tradition* (1983) and John MacKenzie's *Propaganda and Empire* (1984) paved the way for a dramatic reappraisal by historians of the context in which the figure of the nineteenth century explorer (alongside other imperial heroes) developed at home.[8] Although the exact nature of the causal link between exploration and conquest remains a matter of contention,[9] it is beyond doubt that the two were frequently associated, especially when celebrations of exploratory feats took on a national character. Victorian Britain developed a deep attachment to the Empire.[10] This was less obvious on the other side of the Channel, where it was argued for a long time that France had a "colonial Party" but never was a colonial country.[11] However, evidence to the contrary is becoming increasingly available as more research into the subject is undertaken.[12] Our understanding of the networks and institutions that sustained the acquisition and organization of new knowledge about extra-European territories has also significantly improved,[13] placing the history of exploration within the wider context of the ordering and development of western knowledge throughout the nineteenth century. In particular, the history of exploration, through both overviews and individual case studies, has shown how this activity appears as a peculiar mode of interaction of the West with other societies.[14]

Research into the "cultures of exploration"[15] has documented the unique role played by national and provincial geographical societies in promoting awareness of the non-Western worlds, first among the educated elites, then the middle classes, and finally the working classes, disseminating new geographical information through the popular press and literature. The development of geographical societies in Britain and in France shortly after the end of the Napoleonic Wars, and their gradual expansion made them a key transmission belt of knowledge about explorers, making heroic legends of exploration available to the general public and adorning them with the credentials of a scientific institution.[16] Their rise throughout the nineteenth century is inseparable from the gradual recognition of geography as a science, occurring against the backdrop of increased imperial activity.[17]

Historians now have a clearer view of the mechanisms that sustained the development of various nineteenth-century "legends of exploration." Key turning points in this history shape the periodization of the second section of this chapter. From the early 1820s to the 1860s, in what marks a first period, exploration was not directly related to formal expansion. In a second period, coinciding with the wave of New Imperialism, exploration was clearly linked to the European conquest of overseas territories. Finally, this chapter considers a third period, from the turn of the century onwards, when exploration became limited to the remotest places of the earth and the most powerful legends of exploration consisted mainly of the commemoration of nineteenth century explorers.

* * *

The establishment of geographical societies in the early nineteenth century gave explorers specially targeted support and institutional recognition of their fieldwork. The Paris-based *Société de Géographie* (est. 1821), and the Royal Geographical Society in London (est. 1830), served as sponsors for explorers, gave much more visibility to their achievements, and rationalized their activities much more efficiently than the diverse and short-lived associations that stemmed from the "Geography of the philosophers."[18] These societies would become pivotal agents in the promotion of explorers' achievements. The cases of René Caillié and David Livingstone were emblematic of this first moment in the popularization of explorers.

Four years after its launch, the Paris society inaugurated a tradition of patronage and publicity with the publishing of the *Encouragement pour un voyage à Tombouctou et dans l'intérieur de l'Afrique,* in which rewards (from donors, French governmental institutions, and the society itself) were promised to the first traveler to travel safely to Timbuktu and produce detailed observations on the geography, customs, beliefs, and commerce of the city and its environs. At the time, it was known that the Scottish explorer Alexander Gordon Laing had set off for Timbuktu, but the news of his death in 1826 during his return from the famed city did not reach Europe until 1828, the year the Frenchman René Caillié returned in triumph from his own hazardous journey there. Caillié's story was quickly given prominence by the *Société de Géographie,* which organized a solemn exceptional session to celebrate his success. This award ceremony saw René Caillié receiving the Society's gold medal and a 13,000 franc prize, as well as the guarantee of financial support toward the cost of publication of the expedition's report, which appeared in 1830. This son of a convict was also granted a generous state pension and the Legion of Honour.[19] The fact that a French national had succeeded where his Scottish competitor had failed strengthened his enduring heroic reputation.[20] Undertaken half a decade before the French landed in Algiers, Caillié's achievements were celebrated for science's sake: they did not serve as support for any expansionist agenda. Yet, the *Société de Géographie* created the conditions necessary to encourage individual heroism in the field of exploration and ensured the "after-sales" services by widely publicizing his achievements, nationally and internationally.

The practice was repeated, but to a far greater scale and over a longer period, by the Royal Geographical Society with David Livingstone (see Figure 5.1). Above all, it signalled the increasing connection between exploration and imperialism, which added a new dimension to the promotion of exploratory exploits. Whereas the Paris society had lost stamina in the 1830s and 40s,[21] Sir Roderick Murchison's appointment as the head of the RGS in 1843 marked a turning point in the society's development: for twenty-eight years, he made geographical science and imperial expansion compatible pursuits, the outcomes of which were seen as mutually beneficial. Combining patriotism with science and aware of the benefit the society (and geography in general) could get from the heroic feats of explorers, he ensured that the RGS became the nexus of British explorers, with a view that it should reinforce the nation's position worldwide.[22] The RGS hoped to serve patriotic interest by promoting the achievements of British explorers of the moment, as did its offspring the Hakluyt Society (est. 1846) for British explorers of the past.

The immense popularity of David Livingstone resulted from patient promotional work by Sir Roderick Murchison and Livingstone's fellow missionary, the Rev. Horace Waller, who assiduously advanced the cause of Christian expansion in Africa. Livingstone became the best example of the "cultures of exploration" that were in the making in the middle of the nineteenth century. In spite of a long stay in Africa between 1841 and 1856, his reputation at home grew as the reports and letters sent while he was crossing Africa (1852–1856) were eagerly published by the RGS president, who was seeking to revive public interest in the exploration of the interior of Africa at a moment when it was faltering. Murchison's publicity campaign for Livingstone's achievements, as well as his insistence on organizing a special meeting of the society and awarding him the RGS gold medal upon his return, initiated a virtuous circle that has been documented in all biographies of Livingstone, but has rarely been interpreted from the point of view of a promotional system: the swift production of the *Missionary Travels and Researches in South Africa* (the first print run of 12,000 copies was sold out before being released, and 30,000 copies were sold in the five years following its publication[23]), a string of lectures around the country, numerous articles in the press, *honoris causa* doctorates, and an audience with the Queen. Livingstone became a household name in Britain. However, his next expedition on the Zambezi proved much more costly, and less successful, than the first. The publication in 1865 of the *Narrative of an Expedition to the Zambezi and its Tributaries* was in part intended to revive his ailing reputation. Having partly achieved this goal, Livingstone set out on his last

Figure 5.1 British explorer David Livingstone

journey with financial help from the RGS and the British government, an exploration of the hydrographical systems of central Africa. It was during this period, which saw the famous publicity stunt orchestrated by Henry Morton Stanley and the *New York Herald*, that the Livingstone legend was revived. Stanley gave maximum publicity to his meeting with Livingstone through articles in the press and his book *How I Found Livingstone* (1872). As Felix Driver has argued, he had "an unrivalled gift for self-publicity"[24] which, in this instance, also involved the promotion of an earlier hero. However, the revival of Livingstone's fame also resulted from the constant support lent by Murchison (until his death in 1871) and the RGS. The RGS's involvement with the Livingstone legend was so deep that the Rev. Horace Waller informed Livingstone in 1869, while he was away in the field, that

> the interest in this country about you is as intense as I ever would wish it to be and no one has a better chance of grasping it than yourself. The Geographical Society might in short be called the Livingstone Society for the last two years.[25]

The high level of expectation raised by Livingstone's endeavor, and the anxiety surrounding his apparent disappearance in the heart of Africa, ensured that his name remained in the public eye. Waller did not hide his enthusiasm when he saw the explorer's statue at the Royal Academy in 1869:

> You were exhibited in the Royal Academy this year, clad in knicker bockers, gaiters, a huge revolver strapped around your abdomen and a sword by your side—o' you did look so beautiful! and I need not say so, natural![26]

Livingstone's death in Africa and his African servants' decision to carry his remains to the coast gave much material for his sensationalist promoters. The RGS organized a highly publicized and deeply symbolic burial ceremony for Livingstone in Westminster Abbey. The legend was further entrenched by Horace Waller, who took charge of the publication of the *Last Journals* and organized many meetings and conferences to promote his memory. The *Journals* (1874) were heavily pruned, with Waller removing or altering any statement he felt threatened the standing of his hero.[27] Waller was eager to spread a hagiographic vision of Livingstone as an exemplary figure in the cause of the Christian missionary advance and the fight against slavery in Africa.

David Livingstone epitomizes the hero of exploration of the period prior to the New Imperialism, when travelers, explorers, and members of the geographical establishment believed they had a key educational task to perform in society. During his lifetime, Livingstone used his iconic status to promote several ideas he feared were not popular enough in Britain: namely, the abolition of the slave trade, free trade, white emigration to Africa, and the promotion of technology in less advanced societies. Livingstone's example also directly inspired several leading figures in the scramble for Africa, such as Sir Bartle Frere, Sir Harry Johnston, John Smith Moffat, and the Rev. John Mackenzie.[28] With Victorian ministers cautious about embarking upon expensive colonial projects, lobbyists sought to use public opinion to pressure Parliamentary action, and heroes of exploration were particularly good at it. As John Darwin has argued, "foreign policy could easily be derailed by a press campaign or an appeal to patriotic prejudices."[29] Horace Waller and his successors made full use of the evocative power of the Livingstone legend in support of British imperial intervention in tropical Africa (notably Nyasaland and the east African coast).[30] More than twenty years elapsed between Murchison's initial support for Livingstone and Waller's entrenchment of the posthumous legend: this left time for European powers to become more involved in African affairs and to contemplate colonial rule more seriously. From then on, legends of exploration would develop against a much more imperial backdrop.

*   *   *

With informal influence gradually replaced by formal control as the New Imperialism gained momentum, the scene was set for a new generation of heroes who combined exploration with an expansionist agenda. They did not replace the precursors of the first period, who remained powerful embodiments of the "civilizing mission" commonly used to justify the European conquest of the globe, but rather added a new meaning to exploratory activities. Their reputations could be used more straightforwardly to support calls for imperial aggrandizement.

Having made the most of the Livingstone legend, Horace Waller set his sights on General Charles "Chinese" Gordon. Although Gordon never embarked on geographical exploration strictly speaking, his activities in China and the Sudan, not to mention Palestine, often led him to carry out work similar to that of an explorer.[31] Gordon also frequented the same circles as explorers and benefited from the same interest by the geographical establishment. He had joined the RGS in 1858, but decided to resign in 1866 as he felt that "its members were trying to lionize him."[32] However, he still used the logistical benefits the RGS could bestow on him, occasionally borrowing equipment from the society.[33] Gordon's reputation was consciously used by anti-slavery campaigners, and especially Waller, to pressure the British government to intervene against the slave traders. Gordon himself was aware that his name was exploited for this purpose, and he did not hesitate to ask Waller to "kindly keep my property, viz my name out of any letters you may write to the papers."[34] This did not prevent C. H. Allen, the Secretary of the British and Foreign Anti-Slavery Society, from producing a *Life of Chinese Gordon* (1884), priced at one penny to reach the widest possible audience. It met with notable success: the copy available at the Bodleian Library in Oxford reads on the top left corner "300th thousand." Gordon's reluctance to be used by Waller and his colleagues might have stemmed from his own reservations about the work of the Anti-Slavery Society; as he confided to Waller, "*I do not believe in you all*, you say this, and that, and you do not do it."[35] He was struck, however, by the ambiguities of missionary activity, which he sketched out in clear terms to Waller:

> Of course the question is *do men go as simple ministers of Gospel*, or *do they go as civilising agents as well as Ministers of Gospel.* I think all things on the question being answered, is they go as ministers of the Gospel. External things have no right with them if they go as civilising agents. Then of course they must have similar power.[36]

Waller, however, persisted in promoting Gordon in the papers and influential circles. In a letter to the British consul in Zanzibar, Sir John Kirk, in 1880, Sir William MacKinnon, founder of the East Africa Company, acknowledged that Horace Waller "had told [him] everything" about Gordon.[37] Waller had less success with Gordon than with Livingstone and, in the end, it was W. T. Stead, editor of the *Pall Mall Gazette,* who turned "Chinese Gordon" into "Gordon of Khartum." Having twisted Prime Minister William Gladstone's arm into asking Gordon to solve the difficult situation of the Anglo-Egyptian garrison in Khartum—a decision that ultimately led to the general's death in January 1885—Stead was responsible for the chain of events that made the Gordon legend one of the most enduring Victorian myths, and also one that served to justify the Anglo-Egyptian conquest of the Sudan fourteen years later.[38]

In France as much as in Britain, the late 1870s and early 1880s were a turning point in imperial affairs. The increasingly interventionist policies of European powers entailed a significant scaling up of the role of geographical societies and their *protégés*, the explorers. The turning point for the Paris *Société de Géographie* came in 1863–1864 with the arrival of Jules Duval as a member of its committee. Duval orientated the society toward a clearly pro-colonial stance, one that saw exploration as a first step toward annexation.[39] He paved the way for Charles Maunoir, secretary general of the society from 1867 until 1896, whom a key explorer of the time saw as "one of the authorities whose opinion makes the law in the field of exploration."[40] Maunoir, helped by the influential marquess Prosper de Chasseloup-Laubat (Minister of the French Navy and later Minister for Algeria and the Colonies), succeeded in making the *Société de géographie* a key promoter of colonial expansion to the metropolitan public. The society was also soon assisted by the rise of provincial geographical societies. In 1873, the second French geographical society was founded (in Lyons), followed by Marseilles (1876), Montpellier (1878), Oran (1878), Nancy (1879), Rouen (1879), Rochefort (1879), Algeria (1879), Douai (1880), Bourg (1881), and Dijon (1881). As a result, membership of geographical societies rocketed from 600 in 1871 to 9,500 in 1881, making France the leading country in geographical society membership. In 1875, the second international congress of geography met in Paris.[41] This went hand in hand with increased media interest in colonial matters.[42] For instance, the most respectable of French newspapers, *Le Temps*,[43] played a key role in the promotion of the imperial ethos, through a variety of articles on colonial life, dispatches on colonial campaigns, and personal contacts with colonial explorers-cum-military commanders such as Pierre Savorgnan de Brazza, Gustave Binger, and Joseph Gallieni.[44]

Under the French Second Empire, exploration and military activity became closely intertwined. Expeditions to Indochina, such as those by Ernest Doudart de Lagrée, Louis Delaporte, and Francis Garnier in search of the source of the Mekong River (1866–1868), had demonstrated that exploratory work could be undertaken as part of expeditions sometimes bordering on gunboat diplomacy.

In the Sahara, Henri Duveyrier's travels in the late 1850s and early 1860s were very much influenced by the desire to open new trade routes for France and to advance its interests in the region. Duveyrier used the networks of his father to secure support for his ambitious explorations. A serious illness after his return from the Sahara made it impossible for him to produce the book he had intended to write, so his doctor in Algiers, Auguste Warnier, took charge, turning the notes into the book *Les Touareg du Nord* (1864), published under Duveyrier's name. Warnier engaged in hero-making, portraying Duveyrier's exploits in a highly flattering fashion. The doctor stated to Duveyrier's father:

> As Henri lacks experience in the art of writing, he will not be able to produce a work that is worthy of him before undertaking a new journey . . . . I am doing a book to keep the impatient people waiting.[45]

His reputation established with this book, Duveyrier was able to secure the support of the *Société de Géographie* (and particularly of Charles Maunoir, who became a close friend) for his new projects of exploration, compensating for the government's limited enthusiasm for his ideas. The society, of which he became a member in 1864, took care to portray him as a tactful negotiator and an eminent authority on Saharan African affairs in newspapers in the late 1860s and 1870s.[46] Duveyrier subsequently served as an adviser to Saharan explorers (including Charles de Foucauld), and finally managed to influence French colonial policies in North Africa. His appraisal of the Tuaregs as a people friendly to French interests caused many explorers to perish, and he tried to blame these setbacks on the Sanussi Muslim brotherhood.[47] He played an instrumental role in the development of a "black legend" about the Sanusiyya, which ultimately induced France to follow an aggressive expansionist policy in the Sahara.[48]

The Italian-born French explorer Pierre Savorgnan de Brazza exemplifies the hero of exploration who expanded the French empire (see Figure 5.2). His case offers the opportunity to look in detail at the networks of patronage behind a successful legend of exploration. Three expeditions to the Ogoué River in Central Africa won him lasting fame in France not only as an explorer, but also as a liberator of slaves and a benevolent figure for the French empire. Upon his return from his first expedition, in December 1878, Brazza was fêted all over Paris, and "newspapers and politicians made him the man of the hour," notably because he was judged the French answer to Stanley, who had also explored the Congo region.[49] He used his nationwide fame in the newspapers[50] (which he expanded with articles, lectures, face-to-face meetings, and even evocative photographs of himself in explorer's dress romanticizing his role) to fund his second expedition. He had several high-level advocates, including the education minister, colonial lobbyist and soon-to-be Premier Jules Ferry. According to Brazza, Ferry had told him, "Go on. Never restrain your freedom of action. If you succeed, we will support you."[51] The explorer followed the minister's advice. On his second expedition, he concluded on behalf of the French Government (but without any official mandate) a series of protectorate treaties with the Congolese King Makoko, founding the future French colony of the Congo, north of Stanley Pool. The French Chambers were reluctant to approve the treaties of protectorate in principle, but the combined influence of French outrage at British intervention in Egypt and Brazza's charisma won Parliament over to his cause. The unusual enthusiasm of a public generally inclined to stay aloof from colonial questions was a decisive factor. Beyond lobbying geographical societies, the press, and the Chambers, Brazza sent a detailed report to the Minister of Marine Jauréguiberry, making his case for a French colony in the Congo.[52] When the *Société de Géographie de Paris* invited him to give a speech at the *Grand amphithéâtre* of the Sorbonne to an audience that he himself described as "a scientific élite," he made his case for the ratification of the treaties he had signed on behalf of France, and for the construction of a railway line in the Congo. He ended his speech with a vibrant appeal to decision-makers:

> You will lend our project the support of your influence, if you think that it
> may serve the interests of our motherland while serving the causes of science

Figure 5.2 French explorer Savorgnan de Brazza

and civilisation! And as far as I am concerned, the greatest honour you could grant me would be to tell me: 'Go ahead!'.[53]

The "great man of whom everyone talked about those days" cashed in on his successes and led a powerful press campaign to secure government funding for a third expedition.[54] Journalists contributed to the development of the hero's legend. The son of the editor and owner of *Le Phare de la Loire* assured Brazza that his newspaper "had done its best to be useful to you as soon as you came back [from your second expedition]":

> What I wanted to know from you, rather than from one of your friends, was how the newspaper could help you while you are away, what was the overall direction to follow in order to serve your designs, which I feel are patriotic and beautiful. I also wanted to ask you to let us know what you would like the public to know while you are away.[55]

The popularity of Brazza helped give colonial propaganda credibility. Even the socialist leader Jean Jaurès praised Brazza, declaring that "in the Congo, M. de Brazza could cross vast expanses of territories and warlike tribes without a single shot fired, because he knew how to be loved."[56] Brazza also spread colonial ambitions among his Masonic colleagues, to whom he had eloquently defended his own imperial role upon joining them.

> I had been working for a long time to promote peace, civilisation and progress in the Congo, when a pamphlet from the *Grand Orient de France* fell in my hands. The similarity between the ideal of fraternity and tolerance that was advocated and my own aspirations struck me, and that was the reason why I asked to be admitted among you.[57]

A master of self-promotion, Brazza epitomizes the hero of exploration of the age of New Imperialism, who benefited from the vacuum offered by a depressed Third Republic, to become a national hero. A wide network of supporters drawn from the geographical societies, the press, politicians, and Masonry united to produce a long-lasting legend.[58]

Notoriously, the self-promotional dimension was even more developed in the case of Henry Morton Stanley, who made the most of his journalistic status to advance his career and fame. If the Stanley of "Dr. Livingstone, I presume?" still belonged to the period of informal influence rather than outright conquest, his later expeditions bore the imprint of the explorers of New Imperialism, openly aiding European imperial expansion and not shying away from the use of force. Stanley's shrewd use of new communication technologies and new practices in the press, combined with a clear taste for self-promotion, have been widely analyzed.[59]

With the expansion of formal control toward the end of the century, exploration took an even more openly military turn, and the support provided by the geographical establishment became increasingly supplemented by military circles. In Britain, the case of Sir Francis Younghusband illustrates the blurring of the boundaries between exploration and military activity. Most of his expeditions along the frontier of British India and into Tibet were undertaken as a soldier or colonial administrator who enjoyed a strong relationship to the RGS. In 1888, at the age of twenty-five, he had been elected the society's youngest Fellow, and he received the Founder's Medal two years later.[60] Born in India but trained at the Royal Military College of Sandhurst, Younghusband epitomizes the "exploring soldier and imperialist."[61] His leadership of the Tibet expedition of 1903–1904 offers a clear example of a member of the geographical establishment not only intent on filling one of the last remaining blanks on maps, but also directly involved in the imperial aggression that led to the 1904 Lhasa convention, which imposed a protectorate on Tibet.[62] In spite of the expedition's dubious intentions and practices (including the looting of unique artifacts, which did not go unnoticed in the contemporary media in both Britain and India),[63] it strengthened Younghusband's reputation, earning him the Star of India and honorary degrees from the universities of Cambridge and Edinburgh.

France also witnessed a gradual militarization of exploratory activity. Military campaigns of exploration were usually preceded by "campaigns of colonial propaganda,"[64] designed to ensure political and military support for the project. Before embarking upon his two-year long Congo-Nile mission to assert French control over the Upper Nile (under the pretext of exploration), Major Jean-Baptiste Marchand sought the support of influential patrons in Paris, including the ever-present Maunoir, eminent military officers, politicians, and colonial lobbyists.[65] The "Marchand mission" ultimately made its leader a household name in France.[66] Marchand's heroization was made possible for two reasons. First, he appealed to anti-Republicans, who found in him a military hero whose story exposed supposed weaknesses in the Third Republic. Second, the story of his exploration was filled with drama, which attracted many biographers. The nationalist writer Michel Morphy, the author of a *National History of Joan of Arc*, published a serialized account of Marchand's deeds that totaled 2240 pages in 28 volumes, which sold 70,200 copies in a year and a half. [67] Colonial propagandists also seized the opportunity of Marchand's achievement to advance their cause. Paul d'Ivoi's *Marchand* was the opening title of a series entitled *Great Explorers,* which was meant to tell the stories of a "whole host of heroes."[68] The book's opening pages featured an engraving depicting the "heroic explorer" in full colonial officer's gear. The first volume sold 3450 copies by 1900, and 2150 sold of the second volume.[69] D'Ivoi's deep commitment to French colonial expansion was made obvious in his writings for *Le Journal des Voyages,* a weekly dubbed "the eulogist of the French colonial epic."[70] The story of the military explorer sold well, and its geographical content was frequently overshadowed by nationalist considerations.[71]

*   *   *

By the turn of the century, most corners of the globe had been "explored" and many of them conquered. The last wave of explorers directed their efforts to the most remote regions of the earth. Before the First World War, polar exploration made the names of Jean-Baptiste Charcot in France and, in Britain, Captain Robert Falcon Scott, whom some have seen as "a suitable hero for a nation in decline."[72] In the interwar years, a limited number of explorers tested the frontiers of human resistance in deserts: Michel Vieuchange searched for the fabled city of Smara in the Western Sahara and Ralph Bagnold made a name for himself by exploring Egypt's Western Desert.[73] These were among the last representatives of a dying tradition and they never attained the status of national heroes, unlike their glorious predecessors.

Exploration had come to be seen as an activity mostly belonging to the past. Its most salient characteristic in the early twentieth century was the tendency to memorialize the achievements of nineteenth-century explorers, strengthening and expanding preexisting legends, most of which derived from the conjunction of New Imperialism and New Journalism. Heroes of exploration gave readers ethnocentric accounts of strange peoples and customs. Brazza's reputation as a liberator of slaves and a tactful conqueror who was said to have been loved by Africans and made them love the tricolor flag was reiterated in countless schoolbooks and hagiographies. David Livingstone still commanded deep devotion in Britain. Commemorations of his achievements maintained the highly moralizing tone of prewar heroic canons, as can be seen from the following extract:

> Among the great missionaries of the nineteenth century no name ranks higher than that of David Livingstone. Not only is his fame in all the Churches, but also far beyond their borders. He is one of our national heroes, whose memory is honoured by multitudes who own no Church allegiance. He was a great explorer, who did more than any other to 'blaze the trail' in the interior of

the Dark Continent, and in that respect his labours and achievements were of national and international importance. He made contributions to geographical and ethnological knowledge the value of which was gratefully acknowledged by the learned societies of the civilised world.[74]

Finally, the cinema appeared as a key asset to ensure the transmission of the legends of exploration to the new generations. This was a key concern to the director of the Livingstone Film Company, who argued that:

> The presentation of the life of the great Scottish Missionary will, I am confident, not only stimulate interest in missionary work and enterprise, but will revisualize for the present generation one of the finest Christian characters of the Victorian era.[75]

Such a statement anticipated almost exactly what Léon Poirier sought to do in two of his films celebrating key heroes of exploration, *L'Appel du silence* (about Charles de Foucauld, 1936) and *Brazza ou l'épopée du Congo* (1939). The former was meant to contribute to the "recovery of the country" through the "recovery of [national] conscience,"[76] and upon the release of the latter, Poirier reflected that it was "a lesson of energy given by Brazza."[77] At least until decolonization, legends of exploration continued to fulfill the role of exemplary figures to the younger generations. Their remarkable capacity for adaptation to new promotional media, such as the cinema, goes a long way to explaining this longevity.

* * *

The legends of exploration studied here reveal the complex interactions between socio-cultural developments in the metropoles and the evolving relationship between Europe and the non-European worlds. The celebration of exploratory feats started as a rather marginal activity involving a small circle of geographically-minded individuals, but gradually expanded as new means of promotion arose, together with new geopolitical stakes brought about by the New Imperialism, in conjunction with a more fervent nationalism. Besides journalists and biographers, those involved in the promotion of the careers of explorers came to include influential politicians and high-ranking military officers. Explorers themselves came from increasingly varied backgrounds. As the two leading powers of the world in the nineteenth century, Britain and France emulated each other, and the processes that led to the blossoming of legends of exploration in both countries tended to involve comparable actors and to follow similar trajectories.

Ironically, the immediate impact of these explorers seems to have been much more important to the metropolitan public than to African populations. Their actions were powerfully mediated by new journalistic techniques, such as the New Journalism, which hardly looked beyond Europe and America. In the long term, though, they sparked their homelands' interest in overseas lands, often resulting in formal control. It is beyond doubt that their action, and the numerous stories and heroic legends that they inspired, deeply influenced the shaping of the relationship between European and non-Western worlds.

NOTES

1. Robert Cornevin notes that explorers, especially those who operated on the African continent, often served as exemplary figures for European youth from the 1870s: R. Cornevin, "Numa broc et les explorations africaines," in N. Broc, *Dictionnaire illustré des explorateurs français du XIXème siècle, Afrique* (Paris: Editions du CTHS, 1988), xi.

2. See, for instance, Edward Said's appraisal of the role of geography in reinforcing the essentializing character of "Orientalism," in *Orientalism* (New York: Pantheon Books, 1978) and *Culture & Imperialism* (New York: Alfred A. Knopf, 1993). Said's ideas inspired several postcolonial critics to touch on the question of explorers' accounts from a literary point of view, such as D. Spurr, *The Rhetoric of Empire: Colonial Discourse in Journalism, Travel Writing and Imperial Administration* (Durham, N.C.: Duke University Press, 1993).

3. F. Foureau, *D'Alger au Congo par le Tchad* (Paris: Masson, 1902)

4. L. D. Hammond, "Introduction" to *Bougainville's News from New Cythera* (Minneapolis: University of Minnesota Press, 1970), 3. See also M. Thiéry, *Bougainville, Soldier and Sailor* (London: Grayson & Grayson, 1932), 257.

5. R. A. Stafford, "Exploration and Empire," in R. W. Winks (ed.), *Oxford History of the British Empire: Vol. 5, Historiography* (Oxford: Oxford University Press 1999), 290.

6. To borrow a phrase from Geoff Cubitt and Allen Warren in *Heroic Reputations and Exemplary Lives* (Manchester: Manchester University Press, 2000).

7. To use Raymond Williams' concept in *Marxism and Literature* (Oxford: Oxford University Press, 1977), ch. 9.

8. On the influence of Empire and masculinity on imperial heroism, see G. Dawson, *Soldier Heroes* (London: Routledge, 1994). On the role of the press and the printed media in promoting these heroic figures, see Beau Riffenburgh, *The Myth of the Explorer* (London: Belhaven, 1993) and C. Pettitt, *Dr. Livingstone, I Presume? Missionaries, Journalists, Explorers and Empire* (Cambridge, Mass.: Harvard University Press, 2007). S. Venayre offers in *La gloire de l'aventure* (Paris: Aubier,

2002) a genealogy of the concepts of "adventure" and "adventurer," which offers interesting parallels with that of explorers and exploration. For a comparative approach of the promotional processes behind the success of British and French imperial heroes, see B. Sèbe, *"Celebrating" British and French Imperialism: The Making of Colonial Heroes Acting in Africa, 1870–1939*, Oxford University D.Phil. thesis, 2007 (published as *Heroic Imperialists in Africa* (Manchester: Manchester University Press, 2013)); idem, "Porte-drapeaux de l'Empire: la promotion des héros coloniaux français et britanniques de la conquête de l'Afrique à la Seconde Guerre mondiale," *Synergies Royaume-Uni et Irlande* 2 (2009): 81–92; idem, "Colonial Celebrities in Popular Culture: Heroes of the British and French Empires 1850–1914," in R. Clarke (ed.), *Celebrity Colonialism: Fame, Power and Representation in Colonial and Postcolonial Cultures* (Cambridge: Cambridge Scholars Press, 2009), 37–54.

9. An early discussion of this question can be found in R. I. Rotberg, *Africa and its Explorers: Motives, Methods and Impact* (Cambridge, Mass.: Harvard University Press, 1970).

10. See, in particular, John MacKenzie, *Propaganda and Empire* (Manchester: Manchester University Press, 1984), and his edited works, *Imperialism and Popular Culture* (Manchester: Manchester University Press, 1986), *Popular Imperialism and the Military* (Manchester: Manchester University Press, 1991), and *The Victorian Vision: Inventing New Britain* (London: V&A, 2001). See also A. Thompson, *The Empire Strikes Back? The Impact of Imperialism on Britain from the Mid-Nineteenth Century* (Harlow: Longman, 2005). The theory of "popular imperialism" as set out by MacKenzie is challenged by Bernard Porter, *The Absent-Minded Imperialists* (Oxford: Oxford University Press, 2004).

11. To quote the classic work of C.-R. Ageron, *France coloniale ou parti colonial?* (Paris: Presses universitaires de France, 1978).

12. See for instance P. Blanchard, S. Lemaire and N. Bancel (eds.), *Culture coloniale en France* (Paris: Presses du Centre National de la Recherche Scientifique, 2008); O. Saaïdia and L. Zerbini (eds.), *La construction du discours colonial* (Paris: Karthala, 2009) and T. Chafer and A. Sackur (eds.), *Promoting the Colonial Idea* (Basingstoke: Palgrave Macmillan, 2002). For an English-speaking summary of scholarship on popular attachment to the Empire in France, see B. Sèbe, "Exalting Imperial Grandeur: the French Empire and its metropolitan public," in J. M. MacKenzie (ed.), *European Empires and the People* (Manchester: Manchester University Press, 2011), 19–56.

13. On the French case, see E. Sibeud, *Une science impériale pour l'Afrique? La construction des savoirs africanistes en France* (Paris: Editions de l'Ecole des Hautes Etudes en Sciences Sociales, 2002) and S. Dulucq, *Écrire l'histoire de l'Afrique à la période coloniale (XIXe–XXe siècles)* (Paris: Karthala, 2009). On Britain, see H. Tilley (with R. J. Gordon), *Ordering Africa: Anthropology, European imperialism and the politics of knowledge* (Manchester: Manchester University Press, 2007) and J. McAleer, *Representing Africa: Landscape, Exploration and Empire in southern Africa, 1780–1870* (Manchester: Manchester University Press, 2010).

14. For the former, see D. Kennedy, "British exploration in the nineteenth century," *History Compass*, 5, 6 (2007): 1879–1900; for the latter, Riffenburgh, *The Myth of the Explorer* and F. Fernández Armesto, *Pathfinders, A Global History of Exploration* (Oxford: Oxford University Press, 2006) are good starting points.

15. To use Felix Driver's concept.

16. For Britain, see F. Driver, "Geography's Empire: histories of geographical knowledge," *Environment and Planning* 1992 (vol. 10): 23–40; D. N. Livingstone, *The Geographical Tradition: Episodes in the History of a Contexted Enterprise* (Oxford: Blackwell, 1992); F. Driver, *Geography Militant: Cultures of Exploration and Empire* (Oxford, UK and Malden, Mass.: Blackwell, 2001); and J. M. MacKenzie, "The provincial geographical societies in Britain, 1884–1914," in M. Bell, R. A. Butlin and M. Heffernan (eds.), *Geography and Imperialism 1820–1940* (Manchester: Manchester University Press, 1995): 93–124. For France, D. Lejeune, *Les sociétés de géographie en France et l'expansion coloniale au XIXe siècle* (Paris: Albin Michel, 1993).

17. Edward Said reflected in the first chapter of his *Culture and Imperialism* (1993) upon the "overlapping territories" and "intertwined histories" of geographical science and imperialism. For the French side, see Pierre Singaravélou (ed.), *L'Empire des géographes. Géographie, exploration et colonisation XIXe–XXe siècle* (Paris: Belin, 2008) and P. Singaravélou, "De l'explorateur au géographe. La Société de Géographie et l'Afrique (1821–1854)," in D. Lecoq and A. Chambard (eds.), *Terre à découvrir, terres à parcourir* (Paris: Publications de l'université Paris VII, 2000), 258–281.

18. To borrow the term from N. Broc, *La géographie des philosophes. Géographes et voyageurs français au XVIIIe siècle* (Paris: Ophrys, 1975). See also H. Blais, "Les sociétés géographiques, fin XVIIIe—milieu XIXe siècle: quelle institutionalisation pour quelle géographie?," in H. Blais and I. Lesage (eds.), *Géographies plurielles. Les sciences géographiques au moment de l'émergence des sciences humaines (1750–1850)* (Paris: L'Harmattan, 2006), 113–130.

19. Lejeune, *Sociétés de géographie*, 37–40.

20. His birthplace, Mauzé-sur-le-Mignon, organizes yearly celebrations and commemorated the bicentenary of his birth in 1999 with numerous events and exhibitions. For a general appraisal of the myth of Timbuktu, see I. Surun, "La découverte de Tombouctou: déconstruction et reconstruction d'un mythe géographique," *L'Espace géographique* 2:31 (2002), 131–144.

21. Although some notable geographical achievements took place in this period, especially in the Pacific. See H. Blais, *Voyages au grand océan. Géographies du Pacifique et colonisation, 1815–1845* (Paris: Comité des travaux historiques et scientifiques, 2005).

22. For an overview of the role of Sir Roderick Murchison, see R. A. Stafford, *Scientist of Empire: Sir Roderick Murchison, Scientific Exploration and Victorian Imperialism* (Cambridge: Cambridge University Press, 1989).

23. A. D. Roberts, "Livingstone, David (1813–1873)," Oxford Dictionary of National Biography [ODNB]. [Accessed July 10, 2010].

24. F. Driver, "Henry Morton Stanley and his critics: geography, exploration and empire," *Past & Present* 133 (November 1991): 134–164.

25. Rhodes House Library, Oxford [RHL], Waller Papers, MSS. Afr. S. 16, I/B, f. 219, Waller to Livingstone, October 25, 1869.

26. RHL, Waller Papers, MSS. Afr. S. 16, I/B, f. 219, Waller to Livingstone, October 25, 1869.

27. D. O. Helly, *Livingstone's Legacy, Horace Waller and Victorian Myth-Making*, Athens, OH: Ohio University Press, 1987), 26.

28. J. M. MacKenzie, "David Livingstone and the Worldly After-life: Imperialism and Nationalism in Africa," in J. M. MacKenzie (ed.), *David Livingstone and the Victorian Encounter with Africa* (London: National Portrait Gallery, 1996), 201–217.

29. J. Darwin, "Imperialism and the Victorians," *English Historical Review* (June 1997), 623.

30. Roberts, *Livingstone,* ODNB.

31. See for instance A. Moore-Harell, *Gordon and the Sudan. Prologue to the Mahdiyya, 1877–1880* (London: Frank Cass Publishers, 2001).

32. R. Davenport-Hines, "Gordon, Charles George (1833–1885)," ODNB. [Accessed September 3, 2010].

33. RHL, MSS Afr. 16, vol. II, f. 6, Gordon to Waller, January 29, 1874.

34. RHL, Waller Papers, Gordon Manuscript, f. 71, Gordon to Horace Waller, January 31, 1877.

35. RHL, Waller Papers, Gordon Manuscript, f. 88, Gordon to Horace Waller, November 11, 1877.

36. RHL, MSS Afr. 16, vol. II, f. 215, Gordon to Waller, December 16, 1882.

37. National Library of Scotland, Edinburgh [NLS], MS 20311, f. 311, MacKinnon to John Kirk, March 12, 1880.

38. See J. M. MacKenzie, "Heroic Myths of Empire," in MacKenzie, *Popular imperialism and the military,* 109–138, and Sèbe, *Celebrating British and French Imperialism,* 141–151.

39. Lejeune, *Les sociétés de géographie,* 69.

40. Henri Duveyrier quoted by D. Casajus, *Henri Duveyrier, un Saint-Simonien au désert* (Paris: Ibis Press, 2007), 260.

41. A. Murphy, *The Ideology of French Imperialism 1871–1881* (Washington: H. Fertig, 1948), 8.

42. Sèbe, *Celebrating British and French imperialism,* 83–84.

43. V. Goedorp, *Figures du "Temps"* (Paris: Albin Michel, 1943).

44. C. Bellanger, P. Guiral, F. Terrou, (eds.), *Histoire générale de la presse française* (Paris: Presses universitaires de France, 1972), 355.

45. Archives Nationales, Paris, AN 47 AP3, Henri Duveyrier to his father, February 18, 1862, quoted in E. Mambré, "Henri Duveyrier, Explorateur du Sahara (1840–1892)" (*Maîtrise* thesis, University of Aix-en-Provence, France, 1992), 78–79.

46. Mambré, "Henri Duveyrier," 105–118 and 142.

47. Casajus, *Duveyrier*, 137–142.

48. J.-L. Triaud, *La légende noire de la Sanûsiyya* (Paris: Editions de la Maison des Sciences de l'homme, 1995), 99–118.

49. R. West, *Brazza of the Congo, European Exploration and Exploitation in French Equatorial Africa* (London: Jonathan Cape, 1972), 91–92.

50. Archives Nationales d'Outre-Mer, Aix-en-Provence [ANOM], Brazza papers, PA VIII, boxes 1 to 16, press cutting albums.

51. ANOM, Brazza papers, PA 16 VII, box 10, manuscript note from Brazza recounting Jules Ferry's advice to him about the French Congo.

52. H. Brunschwig, *Brazza explorateur, Les traités Makoko 1880–1882* (Paris: Mouton and Ecole pratique des hautes études, 1972), 258–267.

53. Anon., *Réception de Monsieur P. Savorgnan de Brazza au grand amphithéâtre de la Sorbonne le 23 juin 1882* (Paris: Editions de la Sorbonne, 1882), 298–299.

54. C. de Chavannes, *Avec Brazza, souvenirs de la mission de l'ouest africain* (Paris: Plon, 1935), 11.

55. ANOM, Brazza papers, PA 16 III, Box 2, Maurice Schwab to Brazza, January 18, 1883.

56. J. Jaurès, *Discours pour l'Alliance française* in Albi, 1884.

57. ANOM, Brazza papers, folder *"Lettres reçues et brouillons, Commémorations du souvenir de Brazza,"* draft of a letter from Brazza to the Venerable of the lodge *Alsace-Lorraine,* November 23, 1904.

58. I. Dion, *Brazza, au cœur du Congo* (Marseille: Images en Manœuvre éditions, 2007), 129–147.

59. See Driver, "Henry Morton Stanley and his critics"; Pettitt, *Dr. Livingstone, I Presume?*; and J. Newman, *Imperial footprints: Henry Morton Stanley's African Journeys* (Washington D.C.: Brassey, 2004).

60. On Younghusband, see A. Verrier, *Francis Younghusband and the Great Game* (London: Jonathan Cape, 1991), and P. French, *Younghusband, the last Great Imperial Adventurer* (London: HarperCollins, 1994).

61. D. Matless, "Younghusband, Sir Francis Edward (1863–1942)" [ODNB]. [Accessed February 10, 2011].

62. On Younghusband's expedition, see P. Fleming, *Bayonets to Lhasa* (London: Rupert Hart-Davis, 1962) and P. Mehra, *The Younghusband Expedition, an Intepretation* (London: Asia Publishing House, 1968).

63. P. Mehra, "In the Eyes of its Beholders: the Younghusband Expedition (1903–4) and Contemporary Media," *Modern Asian Studies,* 39, 3 (Jul. 2005): 725–739. On the looting question, see M. Carrington, "Officers, Gentlemen and Thieves: the Looting of Monasteries during the 1903/4 Younghusband Mission to Tibet," *Modern Asian Studies,* 37, 1 (2003): 81–109.

64. To use the term coined by P. Venier in "A Campaign of Colonial Propaganda: Gallieni, Lyautey and the Defence of the Military Regime in Madagascar, May 1899 to July 1900," in Chafer, *Promoting,* 29–39.

65. Sèbe, *Celebrating British and French imperial heroes,* 215–220.

66. G. Hanotaux, *Le Général Mangin* (Paris: Plon, 1935), 1.

67. Institut Mémoire de l'Edition Contemporaine, Paris and Caen [IMEC], Hachette Papers, S2/C16B2, "Registres Volumes Retour et Mise en Vente," 1898–1908.

68. Paul d'Ivoi, *Les Grands Explorateurs. La Mission Marchand* (Paris: Fayard frères, 1899–1900), back cover presenting the next title in the series, *General Gallieni: Pacification of Madagascar.*

69. IMEC, Hachette Papers, S2/C16B2, "Registres Volumes Retour et Mise en Vente," 1898–1908.

70. M. Palewska, "Le Journal des Voyages (I)," *Le Rocambole, Bulletin des amis du roman populaire,* Autumn 1998: 9.

71. B. Sèbe, "From Thoissey to the Capital via Fashoda: Major Marchand, partisan icon of the Right in Paris," in J. Wardhaugh (ed.), *Paris and the Right in the Twentieth Century* (Cambridge: Cambridge Scholars Publishing, 2007), 18–42.

72. R. Huntford, *The Last Place on Earth* (London: Pan Books, 1985). On Charcot, see S. Kahn, *Jean-Baptiste Charcot, explorateur des mers, navigateur de poles* (Grenoble: Glénat, 2006).

73. A. de Meaux, *L'ultime désert: vie et mort de Michel Vieuchange* (Paris: Phébus, 2004); T. Monod and J.-F. Sers, *Désert libyque* (Paris: Arthaud, 1994), W. T. Abed, *The Other Egypt* (Cairo; Zarzura publishing, 1998); and A. Goudie, *Wheels across the desert* (London: Silphium Press, 2008).

74. NLS, MS 20318, f.32, "David Livingstone: Centenary of Great Missionary's Ordination," in *The Life of Faith*, November 20, 1940, 643.

75. NLS, MS 7875, letter from J. Aubrey Rees, director of the Livingstone Film Expedition, to W. Smith Nicol, November 10, 1923.

76. L. Poirier, *Pourquoi et comment je vais réaliser L'Appel du Silence* (Paris and Tours: Mame, 1935), 1.

77. Interview of L. Poirier by M. Idzkowski, *Le Jour*, July 15, 1939.

PART II

Territories

6

EXPLORATION IN IMPERIAL RUSSIA

WILLARD SUNDERLAND

In a famous essay, the early eighteenth-century polymath Vasily Tatishchev describes a discussion between two friends about the merits of "science and learning." Some "sciences," they conclude, are "harmful." Others are "curious" but ultimately false (astrology, for example), while still others are entertaining. The best "sciences" of all, however, are the "useful" ones, the ones that help "Man to know himself" and contribute "to the general and individual good." Among these is geography. As Tatishchev says through one of the friends in the dialogue, geography is beneficial because it reveals "not only the location of places and of defenses and approaches . . . of use during times of war and unrest but also the customs of peoples, the natural qualities of the air and soil, the availability (*dovol'stvo*) of products and resources, and the sufficiency and lack in all things."[1]

Tatishchev was a self-conscious "modern" and an ardent *devoté* of the "new learning," so his admiration for "geographical science" is not surprising. But his feelings were also typical of the establishment of his time. Upon coming to the throne at the end of the 1600s, Peter the Great determined that his countrymen were so woefully behind the leading nations of Europe that their only hope for catching up was to imitate much of what the Europeans were doing, including in the area of geography. Indeed, as the tsar and his followers saw it, the adoption of "geographical science" was critical, since the new method would produce more territorial knowledge, which in turn would lead to a better use of territory. Thus the imprecise "sketch maps" (*chertezhy*) used since the sixteenth century were shelved in favor of newfangled scientific ones (*landkarty*) drawn with lines of longitude and latitude, new institutions appeared to gather geographic data, and "learned men" were lured in from Europe to lead geodesic surveys and teach Russian noble boys the joys of triangulation.[2]

Not surprisingly, exploration was an important element in this geographical turn, and, to a degree, the new push built on earlier practices. Russians had been exploring the world around them for centuries, venturing into places like the northern Urals and along the coasts of the Arctic Ocean since at least the 1100s. As recently as the reign of Peter's grandfather, they had penetrated deeply into Siberia, reaching the Pacific by the late 1630s. Yet the Petrine era propelled the country toward a new sort of exploration that in time became far more scientific, systematic, and institutionalized than previous efforts. Peter's reforms effectively laid the groundwork for what would become a bona fide Russian geographical establishment, which then emerged as the all-important command center for exploration, developing and refining it as a distinct arena of state-public expertise.

Like all transitions, the shift to the new exploration was messy and uneven. Though Russian exploration eventually grew into an increasingly professional activity, much of it remained strikingly unscientific in practice, and ordinary folks—long-distance merchants and peasant settlers, for example—never stopped playing a role in the enterprise. The new-style exploration was also driven by a complex bundle of motivations, some of which had little to do with high-minded science. Much as elsewhere, great power politics and imperialism profoundly influenced where and how Russian explorers did their work, and so, too, did the glory-seeking inclinations of individual explorers as well as the Russians' sense of national pride and identity, which became intertwined with the concerns of the "new" Russian exploration from the start. Europe, the thinking went, might crow about its Columbuses and Cooks, but the Russians didn't have to worry about that – they had their own "discoverers" (*otkryvateli*) to be proud of, a point that enthusiastic patriots underscored for their audiences whenever they could.

Does all of this suggest a distinctly "Russian" history of exploration? The sources point to a complicated answer. On the one hand, the Russian case during the imperial era was indeed distinct in important ways from the more familiar European story. For one, as residents of a continental empire, Russians did most of their exploring across land, sending expeditions around their own country or into ill-defined neighboring regions, in contrast to their European contemporaries who ruled maritime empires and explored largely overseas. Overall, Russian exploration was less driven by commercial objectives than some of the European—notably English/

British—explorations, whose experiences tend to be taken as the norm. Exploration in Russia was also much more a state-funded than a privately funded affair.

At the same time, much about Russian exploration is consistent with what we see elsewhere, in particular the way it operated as a scientific and political enterprise as well as the meanings associated with it in Russian culture. Indeed, one of the great developments of the Petrine era was the intensification of Russia's engagement with the world, and, as a result, the explorations that followed were, in a sense, profoundly international and cosmopolitan affairs, closely monitored abroad and themselves influenced by foreign developments. Many "Russian" explorers of the imperial era turn out to have been non-Russian subjects or foreigners in Russian service, while Russian exploration in places like the North Pacific and Central Asia was drivenas much by inter-imperial rivalries as by domestic concerns. Russian exploration was thus many things at once, never purely "Russian" nor somehow uniformly "European" but rather both of Russia and connected to the world at the same time.

Uses and Directions

One of the persistent factors shaping Russian exploration was its close interrelationship with the history of Russian imperialism. By the time it unraveled in the revolution of 1917, the empire of the tsars was second only to the British empire in overall size and included a stunning diversity of peoples, representing ways of life "from the Marble Palace to the cave," as Catherine the Great had once put it.[3] (See Figure 6.1.) The empire acquired this scale and variety as a result of its long historical expansion, and exploration was a direct contributor to this process, both by helping the Russians acquire new territory and by "enhancing the picture" of poorly studied regions already within the state.[4]

Indeed, the empire was fundamental to exploration in another sense as well: it provided the basic geographic orbit for exploration activity. Unlike other European empires that ruled over far-flung colonies and whose explorers, in some cases, ventured onto multiple continents, Russia was a continental state straddling Europe and Asia, and, as a result, the country's explorers tended to work in a Eurasian rather than a global frame. Indeed, the Russians' only truly significant explorations outside of Eurasia unfolded in the Arctic Ocean and North Pacific, and along the coastlines of northwestern North America. Otherwise they explored by land, and mostly in

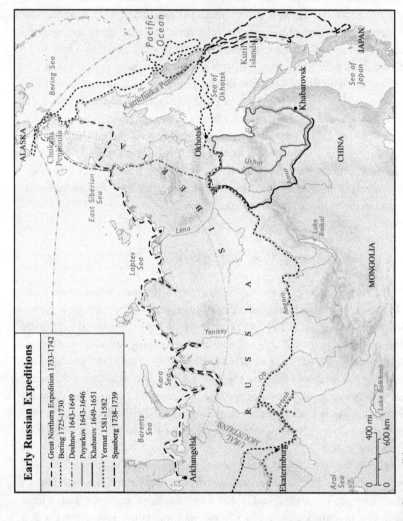

Figure 6.1 Early Russian expeditions

Early Russian Expeditions

- – – – Great Northern Expedition 1733-1742
- ········· Bering 1725-1730
- –·–·–·– Deshnev 1643-1649
- ·—·—·— Poyarkov 1643-1646
- ——— Khabarov 1649-1651
- ••••••• Yermak 1581-1582
- – ·· – ·· – Spanberg 1738-1739

regions to the north, south, and east of the traditional Russian heartland in European Russia rather than to the west, reflecting the fact that the empire's western borderlands—places like Poland, Finland, and the eastern Baltic— were already well known by the imperial era and therefore did not figure as domains of exploration in the strict sense of the word.

Because exploration was so closely tied to the life of the empire, it often led not surprisingly to the imposition—or at least attempts to impose— Russian power in new territories. The Russian ships that nosed around the coastlines of Alaska and the Aleutians in the late 1700s, for example, left behind iron plaques claiming: "This Land Belongs to Russia." In similar fashion, naval commander Gennadii Nevel'skoi combined exploration and empire-building in the Far East in 1849 and 1850 by surveying the Amur River delta and claiming it for the empire at the same time.[5]

In claiming the Amur for Russia, Nevel'skoi did two things that were commonplaces during the imperial era: First, he conveniently disregarded the opinion of the local inhabitants as well as the possibility that the territory might already be claimed by someone else, in this case, the Qing Empire. (The Russians also ignored Japanese claims to the island of Sakhalin just across from the mouth of the river and busily began establishing outposts there as of the 1850s.) Second, he built a fort, which underscored the fact that he and his countrymen—at least in Nevel'skoi's mind—were not just exploring but taking over as well. For centuries the extensive northern, southern, and eastern edges of the empire, including large parts of the Ponto-Caspian and Kazakh steppes as well as much of Siberia, were either only nominally claimed by neighboring states or not formally ruled by any state at all. Exploration was thus a means for the Russians to insist on their right to what they viewed as open territory, which explains why "discovery" as they practiced it so often unfolded in tandem with conquest, functioning in fact as a proxy for the expansion of Russian power.

Of course, this sort of exploration-as-conquest inevitably carried risks and occasionally backfired. One case in point was the expedition of Prince Aleksandr Bekovich-Cherkasskii, who was charged by Peter the Great in 1716 with exploring the upper reaches of the Amu-Darya (Oxus) River in what is today Uzbekistan and Turkmenistan with the double purpose of searching for gold deposits and convincing the local ruler, the Khan of Khiva, to submit to Russian rule. The expedition, which consisted of thousands of soldiers and camels, "two engineers, two merchants, and several naval officers," managed to reach the outskirts of Khiva but was destroyed almost to a man shortly thereafter by the Khivans and their allies, who proceeded to cut off Bekovich-Cherkasskii's head and send it as a gift to their ally, the Khan of Bukhara.[6] (The tsar had instructed the prince to seek a meeting with the Bukharan khan but presumably not quite like this.)

Still, even Bekovich-Cherkasskii's failure was proof of the important shift taking place in exploration in Peter's time. Dispatching military expeditions to dimly known regions had been a state practice well before the Petrine era, in particular to Siberia, where parties of Cossacks had been used to explore and bring new peoples "under the tsar's high hand" during much of the 1600s. But the initiatives of the early 1700s were different in three revealing ways. First, they came to be known by a new name—*ekspeditsiia*—a European loan word that underscored the new regime's interest in borrowing from and keeping up with European practices. Second, they became linked to promoting the new virtue of science. Bekovich-Cherkasskii, for example, was both a military commander and a cartographer who completed the first scientific map of the Caspian shortly before leaving on his doomed expedition. Third, the explorations of the new era became far more regular than before. Even the remarkable Cossack voyages that made their way across Siberia to the Pacific in the seventeenth century had been essentially ad hoc, driven by immediate circumstances and often on the basis of local initiatives, with little in the way of an overarching plan.

With the Westernizing changes of the Petrine era, however, the men in charge of the Russian government, starting with the tsar himself, began to conceive of exploration differently. Rather than something one did by necessity or as opportunity allowed, it now emerged as a virtuous undertaking in its own right, linked not only to what Peter and his lieutenants understood as the essential *raison d'être* of government—the promotion of the state's interest and the common good (*obshchee blago*), which they saw as effectively the same thing—but also to the defining values of the age such as "utility" (*pol'za*), pride in the fatherland (*otechestvo*), and the attainment of a reasoned view of the world based on "learning and science" (*nauka*). Not surprisingly, then, it only stood to reason that exploration needed to be encouraged wherever possible and supported on a systematic basis.[7]

The result of this shift was the emergence of a new exploration culture in Russia in the early 1700s that ultimately led to the country's full participation in the European-driven bonanza of exploration that would define the modern era. Peter's reign was marked by repeated explorations to the southern, northern, and eastern edges of the state, with the most famous coming at the very end of his life in January 1725 as he dispatched Vitus Bering on the first of what became two expeditions to Kamchatka to determine where or whether Siberia touched North America. (Though Bering never actually landed on the American mainland, his ships entered the strait that separated the two continents and that was good enough for Captain James Cook to argue a half century later that the strait should be named after him.)[8] The initiatives of the Petrine era were then followed by numerous others over the rest of the century.

The largest of the eighteenth-century expeditions were huge undertakings involving hundreds or thousands of participants with intertwined military, economic, and scientific objectives, such as Bekovich-Cherkasskii's venture or the more successful (from the state's perspective) Orenburg Expedition assembled in the 1730s to "pacify" the Bashkirs in the Southern Urals and open up trade to Central Asia, while also employing "skilled geodesists" and taking along "a surveyor's wheel . . . astronomical and mathematical instruments and mineralogical and botanical books" to investigate the territory.[9] Others were far smaller and more expressly scientific in their purpose, usually organized around a given scientist-explorer and his team of apprentices. Such were, for example, the five so-called "physical expeditions" dispatched by the Academy of Sciences from 1768 to 1774 to explore the southern and eastern borderlands, the most famous of which was led by the young German naturalist Peter Simon Pallas whose team spent almost six years trekking a vast circuit through central Russia, the Volga, the Urals, and into Siberia as far east as Lake Baikal.

Pallas was twenty-six when he set out. By the time he returned to St. Petersburg some eighteen thousand miles later, he had gone grey and was completely worn out, but he was still driven enough to deliver masses of plant and mineral specimens to the Academy's natural history collections.[10] As a German in Russian service, he also typified the close engagement between Russian and European exploration that had become a commonplace by the time of Catherine the Great and would only grow closer over the remainder of the imperial era.

Indeed, by the 1800s, and especially by the second half of the century, Russian exploration was fully in step with European developments, and a new heyday of activity began in multiple directions. Between 1803 and 1806, a Russian naval expedition completed the first of what would be multiple round-the-world voyages. By the 1820s and 1830s, teams of explorers were making attempts at the highest peak in the Caucasus (and Europe)— Mt. Elbrus—and were foraying into the still largely unknown Altay range in southern Siberia, the Kazakh steppe, and the interior of Alaska. By mid-century, they entered the Amur Region and Central Asia alongside or shortly after the Russian military. By the 1880s, they were exploring the Qing-ruled regions of Manchuria and Mongolia, and by 1900, Gombozhab Tsybikov, a Russian Buryat posing as a Buddhist pilgrim, became the first

"European" to reach Lhasa, the capital of Tibet, a destination long considered one of the holy grails of Western exploration.[11]

As the imperial era came to an end, perhaps the best proof of the great changes in Russian exploration was in the Arctic. The mixed Slavic-Finnic settlers of the White Sea region, the so-called *pomory*, had explored the northern ocean coasts for centuries prior to the imperial era. Building on their knowledge, the Great Northern Expedition—a huge operation, part of which included ships under Bering's command—managed to chart most of the arctic littoral of Siberia by the 1740s, and the preeminent Russian scientist of the day, Mikhail Lomonosov (1711–1765), identified the "Northern Ocean" as "a spacious field for the broadening of Russian greatness."[12]

More northern sailing followed over the 1800s, and by the last decades of the empire, the Russians were fully engaged in the arctic expeditioning and related rivalry for the pole that became such a mesmerizing preoccupation of world culture. Russian explorers craved the glory as intensely as everyone else. As naval commander Georgii Sedov put it, while preparing to launch what turned out to be his unsuccessful bid for the pole from 1912 to 1914, "In recent years, reaching the pole has become something of a struggle between states and it seems that we Russians are the only ones yet to join the international contest . . . I firmly believe in the success of my venture . . . My expedition mates and I are all driven by the same fervent desire—to see the Russian tricolor waving atop the pole."[13]

Structures and Types

Russian explorers thus played a key role in building and consolidating the empire, while at the same time linking the empire to the world. But who exactly were they and what institutions and structures supported their work? It is helpful in answering these questions to draw a distinction between individuals who explored, on the one hand, and self-conscious "explorers" on the other. The former were always a part of exploration in the Russian context, much as elsewhere. But the latter were a special group that coalesced as exploration itself became a specialized activity, supported in turn by institutions that were explicitly designed to promote and collect geographical knowledge.

Among ordinary explorers the most ordinary were peasants who set out to locate new lands for settlement, sometimes crossing thousands of miles in the process. While most of these rural migrants moved to areas that were already known to government officials and geographers,

a great deal of movement in the imperial countryside took place completely removed from any assistance or even contact with the state, which
meant that peasants were indeed exploring new territory. They were simply doing so in their own register, separate from the world of chancellery
plans and scientific categories or objectives.[14] Other plebeian explorers
of this sort were monks and hermits who moved into the wilderness to
seek God, as well as frontier Cossacks, coastal fishermen, and fur trap-
pers (*promyshlenniki*).

Merchants, too, participated in exploration. Much of the information used
by explorers in their reconnoitering came to them first from long-distance
traders working the caravans that ran to regions like Siberia or Central
Asia. Their knowledge also shaped the country's arteries of communication, such as the Siberian Road (*Sibirskii trakt*) whose easternmost section,
the so-called Great Tea Road (*velikiichainyi put'*), connected Russia with
China through the Russo-Mongolian border town of Kiakhta-Maimaicheng.
The road was ordered into being by Peter the Great, but its route followed
the informal information provided by merchants whose experience proved
essential to the whole undertaking.[15]

Merchants were also crucial to the dynamic of exploration in the North
Pacific. Though famous navigators like Bering get the credit, much of the
day-to-day exploring that opened up the route to North America was done
by Siberian merchants and their crews of seal and sea otter hunters venturing out to hunt for "profits" across the water. Regional officials then gathered their findings once they heard about them and sent the information up
the chain of command to St. Petersburg.[16] The founder of the first permanent
Russian settlement in North America, later much celebrated as "the Russian
Columbus," was Grigorii Shelikhov, a merchant from western Russia.[17]

Merchants and peasants aside, the archetype of the explorer in Russia in
the imperial era was either a "man of science" or a military man, or, as was
often the case, both at once. The close connection between the two fields
flowed naturally from the developments of the Petrine period. Peter's interest in exploration was intensely practical. Geographical knowledge was
necessary for answering basic questions: What are the lands of the state
and of the world? What are their features and resources? Who lives in them,
what useful products or habits do they have to offer, and, most of all, how
should they be exploited? It followed from this that explorers needed to be
people with the skills to produce and then deploy this knowledge. Since,
practically speaking, all of this information was quite useful to the military,
it only made sense that military men would be involved as well.

Many Russian explorers thus had a foot in both camps. All the country's prominent maritime explorers, for example, were trained as naval officers—Bering (1681–1741), Johann von Krusenstern (1770–1846), who completed the first Russian circumnavigation, and Stepan Makarov (1848–1904), a well-known oceanographer and Arctic explorer, to name just a few. Still more had army backgrounds. Bekovich-Cherkasskii, who lost his head in Central Asia, was one representative of the type. The best known by far, however, was Nikolai Przheval'skii (1839–1888), a naturalist, geographer, and infantry officer whose evocative descriptions of Central Asia, Mongolia, and Tibet in the 1870s and 1880s—as well as his untimely death in the field—turned him into one of the great heroes of the late imperial era.

Przheval'skii did not lead military expeditions in the formal sense of the word, nor did he claim any new territory for the empire. But by the end of his life he had nonetheless climbed to the rank of major general and managed to occupy a unique position as arguably the country's most compelling spokesman for imperial expansion, using his multiple travels through the empire's newest exotic domains as a platform for extolling the virtues of Russian power in Asia, while at the same time keeping a vigilant eye out for the British, the country's preeminent rivals in the unfolding geopolitical tangle of the Great Game.[18]

One of the keys to Przheval'skii's appeal was his engaging literary style, and the fame he achieved with his pen is a reminder of how the figure of the explorer evolved in Russia over the imperial era. In the eighteenth and early nineteenth century, the aura and influence of explorers rarely extended beyond the limits of Russia's small geographical establishment and a slightly wider circle of educated readers and literati. By the latter part of the tsarist period, however, this had changed as explorers increasingly became figures of mass interest, with their exploits followed—and, depending on the individual, extensively publicized—in the country's expanding public sphere. In the process, the image of the explorer in popular culture shifted accordingly, taking on many of the stock attributes associated with explorers in the West in the same period: stoic manliness and selflessness, love for adventure, dedication to the nation, and quiet confidence in the virtues of progress, science, and empire.[19]

Przheval'skii fit this profile perfectly, almost as if he had invented the code himself. In his best-selling accounts of his expeditions, he repeatedly evoked the mystery of the Orient and the wonder of nature, while naming mountain peaks after tsars and inviting the public to voyage alongside him into a life of simplicity and rewarding hardship in the wilderness: "Transport yourself now in your thoughts, dear reader, and spend a day with us in our camp in the Central Asian desert—once you do, you'll understand how we live on the trail throughout all the days of our journey." This remained his persona—and his image—to the end. As he lay dying of typhus during what turned out to be his last trip to Turkestan, he asked to be buried in his plain expeditionary's uniform and placed under a tombstone with the simple inscription: "Here lies Przheval'skii, traveler" (*puteshestvennik*).[20]

The fame of explorers like Przheval'skii would have been impossible, however, without the institutions and patrons that stood behind them. Though explorers are often cast as intrepid individualists driven by little more than a bold idea, in reality, their work is almost always a collective undertaking that involves extensive planning and funding and depends on far-flung networks of centers and connections that help to gather and relay the explorer's information and reinforce his authority. As the historian of science Bruno Latour has argued, what makes a discovery *a discovery* is less the act of seeing something for the first time than everything that comes next—that is, making a record of what has been found (on maps, in ship's logs, in specimen jars, etc.) and then ensuring that others are informed about the discovery and are able to return. For this to happen, a range of political, financial, and technological supports have to fall in place.[21]

In Russia, this was very much the case. Thus at the same time that Peter the Great and his lieutenants helped to launch a surge of expeditioning, they also laid the keystone for a bona fide geographical establishment of scholars and institutions that would support the extensive activities and capital outlays required. The initial command center for exploration was the Academy of Sciences (est. 1724), which organized expeditions through to the end of the imperial era and hired and trained numerous explorers. The imperial navy, also created upon Peter's direction, became an active sponsor of exploration, as did the army, which established a topographical bureau and other offices to collect and reproduce geographical information beginning in the early 1800s.

Far and away the greatest institutional support for exploration, however, came from the Russian Geographical Society, which was founded in 1845 with the primary purpose of "studying our native land and its peoples" and went on to sponsor tens of expeditions between the middle of the century and 1917. In fact, the society was guided by an ethos of exploration from its inception, given that a number of its founders and first members were explorers, and it was the excitement at the return to St. Petersburg in the spring of 1845 of a two-year Siberian expedition led by the naturalist Alexander von Middendorf that became the immediate catalyst for founding the organization.[22]

The Society sponsored the Amur Expedition that included Nevel'skoi's claiming of the river and Przheval'skii's numerous travels as well as explorations in the Arctic, Sub-Saharan Africa, and Oceania.[23] Like the other national geographical societies on which it was modeled, the Russian one underscored that exploration was a matter of national pride and that explorers themselves were men (and indeed the Society only accepted men as members) with special national obligation. As the explorer and long-term vice-president of the Society Petr Semenov-Tian-Shanskii put it in 1850, "The mark of any scholar who aims to live a common life with his countrymen should be . . . the urge to bring the treasures [of human knowledge] into the life of the nation."[24]

The Academy of Sciences and the military were state bodies. The Russian Geographical Society, by contrast, was a hybrid organization, led by a member of the tsarist family (the society's two presidents prior to the revolution were both Grand Dukes) and favored by the court but with a budget that partly drew on state funds and partly on dues paid by its members.[25] Meanwhile the members themselves were a mixed crew: high-ranking state officials, university professors, naval officers, and artists, as well as businessmen, like the mine owner Aleksandr Sibiriakov and the entrepreneur and banker Fedor Riabushinskii, both of whom donated their own monies to sponsor society expeditions.

Although Russian exploration in the imperial era was overwhelmingly a state-sponsored enterprise, "voluntary organizations" and private sponsors also left their mark. Private monies supported a number of Russian Arctic expeditions, for example, while learned societies, like the Moscow-based Society for the Lovers of Nature, Ethnography, and Anthropology (est. 1863), dispatched expeditions of their own, such as a famous naturalist expedition to Turkestan of 1868–1872 that included the husband-and-wife team of Ol'ga and Aleksei Fedchenko.[26]

Finally, commercial institutions also supported exploration as a way to promote Russian business interests. Trade associations dispatched expeditions of this sort to Mongolia and Persia towards the end of the imperial era, for example.[27] Perhaps the most striking case of a commercial entity providing support for exploration, however, was the Russian-American Company (RAC), which was founded in 1799 to exploit the empire's claims in North America in the style of the colonial joint-stock companies of Western Europe and ended up running the Russian and native settlements of the region for most of the nineteenth century. Indeed, during this period the company became so involved in exploration that it evolved into its own command center for geographical discovery. Together with the navy, it helped to sponsor the great round-the-world voyages of Krusenstern and others in the first part of the 1800s. Additional expeditions ventured into the Alaskan interior. By the 1840s and 1850s, company ships had shifted back to the other side of the Pacific to assist with the "opening up" of the Amur, Sakhalin Island, and the broader Far East.[28]

In fact, one could argue that the RAC ultimately explored so well that it ran itself out of business. Ship's captains, seeking profits for the company and guided by knowledge gained from Native American tribes, probed the islands and mainland coves of Alaska for sea otter and fur seal. Once they found them, they then began hunting so intensely (often with the help of native hunters) that they quickly drove the animals to the edge of extinction. Then, as furs became scarce and their market value declined, the fortunes of the RAC declined as well.

The RAC may well have been able to continue exploiting the empire's American territories by finding new sources of revenue, but its original purpose had been to reap the profits of the fur trade and so, once the trade dried up, it became easier for the government to consider divestment. By the 1840s, St. Petersburg decided to sell off its possession at Fort Ross in Northern California to a local landowner because it no longer made economic sense. It then sold Alaska, with a well-explored coastline but precious few seals or sea otters, to the United States in 1867.[29]

Conclusion

"Wise are those nations and individuals who feel no shame in borrowing the good things they see in others."[30] This statement by Feofan Prokopovich, a close advisor of Peter the Great, could stand as a motto for the Petrine era, and for much of the history of modern Russian exploration as well. The Russians had a long history of exploring prior to Peter's time, but as his reign unfolded in the early eighteenth century, the way they conducted their exploring began to change, with the most important development being a fundamental revalorization of exploration itself as a specialized activity. But as the country borrowed from Europe, in part by hiring the services of European explorers, such as the German Peter Simon Pallas, for example, or the Dane Vitus Bering, what emerged in the process was not "European" exploration but rather an exploring culture that was at once Russian and international at the same time. The Russians, in effect, learned the language of modern exploration from Europe, but came to speak it in their own way.

For example, with a few important exceptions, most notably the great round-the-world voyages of the early 1800s, the Russians concentrated their expeditions within or near their own territory rather than across farther horizons. Their exploration was thus much more Eurasian than global in scope. The Russian practice of exploration also reflected the empire in the direct sense that the country's explorers were often not, in fact, ethnic Russians but rather representatives of other imperial groups. Von Krusenstern was a Baltic German nobleman. Bekovich-Cherkasskii was a Christianized Circassian from the North Caucasus. Przeval'skii was of Polish descent. The first "Russian" to reach Lhasa was a Buryat (see page 141–142), while the first "Russian" to tell Europe about the fabled Chinese caravan town of Kashgar in the late 1850s was Chokhan Valikhanov, a Muslim Kazakh nobleman who became a tsarist army officer and an influential member of the Russian Geographical Society.[31]

Even when Russian explorers openly and self-consciously imitated European ways, they often did so on their own terms. Thus the Russian naval commanders of the round-the-world expeditions of the 1810s and 1820s, many of whom were Baltic German noblemen, made a point of emulating their British counterparts in using elaborate technological displays of instruments and fireworks to impress the non-Western peoples they encountered, but, unlike their Western European peers, they seem to have had misgivings about the practice.[32]

Indeed, perhaps the most distinctive feature of Russian exploration in the imperial era was its complicated relationship with the politics of Russian identity. On the one hand, the leading lights of the Russian geographical establishment eventually became quite satisfied with their achievements and fully confident that their country deserved a place among the world's leading exploring nations. Yet on the other, they were always dogged by a nagging sense of having something to prove. Thus the intense and purposeful cultural borrowing from Europe that defined the Petrine period was accompanied by an equally strong conviction that Russia was nonetheless a great country that would surely become just as great as—if not much greater than—the powers it was trying to emulate.[33] And this included greatness in the sphere of exploration.

It is not surprising, therefore, that mid-eighteenth-century thinkers like Lomonosov were moved to wax lyrical about Russian Columbuses or that slightly later commentators would begin claiming that the country had its own "Cooks" as well (that is, Russian Captain Cooks). In fact, by the late imperial decades comparisons between Russian and Western/European achievements in the exploration arena had become a staple of Russian writing, as if the Russians felt driven to underscore the connection in order to prove a point, as much to themselves as to outsiders.[34] This national sensitivity also became grounds for conflict in the early history of the Russian Geographical Society as Russian members of the organization objected to the idea that so many of its founders and leaders turned out to be Russian Germans. In the end, the society's so-called Russian party won out, and a number of Germans (despite some of them being extremely Russified) had to give up their leadership posts, yet, even with all this, the society never stopped being a cosmopolitan organization, easily as imperial as it was national.[35]

Russians thus found themselves forever on the fence, at once seemingly at home within a shared international club of exploration institutions, practices, and personalities, while at the same time, preoccupied with the need to prove themselves equal to or better than everyone around them, in particular, their European rivals and partners. As the historian Richard Wortman has noted, one of the most obvious signs of Russia's entrée into the "theater of the world" in the early 1700s was the country's engagement with "the European project of world exploration."[36] Another way of putting this is to say that as of the Petrine era exploration became, in effect, a key tool for the Russians to use in trying to prove their Europeanness. This in turn explains both why they took to exploration with such gusto and why they remained so ardent in treating it as a terrain of national achievement.Yet it also explains the self-consciousness that frequently went along with the process, as if Russian explorers were not just trying to make sense of the remarkable territories before them but of their own place in the world as well.

NOTES

1. V. N. Tatishchev, "Razgovor dvukh priatelei o pol'ze nauki i uchilishchakh," in idem, *Sobranie sochinenii* (Moscow, 1996), vol. 8, 51, 91–92.

2. For a comprehensive overview of geography and exploration in Peter's time, see Denis J. B. Shaw, "Geographical Practice and its Significance in Peter the Great's Russia," *Journal of Historical Geography*, 22, 2 (1996):160–176.

3. For Catherine's reference, see "Pis'ma Ekateriny Vtoroi k Baronu Grimmu," *Russkii arkhiv* 16, no. 9 (1878): 93.

4. On exploration's role in "enhancing the world-picture" by documenting lands that were already "discovered" but poorly known, see Felipe Fernández-Armesto, *Pathfinders: A Global History of Exploration* (New York: W.W. Norton, 2006), 289–346.

5. The fort, which Nevel'skoi named *Nikolaevskii post* in honor of Tsar Nicholas I, is now the town of Nikolaevsk-on-the-Amur. On the founding of the fort, see A. I. Alekseev, *Gennadii Ivanovich Nevel'skoi 1813–1876* (Moscow, 1984), 87–88.

6. On Bekovich-Cherkasskii see V. Beneshevich, "Cherkasskii, Aleksandr Bekovich," *Russkii biograficheskii slovar'* (St. Petersburg, 1905) vol. 22,177–183. For the campaign see D. Golosov, "Pokhod v Khivu v 1717 godu," *Voennyi sbornik*, no. 10 (October 1861): 303–364; and A. Popov, *Snosheniia Rossii s Khivoiu i Bukharoiu pri Petre Velikom* (St. Petersburg, 1853), 3–31.

7. On the intellectual culture and sensibilities that informed views of exploration under Peter, see the magisterial survey by Lindsey Hughes, *Russia in the Age of Peter the Great* (New Haven, Conn.: Yale University Press, 1998), esp. 309–316. Much of this was in keeping with developments in other early modern states. See Jacques Revel, "Knowledge of the Territory," *Science in Context*, 4, 1 (1991): 133–162.

8. The most accessible recent summary of Bering's voyages is Orcut Frost, *Bering: The Russian Discovery of America* (New Haven, Conn.: Yale University Press, 2003). Technically speaking, the first European/Russian to sail the Bering Strait was not Bering but rather the Cossack "land-crosser" Semen Dezhnev who led a party there roughly a hundred years before Bering arrived, but Dezhnev lost out in the naming game, alas, because Captain Cook had never heard of him.

9. The quotes here are from the Report by State Counselor Ivan Kirilov to Empress Anna, 1734, *Rossiiskii gosudarstvennyi arkhiv drevnykh aktov* (*RGADA*), f. 248, kn. 750, ch. 3, l.58 (b), 59 (b). For more on the Orenburg Expedition, see Willard Sunderland, *Taming the Wild Field: Colonization and Empire on the Russian Steppe* (Ithaca, N.Y.: Cornell University Press, 2004), 46–49; and Iurii Smirnov, *Orenburgskaia ekspeditsiia (komissiia) i prisoedinenie Zavolzh'ia k Rossii v 30–40-e gg. xviii veka* (Samara: Samarskii Universitet, 1997).

10. Pallas' much reprinted account of his expedition was first published in German: *Reise durch verschiedene Provinzen des Russischen Reichs* (St. Petersburg, 1771–1776), 3 vols.

11. For references and studies relating to some of these expeditions, see Ilya Vinkovetsky, "Circumnavigation, Empire, Modernity, Race: The Impact of Round-the-World Voyages on Russia's Imperial Consciousness," *Ab Imperio*, 1/2 (2001): 191–210; Alexei Postnikov, "The First Russian Voyage Around the World and its Influence on the Exploration and Development of Russian America," *Journal of the History of Discoveries*, 37 (2005): 53–62; Glynn Barratt, *Russia in Pacific Waters, 1715–1825: A Survey of the Origins of Russia's Naval Presence in the North and South Pacific* (Vancouver: University of British Columbia Press, 1981); K. F. Ledebur et al., *Puteshestvie po Altaiskim goram i dzhungarskoi Kirgizskoi stepi* (Novosibirsk: Nauka, 1993); Charles King, *The Ghost of Freedom: A History of the Caucasus* (New York: Oxford University Press, 2008), 101–108, 124; and A. V. Postnikov, *Stanovlenie rubezhei Rossii v Tsentral'noi i Srednei Azii (xviii–xix*

vv.): rol' istoriko-geograficheskikh issledovanii i kartografirovanii; monografiia v dokumentakh (Moscow: Pamiatniki istoricheskoi mysli, 2007).

12. M. V. Lomonosov, "Kratkoe opisanie raznykh puteshestvii po severnym moriam i pokazanie vozmozhnogo prikhodu Sibirskim okeanom v vostochnuiu Indiiu," in his *Pol'noe sobranie sochinenii* (Moscow and Leningrad: Akademiia Nauk, 1952) vol. 6, 420. Lomonosov composed this piece in 1762–1763.

13. G. Ia. Sedov, "Kak ia otkroiu Severnyi Polius," *Sinii zhurnal*, 13 (1912): 7. Sedov ended up dying before reaching the pole, falling ill from scurvy on the northernmost island of the Franz Josef Land archipelago in February 1914. For more on the Russian arctic expeditions of the early 1900s, including two other ill-fated expeditions that also met their end in 1914, see John McCannon, *Red Arctic: Polar Exploration and the Myth of the North in the Soviet Union, 1932–1939* (New York: Oxford University Press, 1998), 18–19.

14. On the impressions of peasant settlers, see Willard Sunderland, "Peasant Pioneering: Russian Peasant Settlers Describe Colonization and the Eastern Frontier, 1880s–1910s," *Journal of Social History*, 34, 4 (2001): 895–922.

15. The most comprehensive study of the Siberian Road is O. N. Kationov, *Moskovsko-Sibirskii trakt i ego zhiteli v xvii–xix v.* (Novosibirsk: Novosibirskii Gosudarstvennyi Pedogogicheskii Universitet, 2004).

16. For an example, see the description of "islands sighted in the open ocean . . . by Selinginsk merchant Andrei Tolstykh," sent to Catherine the Great by Governor of Siberia Denis Chicherin in 1766: RGADA, f. 24, op. 1, d. 34, ll.97–98 (b).

17. The settlement established by Shelikov, which dates to 1784, was at Three Saints Bay on Kodiak Island off the southern coast of Alaska. On the early history of Russian rule on Kodiak, see Gwenn A. Miller, *Kodiak Kreol: Communities of Empire in Early Russian America* (Ithaca, N.Y.: Cornell University Press, 2010). Some scholars contend that the first permanent Russian settlements in North America in fact began on the island of Unalaska a decade or so earlier. See Anatole Senkevitch, Jr., "The Early Architecture and Settlements of Russian America," in S. Frederick Starr (ed.), *Russia's American Colony* (Durham, N.C.: Duke University Press, 1987), 149–153.

18. On Przheval'skii, including references to some of his suspicious remarks about the British, see Daniel Brower, "Imperial Russia and its Orient: The Renown of Nikolai Przhevalsky," *Russian Review*, 53, 3 (1994): 367–381. It's worth pointing out that Przheval'skii's British counterparts had few good things to say about the Russians either. For a general picture of the Great Game and British-Russian mutual perceptions, see Peter Hopkirk, *The Great Game: The Struggle for Empire in Central Asia* (New York: Kodansha International, 1992).

19. On the prevalent image of the explorer in the West in the late nineteenth and early twentieth centuries, see Felix Driver, *Geography Militant: Cultures of Exploration and Empire* (Malden, Mass.: Blackwell, 2001) and Beau Riffenburgh, *The Myth of the Explorer: The Press, Sensationalism, and Geographical Discovery* (New York: Oxford University Press, 1994).

20. The quotes here are provided in E. M. Murzaev, "Nikolai Mikhailovich Przheval'skii 1839–1888," in V. A. Esakov (ed.), *Tvortsy otechestvennoi nauki: geografy* (Moscow: Agar, 1996), 218, 212–213. Despite his personal modesty, Przheval'skii was denied his wish for a humble tombstone. Soon after his death the Russian Geographical Society, with help from the court, commissioned an imposing monument topped by an eagle and an Orthodox cross to stand at the gravesite. A similar monument went up shortly thereafter in St. Petersburg. For images of these monuments, see http://ru.wikipedia.org/wiki/пржевальский,_николай_михайлович (last visited August 2011).

21. Bruno Latour, *Science in Action: How to Follow Scientists and Engineers Through Society* (Cambridge, Mass.: Harvard University Press, 1987), 219–220.

22. Nathaniel Knight, "Constructing the Science of Nationality: Ethnography in Mid-Nineteenth-Century Russia" (PhD dissertation, Columbia University, 1994), 227; Mark Bassin, *Imperial Visions: Nationalist Imagination and Geographical Expansion in the Russian Far East, 1840–1865* (New York: Cambridge University Press, 1999), 98.

23. The best survey of the expeditions of the RGO up to the late nineteenth century is P. P. Semenov (Tian-Shanskii), *Istoriia poluvekovoi deiatel'nosti imperatorskogo russkogo geograficheskogo obshchestva, 1845–1895* (St. Petersburg: V. Bezobrazov i Ko., 1896), 3 vols. For the rest of the tsarist era, see L. S. Berg, *Vsesoiuznoe geograficheskoe obshchestvo za 100 let* (Moscow and Leningrad: Izdatel'stvo Akademii Nauk, 1946).

24. Cited in Bassin, *Imperial Visions*, 97.

25. On the organization of the budget, see the Society's charter, approved in 1849: *Ustav Imperatorskogo Russkogo Geograficheskogo Obshchestva* (St. Petersburg, 1849), 3–4.

26. On the Fedchenkos, see O. A. Val'kova, *Ol'ga Aleksandrovna Fedchenko, 1845–1921* (Moscow: Nauka, 2006); and N. I. Leonov, *Aleksei Pavlovich Fedchenko* (Moscow: Nauka, 1972). On "voluntary associations" during the tsarist era, including the Russian Geographical Society and the Society for the Lovers of Nature mentioned above, see Joseph Bradley, *Voluntary Associations in Tsarist Russia: Science, Patriotism, and Civil Society* (Cambridge, Mass.: Harvard University Press, 2009).

27. See, for example, S. Lomnitskii (Redzhep), *Persiya i Persy: Eskizy i ocherki, 1898–1899–1900* (St. Petersburg, 1902); *Moskovskaia torgovaia ekspeditsiia v Mongoliiu* (Moscow, 1912); and M. I. Bogolepov and M. N. Sobolev, *Ocherki russkoi-mongol'skoi torgovli: ekspeditsiia v Mongoliiu* (Tomsk: Sibirskoe T-vo Pechatnogo Dela, 1911).

28. On the organization of the RAC and some of its exploration activity, see Ilya Vinkovetsky, *Russian America: An Overseas Colony of a Continental Empire, 1804–1867* (New York: Oxford University Press, 2011), 52–72.

29. On Russian Alaska, see the recent studies by Vinkovetsky, *Russian America* and Gwen A. Miller, *Kodiak Kreol: Communities of Empire in Early Russian America* (Ithaca, N.Y.: Cornell University Press, 2010).

30. Quoted in S. A. Mezin, "Petr I kak tsivilizator Rossii: dva vzgliada," in S. Ia. Karp and S. A. Mezin (eds.), *Evropeiskoe prosveshchenie i tsivilizatsiia Rossii* (Moscow: Nauka, 2004), 11.

31. For a Soviet-era biography, see I. Strelkova, *Valikhanov* (Moscow: Molodaia Gvardiia, 1983). For a recent selection of his works, including some of his expeditionary writings, see Chokhan Valikhanov, *Izbrannye proizvedeniia* (Almaty: "Arys", 2009).

32. Simon Werrett, "Technology on Display: Instruments and Identities on Russian Voyages of Exploration," *Russian Review*, 70, 3 (2011): 380–396.

33. On this important aspect of Russian national identity and its origins in the eighteenth century, see Liah Greenfeld, *Nationalism: Five Roads to Modernity* (Cambridge, Mass.: Harvard University Press, 1992), 189–274.

34. For just a few examples of this comparative habit in Russian writing about exploration, see Mikhail Lomonosov, "Petr Velikii" (1761), *Polnoe sobranie sochinenii* (Moscow-Leningrad: Izdatel'stvo Akademii Nauk, 1959), vol. 8: 703; M. S. Al'perovich, *Rossiia i Novyi Svet (posledniaia tret' xviii veka)* (Moscow: Nauka, 1993), 89; and D. Sadovnikov, *Nashi zemleprokhodtsy (raskazy o zaselenii Sibiri) (1581–1712 gg.)* (Moscow: Gramotei, 1874), 176–177. A number of Russian sea captains in the early 1800s self-consciously styled themselves after Captain Cook and had considerable training experience in the British navy. See Werrett, "Technology on Display," 386–387; and Vinkovetsky, *Russian America*, 37–38.

35. On the national politics of the Society in its early years, see Nathaniel Knight, "Science, Empire, and Nationality: Ethnography in the Russian Geographical Society, 1845–1855," in Jane Burbank and David L. Ransel (eds.), *Imperial Russia: New Histories for the Empire* (Bloomington, Ind.: Indiana University Press, 1998), 112–116.

36. Richard Wortman, "Texts of Exploration and Russia's European Identity," in Cynthia Hyla Whittaker (ed.) (with Edward Kasinec and Robert H. Davis, Jr.), *Russia Engages the World, 1453–1815* (Cambridge, Mass.: Harvard University Press, 2003), 91.

7

EXPLORING THE PACIFIC WORLD

JANE SAMSON

Before the successful testing of Harrison's chronometer on Captain Cook's second voyage to the Pacific, explorers of that vast ocean lacked a reliably accurate means of knowing where they were. Their activities seemed unscientific to later generations of explorers. Possible antipodean continents were sketched on maps and globes; island groups were given fanciful names but could not be located again; and the fatal vastness of the Pacific generated both dread and inspiration.[1]

Enlightenment science enabled maritime and overland explorers to navigate more safely, generating a wealth of new information that, in turn, spurred on later generations to fill in the remaining "blanks." Well into the twentieth century, it would have occurred to very few to question the heroism of their accomplishments, or to wonder why the title of "explorer" was given only to white men with the right credentials. Consider the difference and similarities between the first and third editions of J. C. Beaglehole's *The Exploration of the Pacific*. In his preface of 1966, Beaglehole reflected on the way the field had changed since the first edition of 1934. His own views of the importance of non-British expeditions, notably those of Ferdinand Magellan and various Dutch explorers, had been challenged, and he wished he could have included more about them. He also noted how recently many of the Pacific islands had been charted and identified to Western scientific satisfaction. Nevertheless the task remained the same: "To give an account of European exploration of the Pacific from Magellan to Cook."[2] Andrew Sharp, also writing in the 1960s, took a similar approach in *The Discovery of the Pacific Islands* in which he traced "the first European or American discovery of the various Pacific Islands."[3]

One of the many accomplishments of the Pacific Studies movement of the 1960s was to highlight the historical activities of explorers who were not necessarily the first official European or American discoverers. Indigenous peoples, traders, sailors, and missionaries—women as well as men—received long overdue investigation. Like other "area studies" movements, Pacific Studies highlighted local archives and contexts. Led by J. W. Davidson and others, Pacific-based scholars uncovered and catalogued local source material traditionally neglected in favor of research into manuscripts at European or American archives. Initiatives such as the Pacific Manuscripts Bureau (based at the Australian National University) made readily available, often for the first time, local church and mission records, private papers, business archives, and the holdings of archives from former colonial governments in the islands.[4] The Australian Joint Copying Project (also based at ANU) began to microfilm exploration and colonial records from U.K. repositories as well as manuscripts in private hands.[5]

Antipodean-based scholars were now able to consult wide-ranging primary source material without facing the often prohibitive cost of travelling to Europe or the United States. A new interest in unconventional characters such as beachcombers or traders was reflected in collections like H. E. Maude's *Of islands and men; studies in Pacific history* (1968). The great men of conventional exploration history were not necessarily the first to have reached various part of the Pacific: first contact with indigenous peoples was just as likely to have been made by an escaped sailor or an adventurous trader. Thanks to the lengthy process of European contact with the western Pacific islands, the "exploration" of the Pacific lasted well into the twentieth century.[6]

Pacific Studies was also characterized by a multidisciplinary approach to training and research, notably a collaboration between history and anthropology. This helped scholars to incorporate indigenous oral history and to appreciate neglected voices from the archives. Greg Dening, a Pacific Studies pioneer, was trained in both anthropology and history, and his studies of interactions between Europeans and Marquesan islanders emphasized the need to understand Marquesan histories and cultures in their own right. He conceptualized culture contact in terms of "Beaches," where islanders and strangers met and interacted. Sometimes these were literal beach encounters, as when a European explorer came ashore for the first time. Other beach encounters were abstract, as when an historian, distant in time and space from the events under study, encountered those events in the archive. In other cases the Beach could act as a trans-geographical concept reflecting political, social, and cultural identities with complex histories.

Islanders played a direct and active role in shaping these histories through "the islands men and women make by the reality they attribute to their categories, their roles, their institutions and the beaches they put around them with their definitions of 'we' and 'they.'"[7] Critical and deeply personal historiography became typical of Dening's work, making his pioneering book *Islands and Beaches* (1980) "an inspiring and enlightening achievement" in both Pacific Studies and in what postmodernists would later call "reflexive" historical methodology.[8]

Of fundamental importance in Pacific Studies was an affirmation of indigenous peoples as active agents in their own history. Dening's work, for example, hoped to

> redress the imbalance of one-sided history that describes the two-sided events of contact and expansion as if it were merely the story of Western politics and diplomacy, exploration and adventure, settlement and administration.[9]

Scholars today would question the "two-sided" nature of these events, pointing out that race, class, gender, and many other factors produced far more than two sides to every story. Also, as David Chappell has pointed out, we should "counter-explore" how Pacific islanders themselves launched a "second diaspora" across the Pacific and beyond, working as translators or crew on exploration and mission vessels, and voyaging widely along globalised trade routes opened up by European maritime commerce.[10]

Meanwhile, European explorers themselves wondered about the prodigious voyages that must have taken place to colonize the islands in prehistoric times. Ethnologists had speculated about the ultimate origins of Pacific peoples and their cultures. Were they part of the "lost tribes" of Israel? Were their languages derived from Sanskrit? As Kerry Howe has pointed out, by the 1960s, "In spite of 200 years of study and speculation, the broad picture was not fundamentally very different from that offered by Captain Cook—that the Polynesian homeland lay to the west."[11]

During the 1960s and 1970s, technological advancements in archeology, notably radiocarbon dating, coincided fruitfully with the willingness of Pacific Studies scholars to highlight indigenous agency. Plenty of information was now available to conduct a multi-disciplinary assessment of the skilled and astonishingly lengthy voyages—by islanders, not Europeans—that had originally colonized the Pacific. Writing in 1977, Oskar Spate noted that "until our own day the Pacific was basically a Euro-American creation" and, although this was already changing, it would "demand a new historiography."[12] It is to this period that Kerry Howe traces a "post-imperial study of indigenous cultures," in this case "the achievements and adaptive progress of indigenous peoples."[13] Ben Finney, one of the first to take this new approach, did his own fieldwork to challenge generations of historical work based on archives often distant from the islands and activities they described. Applauding the "New, Non-Armchair Research," Finney and others mounted a decisive challenge to the idea, most recently promoted by Andrew Sharp's *Ancient Voyagers in the Pacific* (1956), that prehistoric indigenous voyaging had involved "drifting" and chance landfalls rather than skilled exploration.[14] Instead, Finney explained, recent multidisciplinary research revealed indigenous navigational skills "of considerable antiquity, perhaps extending as far back as the second millennium B.C." and astonishing feats of deep-sea exploration, which reproached the "gross conjecture" of earlier historiography.[15] Europeans were not the only ones to have entered the vast Pacific with both skill and intent. This viewpoint is now taken for granted: the 2007 *Oxford Companion to World Exploration* begins its Pacific section with indigenous exploration, settlement, and trade. Not until halfway through the section are European activities discussed.[16] A comparison of the scope of Pacific navigation with the tracks of Captain Cook reveals the exceptional nature of the Great Navigator's achievements. It also underlines the vast skill and courage of prehistoric Pacific explorers (see Figure 7.1).

What about land-based exploration in the Pacific? Radiocarbon dating generated significant debate concerning the length and scope of aboriginal exploration and settlement on the Australian continent. Reflecting on his long career in Australian pre-history, archaeologist John Mulvaney described a pervasive Eurocentricity that plagued attempts to convey the legitimacy and implications of new research. In the early 1960s most scholars believed that humans had been present in Australia for only 13,000 years; by the end of the 1970s, Mulvaney and his colleagues were contending that 40,000 years was the probable span.

So entrenched were the old chronological framework, and so enduring the anti-Asian prejudices in Australia, that sometimes the radiocarbon results processed by cutting-edge Asian labs were dismissed because they were "made in Japan."[17] European and North American scholars, in turn, were reluctant to accept the professionalism of their Australian or New Zealand counterparts. In Australia there was an additional problem: the implications of such a lengthy presence for Aboriginal land claims, and its evidence of the strength and durability of Aboriginal societies and cultures generally. Even though pre-historians continue to be mainly sympathetic to Aboriginal causes, Aboriginal activists themselves object to the term "pre-history," demanding instead "equal status 'history' with Europeans."[18]

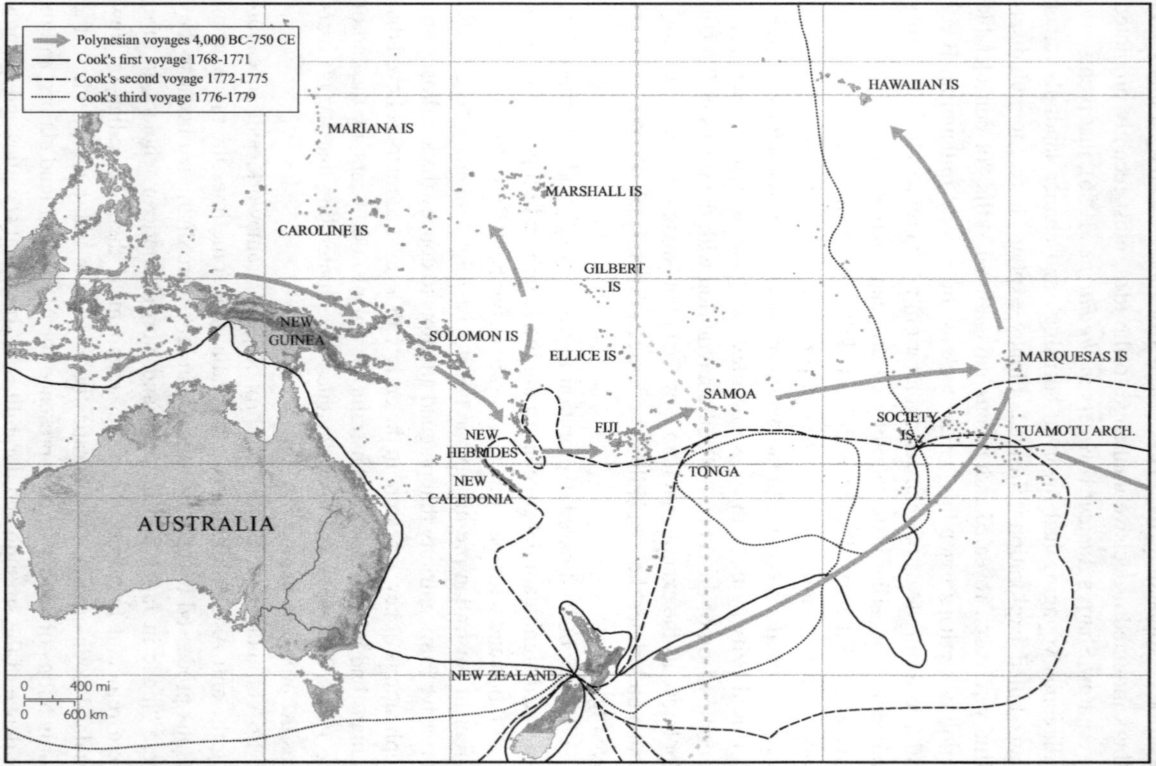

Polynesian voyages 4,000 BC-750 CE
Cook's first voyage 1768-1771
Cook's second voyage 1772-1775
Cook's third voyage 1776-1779
HAWAIIAN IS
MARIANA IS
MARSHALL IS
CAROLINE IS
GILBERT IS
NEW GUINEA
SOLOMON IS
ELLICE IS
MARQUESAS IS
SAMOA
SOCIETY IS
TUAMOTU ARCH.
FIJI
NEW HEBRIDES
TONGA
NEW CALEDONIA
AUSTRALIA
NEW ZEALAND
0 400 mi
0 600 km

Figure 7.1 Map of Polynesian expansion and Cook's voyages across South Pacific

Historians of exploration have been slow to respond to the call for "equal status history" even in the fashionable field of first contacts and early European colonization. As historian Elaine Thompson notes, "Until very recently the words 'discovery' and 'exploration' were used freely to describe the relatively short history of European relations with Australia," rather than the activities, prehistoric or otherwise, of Aboriginal people.[19] Aboriginal members of Australian exploration parties remain marginalized even in recent postcolonial scholarship. In a collection of essays on new approaches to the history of Britain's settler colonies, editor Lynette Russell underlines the deconstruction of the traditional two-sided "frontier."[20] The contributions on Australia, however, are dominated by two pieces on Edward Eyre, a well-known Victorian explorer and colonial governor. Both call for a postcolonial critique of Eyre's humanitarian reputation concerning Aboriginal Australians, emphasizing the racism and unequal power relations that dominated his views, rather than Eyre's dependency on Aboriginal assistance. His power as a white, imperial male remained the centre of attention.

The politics of this situation demand attention because, as historian Henry Reynolds explains, "Explorers walk tall through the pages of Australian historiography."[21] Although generations of scholars have critiqued their heroism from a variety of perspectives, this has not displaced European explorers from the main focus of debate. As a result "the contribution of the Aboriginal peoples to the exploration of Australia" has not been fully or properly recognized.[22] One reason for this, perhaps, is the relative scarcity of Aboriginal and other indigenous scholars of exploration in Australian or Pacific history. Donald Denoon has noted that the field continues to be dominated by non-indigenous scholars who, for the most part, pursue their careers outside the Pacific region.[23] Another explanation suggested by Denoon is a nationalism that prompts many indigenous scholars to focus on the history of their own homelands, rather than conducting more broad-based international or regional research: "This imbalance poses the question how best to harmonize the regional perspectives of much expatriate research, with the mainly national focus of most indigenous discourse."[24] This question remains largely unanswered.

Indigenous academics do indeed insist upon setting their own research agenda, sometimes in open defiance of the preoccupations of Western scholarship. Following a conference commemorating the world tour of a replica of Cook's first Pacific ship, the *Endeavour*, Aboriginal Australian

activist Jackie Huggins closed the proceedings with a provocative statement
that called the whole enterprise into question:

> The history of the Australian continent did not commence when Captain Cook
> first landed on the eastern coast but 50,000 years before that . . . . Aboriginal
> publications and education programs are exploring the reality of their history.
> 'BC' now means 'Before Cook.'[25]

Unfortunately for Huggins and her Aboriginal colleagues, non-indigenous
scholars remain as preoccupied as ever with Captain Cook. Perhaps no
other geographical area features such ongoing emphasis on the voyages of a
single explorer, although some Native Studies scholars in Canada, speaking
of the prominence given to Sir John Franklin in Arctic historiography, tend
to groan "Not Franklin again!" after the appearance of each new biography
or TV documentary.[26] After a generation of postcolonial scholarship, with
its emphasis on scrutinizing the power relations of both history and historiography, this state of affairs needs to be investigated. It is not only a question of who "owns" the history of Pacific exploration,[27] whether indigenous
or non-indigenous scholars, but also who gets to privilege certain topics as
uniquely important, and why.

The leading Pacific history debate of the last two decades has concerned
Captain Cook, specifically his death at the hands of Hawai'ians in 1779.
Earlier historians have tended to focus on Cook's own actions or those
of his crews, but recent scholarship has mined the vast documentation of
Cook's voyages for information about Pacific islanders in general, and
especially for clues to Hawai'ian motivations for killing Cook.[28] By the
1990s, two non-indigenous scholars began battling for Pacific moral high
ground from their distant American campuses. Marshall Sahlins, a Pacific
anthropologist based in Chicago, had been for many years an advocate of
taking seriously the structures and internal integrity of indigenous Pacific
societies. Moving in the 1980s from more theoretical work to explorations
in history, Sahlins produced two particularly important books: *Historical
Metaphors and Mythical Realities* (1981) and *Islands of History* (1985).
In them he proposed that Captain Cook had been killed for appearing to
be the Hawai'ian deity Ono, but failing to behave in the expected way.
Gananath Obeyesekere, an anthropologist at Harvard new to the Pacific
field, disagreed in almost every respect, claiming that all indigenous peoples share a practical rationality that allowed decisions to be made for
pragmatic reasons.[29] His Sri Lankan ancestry, Obeyesekere argued, gave
him an advantage in understanding these matters. To suggest as Sahlins

did, that indigenous peoples found meaning from within their particular cultural context, was racist.

The controversy reached the mainstream press and rebuttals were published by both men.[30] Academics produced a stream of articles and books assessing the state of play and locating their own academic politics accordingly.[31] As we have seen, Jackie Huggins had wondered when the same energy would be devoted to the period "BC"—"Before Cook." For the Hawai'ian scholar Haunani-Kay Trask, the significance of Cook's voyages lay elsewhere: in "the toll introduced diseases [have] been taking on the Native people" and in other aspects of colonialism in the islands.[32] The Tongan anthropologist Epeli Hau'ofa was critical of both the valorization and the demonization of Cook. Blaming Cook for the evils of colonialism was merely sending him "to the wings to await our summons when it is necessary to call in the Plague. . . ."[33] Hero or villain, "As long as this particular spirit struts the centre stage, our peoples and institutions will remain where they are now: as minor characters and spectators".[34] Donald Denoon had suggested that indigenous and non-indigenous approaches should somehow be harmonized, but is there not a legitimate critique of the ongoing historiographical focus on Cook's voyages and those of other famous Europeans? On the other side of the coin, have not various historiographical developments brought new perspectives to the study of familiar explorers and their activities?

In his pioneering volume *European Vision and the South Pacific*, first published in 1960, Bernard Smith began to explore "the relation between art and science," understanding that ways of seeing (artistic or otherwise) involved rendering the experience of the Pacific into forms comprehensible in Europe.[35] By the second edition in 1985, Smith wrote that "the assured posture of the 'scientific' observer, secure in his own capacity to view the other with a wholly objective and neutral gaze, is much less common in academic circles today than it was then."[36] Smith's own contribution back in 1960 had facilitated this sea change, analyzing the artwork of a range of European visitors to the Pacific, including settlers and missionaries, and decisively critiquing its "objectivity."

With literary deconstruction and other postcolonial methodologies in the air from the 1980s onward, the terms and extent of critique widened. Paul Carter's work proclaimed history to be "imperial" through its failure to examine how language creates knowledge; knowledge was not somehow objectively acquired and then communicated through language. Instead, language was contingent and so therefore was knowledge; geographical spaces, for example, were not free standing realities, but instead were created by the process of exploration and knowledge production and dissemination.[37] Carter's worked sparked an interest in the deconstruction, or "fragmentation," of Pacific explorers, questioning their heroic status by including indigenous voices, roles, and contexts. As Simon Ryan noted in his 1996 survey of exploration historiography in Australia: "The rewriting of exploration, then, cannot simply be a matter of reversing an attitude towards another historical period, changing the image of the "heroic explorer" to ravenous agent of imperialism."[38] Either way, the focus would remain on the European explorer. The rewriting Ryan calls for would ensure that Pacific peoples were more than bystanders whose colonial victimization was all that could be discerned in all-powerful tropes and discourses of European texts.

Nuanced works such as Anne Salmond's study of indigenous/European interactions in New Zealand, *Two Worlds*, featured the concept of "mirror-image ethnography—in which each side saw the other through a haze of their own reflections."[39] Existing work on the complexities of indigenous/European interactions had given a head start to postcolonial literary scholars eager to explore discursive complexities in the texts of exploration. Not only could they easily access the published official accounts of the most famous expeditions—already edited and published by an earlier generation—but they could also compare those accounts with the lesser-known journals or letters of sailors, beachcombers, and missionaries that had been unearthed in the Pacific Studies era.

As writer Neil Hegarty has observed: "The more a single voyage is analysed in its textual multiplicities . . . the more unstable and plural become the narratives."[40]

Which "single voyage" to study in this way, however, has tended to yield rather predictable results. A few indigenous explorers had been brought to light in the Pacific Studies era, such as Ta'unga of the London Missionary Society.[41] More recently, further attention has been given to islanders associated with the most famous explorers. European texts have scoured for information about the two Raiateans, Tupaia and Mai, taken aboard by Captain Cook. Tupaia, a priest, proved an invaluable authority on navigation in the Society Island group and found that he could be understood by the indigenous Maori when the expedition reached New Zealand. Tupaia died before reaching Britain but Mai did not. A celebrity in his day, Mai (known then as Omai due to mistranslation) has been studied recently as "a curiosity, a visually striking personality, and a living experiment."[42] All of this is true, but the vast majority of Pacific peoples took ship under less famous captains and have remained largely unknown to history.[43] So have the many Pacific peoples killed by Europeans during (or after) early contacts.[44]

Interest in the careers of lesser known European explorers has also been scarce. Retired naval hydrographer Andrew David has produced the only extensive account of the neglected 1852–1861 voyage of HMS *Herald*, understanding, as relatively few have, that the lateness of European contact with the western Pacific means that the Victorian period is just as important for the history of exploration as the officially-designated "Age of Exploration" in the eighteenth century.[45] Jordan Goodman of the Wellcome Institute has recently produced the first major study of HMS *Rattlesnake* in New Guinea and other areas of the southwest Pacific.[46] Given Queensland's early interest in southeastern New Guinea, and subsequent British and Australian rule in the area, *Rattlesnake*'s explorations and mapping were crucial factors in later colonial claims.

Earlier activities have fared little better than the Victorian voyages. Glyndwr Williams, who has published his share of work on Cook, has also labored to draw greater attention to the earlier English and British voyages, especially in his books on the buccaneers, the wild speculations of the "South Sea Bubble" era, and the neglected voyage of Commodore George Anson in 1740–1744.[47] Williams notes the "practical, literary and philosophical" fascination produced in England by early Pacific voyage texts which were "studded with images and descriptions that took root in the English folk memory."[48] New editions and compilations joined ballads, plays, and artwork to form a culture of Pacific exploration that must be considered alongside the well-known voyage texts. Given postmodern critiques of narratives of progress, especially those generated by the Enlightenment, one might expect recent scholarship to give at least as much attention to earlier voyages as they do to Cook's. Cook's voyages ushered in a new era of greater scientific rigor, to be sure, but why should this be driving the academic agenda so strongly in these postmodern and postcolonial times? Instead, writing in 1997, Williams felt that he had to make a case for why the earlier voyages had a place "important enough to deserve a book of [their] own."[49]

Meanwhile, if the gist of the Sahlins/Obeyesekere debate really was the search for a greater understanding of indigenous motives for the killing of a European explorer, why the lack of interest in other Pacific deaths during the exploration period? Preliminary research into the killing of Commodore James Goodenough in 1875, for example, reveals the type of "textual multiplicity" extolled by Neil Hegarty. It was simply a question of being prepared to explore less well-trodden archival and historiographical ground.[50] The value of exploring oral traditions is demonstrated by a very recent article by Thorgeir Kolshus and Even Hovdhaugen on "Reassessing the death of

Bishop John Coleridge Patteson." Patteson was killed by Nukapu islanders in 1871 but, although Patteson was one of the most famous missionary martyrs of the Victorian period, only one anthropologist had studied
Nukapu since his death.[51] Kolshus and Hovdhaugen's fieldwork, combined
with a reassessment of written records, allowed them to explore beyond the
Melanesian Mission's official version of events, revealing the "one element
that, quite remarkably, has been ignored by scholars . . . the role played by
[Pacific island] women."[52] Oral testimony, both that recorded after the fact
by later missionaries and that still present among Nukapu islanders, indicates that high-ranking island women opposed the attack on Patteson, and
organized the respectful return of his body afterward. Sociologist Michael
Gilding had written back in 1982 that "for all the generalizations that have
been made about massacres [in Melanesia] during the contact period there
has been no close study of any single case."[53] The intervention of Kolshus
and Hovdhaugen confirms that there is much to learn by accepting Gilding's
longstanding invitation.

Historians once gave rather uncritical praise to such European triumphs
as the chronometer, highlighting the superiority of Western science and its
ability to conquer the vast "unknown" reaches of the Pacific. Nevertheless,
as historian Tony Ballantyne has pointed out, modern Pacific historiography
has long featured the critical study of the relationship between science and
empire because "the explicit entwinement of knowledge and empire in the
European 'opening up' of the Pacific has meant that historians of the region
have been much less sanguine about the connections between science and
power than many of their contemporaries working on North American and
European history."[54] For example, historians have long debated Joseph
Banks's role on Cook's first expedition. A man of empire in the broadest
sense, Banks combined scientific interests with his personal wealth and
political connections to create a truly global network of scientific researchers and collectors. Work on Banks by Harold Carter, John Gascoigne, and
others provided landmark investigations of the imperialism of science in the
Pacific, demonstrating not only the familiar theme of Western expansionism
and its impact on the Pacific world, but also the impact of the Pacific world
on Europe itself (and later the United States).[55] Others have expanded the
definition of "scientist" to include scholarly missionaries, who were often
the first sustained observers of Pacific peoples.[56]

Non-British voyages have generated relatively little debate in Pacific historiography. The occasional comparative study appears, such as *Pioneers
of the Pacific* (2005) published by the National Maritime Museum "to
introduce the general reader to six of Cook's followers," thus reducing

(in fine imperial style) several continental European voyagers to the status of "followers" of the British paragon. The collection includes a study
of Jean-François de Galaup, Comte de La Pérouse, whose expedition
arrived at Botany Bay in Australia only a few days after the First Fleet.
Texts from La Pérouse's voyage have been used to some limited extent,
usually in debates about early contacts between Samoans and Europeans.[57]
The case of Alejandro Malaspina is another story. An Italian nobleman who
explored the world with the Spanish Royal Navy, he was later neglected by
the Spanish government for political reasons. The records of his voyages
have been published for the first time only recently, edited (among others)
by Andrew David and Glyndwr Williams.[58]

Why highlight the work of those who bring new archives to light, or
translate them to improve accessibility? In his multi-volume work on Russia
in the Pacific, Glynn Barratt demonstrates the wealth of ethnographic and
other information contained in neglected Russian records. In the latter days
of the Cold War, Barratt explains, Soviet historians became interested in
the long history of Russian involvement in the Pacific region but others
did not: "It is as though we refuse to recognize that Soviet vessels are not
Johnny-come-latelies on the South Pacific scene."[59] Later, he reinforced this
critique, noting that his own translations were often the first into English
of important Russian exploration accounts. "If I emphasize the fact that
Russian sources ... may be of value to the student of Tahiti and other islands,
it is because the very fact that they exist is largely ignored throughout the
West."[60] The postcolonial turn has generated interest in a globalized, multidisciplinary exploration of encounters between the colonial powers and
non-European peoples in other fields, but the "transnational" dimension
seems to have found little traction in the Pacific context.

Little of this international archival effort has been undertaken by historians who identify themselves as postcolonial scholars, despite the attention
drawn by Edward Said to the crucial role of French ethnography in the construction of "orientalism." A distinguished exception is Bronwen Douglas,
who produced a series of articles and chapters on comparative British and
French ethnography in the eighteenth century and beyond. Douglas contends
that we should speak broadly of "Oceania," including coastal Australia and
Aotearoa/New Zealand, a term which "reinstates the cartographic vision of
the French geographers and naturalists who invented the term and transcends
its restriction to the Pacific Islands in much later Anglophone usage."[61] So
fundamental is French ethnography to Pacific historiography that we reveal
its importance every time we speak of "Polynesians" or "Melanesians,"
terms coined by the French explorer Dumont d'Urville.[62]

Meanwhile the Cook Books continue to pour from the presses.[63] The point here is not that there is nothing new to say about Captain Cook. The point, if I may paraphrase historian Kerry Howe, is to ask whether we are learning more and more about less and less? Ever since the emergence of Pacific Studies in the 1960s, the status of European explorers as "heroes" has been in question. As Howe has noted:

> Pacific history since the 1950s and 1960s has been relatively nonauthoritarian, relatively relative, consciously inclusive, aware of pluralities, and certainly deeply reflexive. The alleged sins of modernist history—its singleness, stability, exclusiveness, determinacy—have not been so obvious as perhaps in some other fields of history.[64]

Meanwhile, however, the privileged position of certain voyages, especially those of Captain Cook, seems to have gone largely unnoticed. Despite the best efforts of indigenous scholars and activists, and of those postcolonial theorists seeking to "provincialize" Europe,[65] famous European explorers and their activities continue to dominate academic attention. Historical geographer Felix Driver has warned of a recent "narrowing of perspective, especially, I would add, in the context of the history of exploration and travel."[66] Perhaps nowhere else is this better exemplified than by the Great Navigator's long shadow over the Pacific world.

NOTES

1. In an attempt to contain the potential scope of historiography for the entire Pacific region, this essay will focus on the southern Pacific. For various reasons, the history of north Pacific exploration has remained largely aloof, located within the disciplines of Asian, Russian, Canadian, or American studies rather than forming an academic identity of its own. The reasons for this are too complex to investigate there.

2. J.C. Beaglehorn, The Exploration of the Pacific, 3rd ed. (London: Adam and Charles Black, 1966), vii.

3. Andrew Sharp, *The Discovery of the Pacific Islands* (Oxford: Clarendon Press, 1960), 1.

4. See http://asiapacific.anu.edu.au/pambu/ (accessed November 12, 2012).

5. See http://www.nla.gov.au/microform-australian-joint-copying-project (accessed November 12, 2012).

6. See Bob Connolly and Robin Anderson, *First Contact: New Guinea's Highlanders Encounter the Outside World* (New York: Penguin, 1988) concerning

the neglected archives of a Australian exploring expedition to New Guinea in the 1930s.

7. Greg Dening, *Islands and Beaches. Discourse on a Silent Land. Marquesas 1774–1880* (Honolulu: University of Hawai'i Press, 1980), 3.

8. Ivan Brady, "On Dening's *Islands and Beaches*" in Doug Munro and Brij V. Lal, eds. *Texts and Contexts. Reflections in Pacific Island Historiography* (Honolulu: University of Hawai'i Press, 2006), 215.

9. Dening, *Islands and Beaches*, 37.

10. David Chappell, *Double Ghosts: Oceanian voyagers on Euroamerican ships* (Armonk, NY: M.E. Sharpe, 1997), xv.

11. K. R. Howe, *The Quest for Origins. Who First Discovered and Settled New Zealand and the Pacific Islands?* (Auckland: Penguin, 2003), 60.

12. O. K. H. Spate, *The Spanish Lake*, vol. 1 of *The Pacific since Magellan* (London: Croom Helm, 1979), x.

13. Howe, *Quest for Origins*, 62; also see Ben Finney; *Pacific Navigation and Voyaging* (Wellington: Polynesian Society, 1976).

14. Finney, *Pacific Navigation and Voyaging* 6–7. By the 1990s so much specialist work had accumulated that an encyclopedia was needed to survey the field; see Nicholas J. Goetzfridt, ed. *Indigenous Navigation and voyaging in the Pacific: a reference guide* (New York: Greenwood, 1992).

15. Finney, *Pacific Navigation and Voyaging*, 10, 11.

16. David Buisseret, ed. *The Oxford Companion to World Exploration*, 2 vols. (Oxford: Oxford University Press, 2007).

17. D. J. Mulvaney, "Archaeological Retrospect", *Antiquity* 60 (1986): 102.

18. Mulvaney, "Archaeological Retrospect," 104.

19. Elaine Thompson, *Fair enough: egalitarianism in Australia* (Sydney: University of New South Wales, 1994), 97.

20. Lynette Russell, ed. *Colonial Frontiers: Indigenous-European encounters in settler societies* (Manchester: Manchester University Press, 2001).

21. Henry Reynolds, "The land, the explorers and the Aborigines," *Historical Studies* 19:75 (1980): 213.

22. Thompson, *Fair enough*, 102.

23. Donald Denoon, "What is to be done, and who is to do it?," in Brij V. Lal and Hank Nelson, eds. *Lines Across the Sea. Colonial Inheritance in the Post Colonial Pacific* (Brisbane: Pacific History Association, 1995), ix.

24. Denoon, "What is to be done," ix.

25. Jackie Huggins, "Cook and the New Anthropology," in Margarette Lincoln, ed. *Science and Exploration in the Pacific* (Woodbridge, U.K.: Boydell Press, 1998), 206.

26. My thanks to Ellen Bielawski, Dean of Native Studies at the University of Alberta, for this particular insight.

27. See Doug Munro, "Who 'Owns' Pacific History: reflections on the insider/outsider dichotomy," *Journal of Pacific History* 29:2 (1994): 232–237.

28. Compare George Gilbert, *The death of Captain James Cook* (Honolulu: Paradise of the Pacific Press, 1926) and J. C. Beaglehole, "The Death of Captain Cook," *Historical Studies* 11:43 (1964): 289–305, with Greg Dening, "Sharks that walk on the land: The death of Captain Cook," *Meanjin* 41 (1982): 427–437 and the work of Marshall Sahlins cited below.

29. Gananath Obeyesekere, *The Apotheosis of Captain Cook: European mythmaking in the Pacific* (Princeton, N.J.: Princeton University Press, 1992).

30. The principal rebuttals by Obeyesekere are "Anthropology and the Cook myth: A response to critics," *Social Analysis* 34 (1993): 70–85, "How to write a Cook book: Mythic and other realities in anthropological writing," *Pacific Studies* 17 (1994): 136–155, and the second edition of *The Apotheosis of Captain Cook: European Mythmaking in the Pacific* (Princeton: Princeton University Press, 1998). For Sahlins see *How 'Natives' Think: About Captain Cook, for Example* (Chicago: University of Chicago Press, 1995). Also see the contributions by both men to Robert Borofsky's forum "Cook, Lono, Obeyesekere and Sahlins," *Current Anthropology* 38:2 (1997): 255–282.

31. The review literature is massive; for some of the most substantial assessments see Robert Borofsky, "Cook, Lono, Obeyesekere and Sahlins," *Current Anthropology* 38:2 (1997): 255–282; Brian Fagan, "The Captain Cook Debate, cont'd," *Washington Post Book World* August 3, 1995; David Hanlon, "On the practical, pragmatic, and political interpretations of a death in the Pacific," *Pacific Studies* 17 (1994): 103–111; K. R. Howe, "The making of Cook's death," *Pacific Studies* 31 (1996): 108–118; Bruce Knauft, "Monument of miscast error: Obeyesekere versus Sahlins and Captain Cook," *Social Analysis* 34 (1993): 34–42; Jonathan Lamb, "Social facts, political fictions, and unrelative events: Obeyesekere on Sahlins," *Social Analysis* 34 (1993): 56–60; Samuel Parker, "The revenge of practical reason?," *Oceania* 65 (1995): 57–67; Deborah Rose, "Worshipping Captain Cook," *Social Analysis* 34 (1993): 43–49; David R. Stoddart, "Captain Cook and How We Understand Him," *Geographical Review* 87:4 (1997): 537–542; Nicholas Thomas, "Commonsense sorcery," *Pacific Studies* 17 (1994): 118–124. For a book-length assessment and fresh contribution see Glyndwr Williams, *The death of Captain Cook: a hero made and unmade* (Cambridge Mass.: Harvard University Press, 2008).

32. Haunani-Kay Trask, *From a Native Daughter*, 2d ed. (Honolulu: University of Hawai'i Press, 1999), 9.

33. Epeli Hau'ofa, *We Are the Ocean: Selected Works* (Honolulu: University of Hawai'i Press, 2008), 65.

34. Hau'ofa, *We Are the Ocean*, 65.

35. Bernard Smith, *European Vision and the South Pacific* (Oxford: Clarendon, 1960), preface.

36. Smith, *European Vision and the South Pacific*, vii.

37. Paul Carter, *The Road to Botany Bay: an exploration of landscape and history* (London: Faber and Faber, 1987).

38. Simon Ryan, *The Cartographic Eye. How Explorers Saw Australia* (Cambridge: Cambridge University Press, 1996), 14.

39. Anne Salmond, *Two Worlds: First Meetings between Maori and Europeans 1642–1772* (Auckland: Viking, 1991), 15.

40. Neil Hegarty, "Unruly Subjects. Sexuality, Science and Discipline in Eighteenth-Century Pacific Exploration," in Margarette Lincoln, ed. *Science and Exploration in the Pacific. European voyages to the southern oceans in the eighteenth century* (Woodbridge, U.K.: Boydell Press, 1998), 184.

41. R. G. and Marjorie Tuainekore Crocombe, *The works of Ta'unga; records of a Polynesian traveler in the South Seas, 1833–1896* (Canberra: Australian National University Press, 1968).

42. Rüdiger Joppien, "Philippe Jacques de Loutherbourg's Pantomime 'Omai, or, a Trip round the World' and the Artists of Captain Cook's Voyages," in T. C. Mitchell, ed. *The British Museum Yearbook: Captain Cook and the South Pacific*, vol. 3 (London: British Museum Publications, 1979), 82.

43. See Chappell, *Double ghosts*.

44. For a critique of longstanding views about "gunboat diplomacy" and its impact on Pacific peoples, see Samson, *Imperial Benevolence*.

45. Andrew David, *The Voyage of HMS Herald* (Carlton, Victoria: The Miegunyah Press, 1995); on the neglect of Cook's successors see Jane Samson, *Imperial Benevolence*.

46. Jordan Goodman, *The Rattlesnake: a voyage of discovery to the Coral Sea* (London: Faber and Faber, 2006).

47. Glyndwr Williams, *The Great South Sea. English Voyages and Encounters 1570–1750* (New Haven, Conn.: Yale University Press, 1997) and idem, *The Prize of All the Oceans: The Triumph and Tragedy of Anson's Voyage Round the World* (London: HarperCollins, 1999).

48. Williams, *The Great South Sea*, xiv.

49. Williams, *The Great South Sea*, xv.

50. Jane Samson, "Hero, fool or martyr?: The many deaths of Commodore Goodenough," *Journal of Maritime Research* (2008) online http://www.jmr.nmm.ac.uk/server/show/ConJmrArticle.243 (accessed November 12, 2012).

51. Thorgeir Kolshus and Even Hovdhaugen, "Reassessing the death of Bishop John Coleridge Patteson", *Journal of Pacific History* 45:3 (2010): 332.

52. Kolshus and Hovdhaugen, "Reassessing the death of Bishop John Coleridge Patteson," 331.

53. Michael Gilding, "The Massacre of the *Mystery*," *Journal of Pacific History* 17:2 (1982): 66. Peter Corris and Roger M. Keesing had already published a study of the 1927 killing of a district officer in Solomon Islands, but this does not constitute an early contact situation. Four years after Gilding's challenge, Roger M. Keesing published "The 'Young Dick' Attack: Oral and Documentary History on the Colonial Frontier," *Ethnohistory* 33:3 (1986): 268–292. The subsequent postcolonial critique of ethnohistory, perhaps, threw the baby out with the bathwater.

54. Tony Ballantyne, ed. *Science, Empire and the European Exploration of the Pacific* (Aldershot, U.K.: Ashgate Variorum, 2004), xv.

55. For example see Harold B. Carter, *Sir Joseph Banks, 1743–1820* (London: British Museum, 1988); John Gascoigne, *Science in the Service of Empire: Joseph Banks, the British state and the uses of science in the age of revolution* (Cambridge: Cambridge University Press, 1998) and the multiple volumes of Banks correspondence edited by Carter and by Neil Chambers. The State Library of New South Wales has undertaken a major initiative to make its Banks collections available online, see http://www2.sl.nsw.gov.au/banks/ (accessed November 12, 2012).

56. Niel Gunson, *Messengers of Grace: evangelical missionaries in the South Seas, 1797–1860* (Oxford: Oxford University Press, 1978); Jane Samson, "Ethnology and Theology: Nineteenth Century Missionary Dilemmas," in Brian Stanley, ed. *Christian Missions and the Enlightenment* (Grand Rapids, Mich.: Eerdmans, 2001): 99–123; "Pacific: Missionary Accounts," in David Buisseret, ed. *The Oxford Companion to Exploration* (Oxford: Oxford University Press, 2008); and Helen Gardner, "The 'Faculty of Faith': Evangelical missionaries, social anthropologists, and the claim for human unity in the 19th century," in Bronwen Douglas and Chris Ballard, eds. *Foreign Bodies. Oceania and the Science of Race 1750–1940* (Canberra: ANU E-Press, 2008): 259–282.

57. See Jocelyn Linnekin, "Ignoble Savages and Other European Visions: The La Pérouse Affair in Samoan History," *Journal of Pacific History* 26:1 (1991) and Serge Tcherkézoff, *"First Contacts" in Polynesia: the Samoan Case (1722–1848): Western misunderstandings about sexuality and divinity* (Christchurch: The Macmillan Brown Centre for Pacific Studies, 2004).

58. The first volume appeared in 2002; see Andrew David, Felipe Fernandez-Armesto, Carlos Novi and Glyndwr Williams, eds. *The Malaspina Expedition 1789–1794: The Journal of the Voyage by Alejandro Malaspina, Volume I, Cadiz to Panama.* (London: The Hakluyt Society [Series III, Volume 8], 2002).

59. Glynn Barratt, *Russia and the South Pacific 1696–1840*, vol. 2 *Southern and Eastern Polynesia* (Vancouver: University of British Columbia Press, 1988), xii.

60. Barratt, *Russia and the South Pacific*, xvii. French voyages are better known than most of their European counterparts; see Glynnis M. Cropp, Noel R. Watts, Roger D. J. Collins and K. R. Howe, eds. *Pacific Journeys: essays in honour of John Dunmore* (Wellington: Victoria University Press, 2005).

61. Bronwen Douglas and Chris Ballard, eds. *Foreign Bodies. Oceania and the Science of Race 1750–1940* (Canberra: ANU E-Press, 2008), 5.

62. See the special issue devoted to this topic in *The Journal of Pacific History* 38:2 (2003).

63. For a sampling from the last decade alone see Frank McLynn, *Captain Cook: Master of the Seas* (New Haven, Conn.: Yale University Press, 2011); Maria Nugent, *Captain Cook Was Here* (Cambridge: Cambridge University Press, 2009); Geoffrey Blainey, *Sea of Dangers: Captain Cook and his rivals*

in the South Pacific (Chicago: Ivan R. Dee, 2009); John Gascoigne, *Captain Cook: voyager between worlds* (London: Hambledon Continuum, 2008); Harriet Guest, *Empire, Barbarism, and Civilisation: Captain Cook, William Hodges and the Return to the Pacific* (Cambridge: Cambridge University Press, 2007); Dan O'Sullivan, *In Search of Captain Cook* (London: I. B. Taurus, 2008); Nigel Rigby, Pieter van der Merwe and Glydwr Williams, *Captain Cook in the Pacific* (Greenwich, U.K.: National Maritime Museum, 2005); John Robson, *The Captain Cook Encyclopedia* (London: Chatham, 2004); Anne Salmond, *The Trial of the Cannibal Dog: Captain Cook in the South Seas* (London: Allen Lane, 2003); Glyndwr Williams, *Captain Cook: explorations and reassessments* (Woodbridge U.K.: Boydell Press, 2004); Martin Dugard, *Farther than any man: the rise and fall of Captain James Cook* (New York: Pocket Books, 2001). Nicholas Thomas's *Discoveries: The Voyages of Captain Cook* (Allen Lane, 2003) was published in the United States under a different title, *Cook: the extraordinary voyages of Captain James Cook* (New York: Walker & Co., 2003). This list is by no means exhaustive.

64. Howe, *Nature, Culture, and History*, 68–69.

65. Dipesh Chakrabarty, *Provincialising Europe: Postcolonial thought and historical difference* (Princeton, N.J.: Princeton University Press, 2000).

66. Driver, *Geography Militant*, 7.

8

DECENTERING EXPLORATION IN
EAST AFRICA

STEPHEN J. ROCKEL

Mid-nineteenth-century East Africa[1] was much better connected to the Indian Ocean region and the wider world of transcontinental capitalism than is generally assumed.[2] The first European explorers who travelled through the interior of East and Central Africa had to come to terms with spatial networks and traveling cultures that connected many regions of the vast interior of the African continent with the cosmopolitan and maritime world of the Indian Ocean coast. (See Figure 8.1.) When Richard F. Burton and John Hanning Speke departed Kaole on the mainland opposite Zanzibar in June 1857 on their famous East African Expedition to the central African lakes, the caravan system they relied on for transportation and survival was well established. A transregional and multiethnic culture had long facilitated trade, communication, and the movement of people, commodities, and ideas. A spatial infrastructure of route networks, market towns, caravan stops, and provisioning systems provided a material foundation. Those Africans, Arabs and Indians who traded cloth and brass wire, beads, ivory, hippo teeth, gum copal, guns, iron tools, livestock, and luxury goods at various points along the main caravan routes had accumulated an enormous reservoir of specialist knowledge about the logistics and culture of travel, about the local demand for imported manufactured products among the many peoples of the East and Central African interior, and about the sources of ivory and slaves. They learned the trading languages of Kinyamwezi, Kiswahili, Maa and others. Over the course of their travels they spread new crops, aesthetics, fashions, and ideas of wage labor and entrepreneurship. In the minds of the merchants, small traders and caravan porters of the central

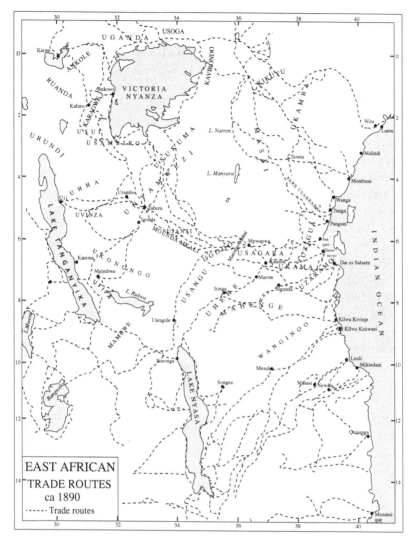

Figure 8.1 Map of East African caravan routes in the nineteenth century [From Stephen J. Rockel, *Carriers of Culture: Labor on the Road in 19th Century East Africa* (Portsmouth N.H.: Heinemann, 2006), xvii]

caravan routes followed by Burton and Speke, there were no maps filled with large blank spaces, only long journeys and distant destinations.[3]

European and other western explorers in East Africa followed well behind the footsteps of African (Nyamwezi, Sumbwa, Yao, Kamba and Swahili) elephant hunters, traders, caravan operators, and professional long-distance porters and, from the early 1800s, Arab, Indian, and Beluch traders. By the time Burton and Speke reached Lake Tanganyika in February 1858, the penetration of eastern Africa by merchant and industrial capitalism was well under way, as African- and Asian-led caravans carried cloth, guns, metal goods, and other industrial imports thousands of kilometers into the interior in exchange for ivory and other African products. They were drawn into the vast interior by the expansion of the elephant frontier as ivory prices rose dramatically (fueled by the rise of the western middle classes) and industrial production cheapened cloth imports.[4] This late eighteenth and nineteenth-century commercial system itself overlay much older patterns of regional trade carried out by African groups in copper, iron implements, salt, and cattle.[5]

The widespread presence of sleeping sickness in the region, caused by trypanosome parasites and transmitted by the tsetse fly, made the use of domestic and draft animals almost impossible. Thus, Western explorers, like the African and Arab pioneers, became completely reliant on human porterage, with its corresponding labor markets, route networks, market towns and caravan stops, provisioning systems, lodgings and security, as well as knowledge of all kinds gained from African and coastal Muslim travelers. Slave labor supplemented the voluntary labor of professional porters and peasant food producers and provided domestic labor in the households of African and Muslim traders. Over time, European travelers adjusted to East African realities and incorporated most aspects of the caravan system and its labor practices into an apparently systematic and scientific approach to travel.[6]

Western exploration came relatively late to the interior of East Africa. There was no counterpart of Mungo Park's journey to the Niger River (1795–1797), representing an earlier and perhaps more romantic age. Exploration was a multinational enterprise involving German, English, Scottish, Austrian, Welsh-American, Swiss, French, Belgian, Portuguese, and Irish travelers and, later, Canadians, Americans and Italians. Missionary travelers like the Germans J. L. Krapf, Johann Rebmann, and Jakob Erhardt made important early contributions to the exploration of the region as well, as did a few women, such as the remarkable Annie Hore, who traveled as far as Lake Tanganyika with her husband, Edward Coode Hore, of the

London Missionary Society.[7] During the pivotal decades from the 1850s to the 1870s, however, the British dominated exploration of the region. They were obsessed with exploration of the sources of the Nile and the Great Lakes watersheds of East and Central Africa.[8]

Much of what is known about African societies in this period relies on explorers' writings. Many fine works, some published posthumously, emerged from the pens of nineteenth-century explorers and travelers. Almost all were inflected with the racial theories of their day and some-times by their own personal antagonisms toward Africans—including the most brilliant (Burton) and blustering (Samuel Baker).[9] Their writings reveal five themes that run through European exploration in East Africa. First, in the generation after Krapf, Rebmann, Erhardt, Burton, Speke, and James A. Grant, close connections developed between the explorers and positivist and imperialist enterprises linked to the partition of Africa.[10] Yet the exploration enterprise had uneven results. Rwanda was not visited by a European until the 1890s.[11] Second, some explorers were connected to anti-slavery movements or used antislavery rhetoric, which was fully exploited by the imperialists. Third, the long rivalry of Christian Europe with the Islamic world influenced the perspectives of European travelers. For all the pro-Arab sympathies of Burton, most explorers as well as missionaries con-nected slavery to Islam and the Arabs, contributing to the manipulation of latent anti-Arab sentiments in Europe. Fourth, the relationship between dis-covery and violence marred the achievements of some of the more famous explorers, the best-known case being Henry Morton Stanley. Fifth, the explorers' collective documentary and other works shifted the epistemo-logical foundations of European knowledge about Africa in new directions with consequences extending into the twenty-first century.[12]

* * *

In early 1845, a great "Arab" caravan with a large armed escort left Bagamoyo, on the Indian Ocean coast of modern Tanzania, for the interior.[13] By the time it crossed Lake Tanganyika and entered the Congo basin— a difficult journey to that point of about 1,500 kilometres—it consisted of several Arabs and Swahilis and "two hundred armed slaves," no doubt Waungwana, the Islamicized slave and freed slave porters of the coast. One of these Arabs was Said bin Habib of Zanzibar. Seven years later, a section of this great expedition under the leadership of Said bin Habib arrived at Benguela on the west coast of the continent. François Bontinck, the his-torian of this epic story, writes of the climax: "The arrival at Benguela, on April 3 1852, of three 'Moors' of Zanzibar, leading a caravan of forty porters, was without doubt a sensational event for the inhabitants of that important port."[14] Said bin Habib continued his ivory and slave trading business in the interior of the continent for several more years, at Kazembe, Katanga, and the Zambezi Valley, among other places, and visited Luanda three times in the process. In 1860 he returned to Zanzibar, completing a double-crossing of the continent that had taken sixteen years.[15]

Most accounts of Victorian exploration in East and Central Africa ignore the precedents of African and Arab travelers such as Said bin Habib, and the complexities of the caravan systems established and extended by the Yao, the Nyamwezi, the Kamba, the Swahili and other travelling peoples, on which European explorers were completely reliant. By way of example, consider the otherwise splendid *David Livingstone and the Victorian Encounter with Africa*, a companion volume to a major museum exhibit.[16] In this book (1996), Africans typically remain the objects of Exeter Hall[17] concern or the practical endeavors of missionaries, or are condemned for their involvement in the slave trade.[18] Overlooked are the African traders and empire builders, along with professional caravan leaders and porters, who opened up vast territories to commerce and new ideas. They carried African and imported products across a region as big as Europe. They invented new ethnicities and trans-regional cultures. Yet the only hint of their role in the Livingstone volume appears in its copious illustrations, which include images of Livingstone's African companions, Abdullah Susi and James Chuma.[19] These two Africans have achieved recognition in what historian John MacKenzie refers to as the "biographical industry" on Livingstone and his travels only through their status as "faithfuls" on his famous last journey.[20]

Livingstone was familiar with the realities of East African trade and the caravan system that sustained it, and he had met Said bin Habib more than once. In his *Last Journals* he commented repeatedly on the efficiency of caravans along the route through what is now Tanzania and the massive loads carried by the strongest of the professional porters. He praised the "Banyamwezi" porters who "as usual" carried goods "honestly to Unyanyembe" in advance of himself.[21] His own porters and servants were familiar with the caravan culture of the trading routes created by the Nyamwezi and other traveling peoples. Livingstone described the emotional impact of the safari drum and the *barghumi* (kudu horn) that sounded at the start of a march: "These sounds seem to awaken a sort of *esprit de corps* . . . . My attendants now jumped up, and would scarcely allow me time to dress when they heard the sounds of their childhood, and all day they were among the foremost."[22] The honor of professional caravan personnel required them to make an appropriate impression at the departure and conclusion of a long journey. Appearances were so important that caravan leaders took on the responsibility of making sure that their porters were correctly attired when entering their home town. Swahili trader Selemani bin Mwenye Chande wrote in advance to his creditor requesting clothes to wear when his caravan entered Bagamoyo.[23] Before entering Ujiji on Lake Tanganyika, the mud-stained porters of a London Missionary Society expedition stopped to rest and refresh themselves, and "from carefully preserved little bundles, brought forth clean white garments, and various array, for the entry into the town." Thus, the "nearly naked, and starving" followers of Livingstone, bearing his body, made an attempt to present themselves in the usual style of a caravan making a grand entry at the end of a journey when they reached the trading centre of Kwihara, near Tabora. On such occasions, the townspeople gathered to welcome the newcomers and join in the celebrations, shouting and firing guns.[24] Livingstone was also familiar with the vital role of caravan women on long journeys, though he disapproved of the widespread practice of temporary "marriage" of porters and headmen to their caravan "wives."[25]

Explorers' and missionaries' reports[26] and modern histories contain a plethora of information on exploration in the context of the nineteenth-century caravan system and East African traveling cultures.[27] Finding experienced caravan leaders and ensuring access to enough porters to carry baggage and trade goods was a constant preoccupation of all foreign travelers in the interior, whether Arab, Indian or European. According to Cornelia Essner, "the *Leitmotiv* in their [Europeans'] writings is the long-winded discussions of complaints concerning the question of porters."[28] Some of the more perceptive explorers and other early European travelers went beyond mere complaints to acquire an understanding of the spatial organization of the caravan system, the logistics of travel, and other aspects of caravan culture. A few explorers' published works included appendices that listed caravan personnel, thus recognizing individually the importance of caravan leaders, headmen, porters and guides to the success of their expeditions.[29] But popular histories of African exploration and travel—Tim Jeal's biography of Henry Morton Stanley is a prominent example—often persist in portraying the region in terms of the caricature Stanley himself did so much to create, that of "Darkest Africa," and largely ignore the literature on the caravan system that Livingstone, Stanley, and all other foreign travelers in Central and East Africa relied upon.[30] In Jeal's book, the life of "Africa's greatest explorer"[31] can still be written without engagement with the mature field of African history. As the Africanist and imperial historian A. G. Hopkins concludes in a withering critique: "Decades after the foundation of the lead-ing journals in the field, it is still possible to produce a widely publicized book that bypasses modern research on the partition of Africa, conveys a wholly dated image of the continent to a new generation of general readers, is waved through enthusiastically by a bevy of reviewers and is honoured by prize-giving pundits."[32]

Hence, it remains as essential as ever to locate African explorers and exploration in the wider context of commerce, caravan culture, and the infrastructure of caravan travel in the region, much as the best recent work on exploration places it in the context of scientific, economic and cultural change in Europe. Two key groups of caravan workers—the Nyamwezi and the Waungwana—are central to this enterprise. The following section will consider the spatial infrastructure of travel: the trade routes, caravan towns, and provisioning systems that facilitated European exploration as well as all other travel in East and Central Africa.

*   *   *

When studying interactions between Europe and Africa in the age of explo-ration and empire, historians typically utilize terms like "race," "gender," "development," "labor," "slavery" and "freedom," which reflect a western intellectual lineage. To apply these terms to Africa as unproblematized uni-versal categories, or to suggest that Africa was irrelevant to globalization in the eighteenth and nineteenth centuries, is to distort the African expe-rience; hence it is essential to deconstruct and historicize them.[33] I wrote elsewhere that many colonial sources and indeed some modern histories assume that long-distance caravan porters were either captive or slave labor-ers and, at best, unsophisticated sojourners at the coast. Late nineteenth century imperial discourse justifying conquest and subjugation underlies such notions. My argument opposes such views. Professional caravan por-ters were innovators at the forefront of East African engagement with the international capitalist economy. They were key players in the development of new social, economic and cultural networks across East and much of Central Africa during the late precolonial period. Indeed, they helped create the framework for the integration of modern Tanzania.[34]

The Nyamwezi of western Tanzania were the most important traveling and trading people in East Africa and their innovations most shaped the car-avan system that European travelers eventually utilized. There is strong evi-dence that some Nyamwezi elephant hunters had reached the rich hunting grounds in the Luangwa Valley west of Lake Malawi and begun to transport ivory to the coast as early as the mid-eighteenth century.[35] Characteristics of Nyamwezi caravan culture included standard practices related to labor specialization, marching patterns, the order of precedence and rank, customary law regulating authority and discipline, and a porter code of honor.[36] It recognized a standard cloth wage in *doti merikani* for upcountry journeys, that is, for caravans leaving the coast for the interior.[37] Trade and hospitality between various groups along the trade routes were promoted through the practice of blood brotherhood, joking relationships (*utani* in Kiswahili), and the spread of a lingua franca: [38] first Kinyamwezi, then, as coastal caravans became more common in the interior, Kiswahili. As coastal traders became large employers of caravan labor, more standardized provisioning systems—based either on a fixed grain ration (the *kibaba*) or defined allowances for porters of cloth or beads to buy provisions along the routes (*posho*)—became typical.[39] The presence of women in the caravans was crucial for the spread of this caravan culture in a multi-ethnic environment, as well as the well-being of male porters.

Nyamwezi caravan culture influenced the Swahili of the coast and in turn was affected by them. In the interior Nyamwezi social and cultural norms prevailed because the peoples of the western interior pioneered the caravan system, and the majority of porters and caravans working the central routes were Nyamwezi. Nearly all explorers (including Burton, Speke, and Grant) hired Nyamwezi porters at some point, even if their expeditions set out from the coast with a locally recruited labor force of Waungwana porters. (See Figure 8.2.)

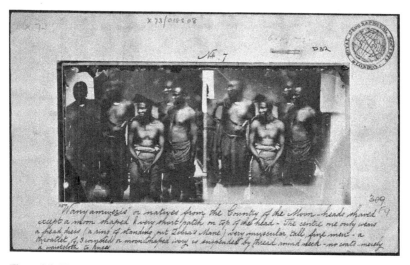

Figure 8.2 Nyamwezi caravan porters, photographed by James Augustus Grant in Zanzibar, 1860. Permission of the Royal Geographical Society, London.

Most Nyamwezi trading ventures were small to medium in scale, with caravans consisting of thirty or forty to two or three hundred members. During the last decades before colonial conquest the Nyamwezi also operated much larger caravans of up to 2,500 or 3,000 porters. These conveyed the commercial status of the members of the trading elite of Unyanyembe and other large chiefdoms, or represented combined ventures that joined together to create a formidable force on the road. The more powerful chiefs such as Mirambo could mobilize a huge work force, drawing on their status as chiefs, rich traders, and warlords.[40]

All of the labor specialization and customs that had characterized caravan culture prior to the arrival of European explorers would persist in the parties that took them into the interior of East Africa. The most important caravan officers were the *wanyampara*, literally "grandfathers," meaning headmen or elders. According to C. T. Wilson of the Church Missionary Society (CMS), "It is under these *niamparas* that the porters or *pagazi* go down to the coast to engage in caravans going up into the interior." Coastal porters also used the title, showing how Nyamwezi terminology was incorporated into a multiethnic environment, although with a slightly different meaning. One historian writes, "The leaders of the porters, the *wanyampara*, were self-made men of great physical strength endowed with moral stamina and a sense of justice. Famous leaders spent their best years on the caravan paths, passing from one expedition to another."[41]

Another caravan official was the *mganga*, a traditional doctor or diviner, who provided ritual protection against the dangers of the road and acted as an advisor to the caravan leader. Apart from protecting caravan personnel, the *mganga* ritually cared for the ivory. The final important caravan office was that of the *kirangozi*, the guide or leader on the march. The *kirangozi* was often elected by the porters from among their ranks, based on his experience and knowledge of the roads. He led the caravan along the correct route and marked off paths to avoid so that stragglers would not lose their way. He might also negotiate *hongo* (taxes, fees) with chiefs along the route. The *kirangozi* were experts on caravan travel and had wide knowledge of the peoples and customs of the road.[42]

Caravan labor was arduous, and the daily march averaged about twelve to fifteen miles, usually completed by late morning due to the heat. Each porter typically carried a load of about sixty to seventy pounds of trade goods or ivory, but in addition to this he carried a weapon, a sleeping mat, cooking pots, and rations. The total load might be one hundred pounds but the strongest men carried large tusks weighing much more. Double loads carried by two men were not uncommon but they were unpopular, as they were difficult to maneuver along the narrow paths. Women and children carried camp equipment and extra provisions.[43] In camp, porters ate in messes of four or five men who were usually close friends. Each member was allocated a task such as preparing shelter, cooking, or collecting firewood. The routine of hard work was broken by the excitement of the hunt, occasional skirmishes, sexual adventures, storytelling, the consumption of tobacco, cannabis (*bangi*), and beer (*pombe*). Music and dance was shared with local communities en route.[44]

The Swahili and their coastal predecessors had traded with neighboring peoples for at least two thousand years, but only toward the end of the eighteenth century did they journey very far into the interior. By the early 1800s, the Nyamwezi and the coastal Swahili were partners in long-distance trade and by the 1820s coastal traders had reached Unyamwezi, five hundred miles into the interior.[45] The majority of their porters were Waungwana (literally "gentlemen"), wage-earning slaves, and freed slaves, most of whom had been enslaved in early childhood in the regions around Lake Malawi or southern Tanzania and brought to the coast, but who subsequently claimed coastal Muslim identity.[46] C. T. Wilson and R. W. Felkin defined the term Waungwana as follows:

> The word Wang'uána [sic] means gentlemen, and has been appropriated by these negroes to distinguish themselves from the slaves who work on the mashamba or plantations. . . . A few of them have obtained their freedom but the majority are still slaves, allowed by their owners, on condition of their receiving a part of their wages, to engage in the service of European travellers.[47]

Clearly the Waungwana, of servile and marginal origins, used a strategy of identity appropriation in order to claim some kind of status in coastal society. They adopted from Swahili patricians key elements of coastal civilization—fluency in Kiswahili, Islam, and an urban life—which gave them, they believed, higher status than coastal society's domestic and agricultural slaves, farmers, fishermen, artisans, and the thousands of caravan porters and traders who descended seasonally from the interior. In contrast, visitors from upcountry were disparaged as *washenzi* (barbarians) because of their animist beliefs, upcountry speech, and different clothing and habits.[48]

The Waungwana became major players in the caravan system and the emerging centers of urban modernity along the main routes such as

Bagamoyo, Tabora, and Ujiji. As Speke noted, they served as armed retainers of coastal traders:

> The Arabs travel in bodies, consisting of several caravans joined together, for mutual protection, of a number averaging from 200 to 800 men, of which a considerable portion, their own domestic slaves, carry muskets, very often the condemned Indian Arab ones . . . whilst the common porters, like all the natives of the interior, carry a bow and a spear.[49]

It was not uncommon for a Mwungwana (singular of Waungwana) to develop an independent career once freed upon the death of his merchant master. He might work as a porter for some years and accumulate a little capital and then begin trading on his own account.[50] Some might become big traders and caravan operators in their own right. Given that virtually all European explorers began their journeys at the coast it was inevitable that they employed large numbers of Waungwana porters, a pattern that persisted from the East African Expedition of Burton and Speke into the conquest period of the 1890s.[51]

European exploration in East Africa rested not only on the expertise and experience of the Nyamwezi and Waungwana, but also on a complex spatial and institutional infrastructure. Its most obvious features were the new market and caravan centers of the main routes, most notably along the central route that ran from the Mrima coast opposite Zanzibar to Tabora and Ujiji, the same route taken by so many European explorers and missionaries. The historical experience of towns such as Bagamoyo, Mpwapwa, and Tabora was similar to all of the urban settlements along the central trade routes, even though local and regional characteristics gave each of these centers its own identity.[52] According to Walter and Beverly Brown, the pioneer urban historians of nineteenth-century Tanzania, "They embraced many of the same immigrant groups; they developed an economic interdependence that involved the same commodities, personnel, and commercial practices; they acquired a common cultural life that was expressed linguistically, religiously, and materially."[53]

Typical urban settlers included Arab, Swahili, and Indian traders, Muslim clerics and Christian missionaries.[54] Traders and missionaries established large households of employees and retainers, often numbering in the dozens. Porters sometimes put down roots locally, far from home, setting up a homestead with a local woman or working the land through the wet season. Others made a living until the next caravan season by selling firewood or building materials. The urban populations of each town included local people and immigrants drawn by ties of marriage, clientage, or economic advantage, as well as slaves and freed slaves of heterogeneous origins.[55] In Mbwamaji, on the coast, informants still remember the Manyema ancestry of some neighbors, probably descendents of slaves and free people arriving with caravans from the eastern Congo in the nineteenth century.[56] In Mpwapwa a community of Christianized ex-slaves established itself beginning in the late 1870s, creating a new multi-ethnic identity comparable to other settlements of former slaves along the main caravan routes. The emergence of such slave and ex-slave communities at the heart of many of the new urban centers of the nineteenth century paradoxically helped create more open, heterogeneous, multiethnic social environments.[57]

Burton, Speke and Grant, as well as Livingstone, Stanley, and Cameron, all spent extended periods of time in Tabora or Ujiji restocking trade goods, reorganizing their caravans, waiting for supplies, collecting information on the next regions to be traversed, hiring porters, organizing botanical and other collections, and writing letters and reports. In many of these tasks they had little choice but to do as other travelers did. As Adrian Wisnicki has noted, for example, the experience of the East African Expedition was shaped and its discoveries limited by the patterns set by African and Arab travelers before them.[58]

If the main caravan junctions and termini had their histories, so too did the routes themselves.[59] It is a misconception to envisage a single road or pathway to a particular destination. Rather, caravan routes consisted of a web of tracks that connected the main trade entrepots with all the "viable communities" in the general direction of the line of march.[60] These networks of footpaths existed in part so that the thousands of porters passing through each year did not overwhelm peasant and pastoralist communities with their food requirements. The caravan trade rested upon the most basic human requirements of food and water, as much as it did on political conditions and commercial calculations. Thus, drought, famine, agricultural and pastoral production, disruptions to food production caused by political conflict, as well as changing African consumption patterns, all shaped African travel and exploration.[61]

*   *   *

This was the world that Burton, Speke and Grant, Karl Klaus von der Decken, Livingstone, V. L. Cameron, Stanley, and others entered. Most explorers prior to the 1890s, a period of violence, famine, and disease associated with colonial conquest, more or less conformed to the customary standards and practices of East African travel. When they ran into difficulties they negotiated, argued, persuaded, and compromised with their porters and local political leaders. Often they backed down. On occasion, like other caravan leaders, they disciplined refractory porters through corporal punishment. Fines were resented as were cuts in rations, which had the effect of hindering efficient travel.[62] A handful of Europeans went well beyond recognized standards. CMS missionary A. M. Mackay took to shooting porters when frustrated, as did Stanley. Unfortunately, some recent writing on Stanley presents a sanitized account of his caravan management and dealings with African communities.[63]

In the era of exploration that preceded the partition of Africa, caravan travel generally involved trade with communities en route. Access to food, water, porters, and trading opportunities depended on the cooperation of local rulers, who generally held the balance of power. Alliances between big coastal traders and upcountry chiefs were common and were sometimes cemented by marriage.[64] Where caravan leaders took a high hand, their expeditions, whether for trade, exploration, or missionary enterprise, could be wrecked or their prospects for success severely damaged. Indeed, survival depended on moderation, in contrast to the late 1880s and 1890s when a new and more belligerent attitude typified the imperial expeditions of treaty making, station building, and conquest.[65] Stanley's expeditions were in part responsible for establishing the new pattern, in particular the infamous Emin Pasha Relief Expedition. The expedition's Advance Column, wrote William Stairs, one of its officers, had made its way through the Ituri forest "by *rifle alone*, by shooting and pillaging. . . . Stanley is not a 'cloth giver.' He prefers leaden means of securing respect and food."[66] It should not be forgotten that a large proportion of the expedition's loads consisted of weapons, gunpowder, and boxes of ammunition, an aberration in East African travel.[67] Yet ominous signs of future behavior were present much earlier. During his first East African journey, Stanley sometimes chained resisting porters and wrote that he would "never travel in Africa again without a good long chain." For the rest of his African career a set of chains was an indispensable tool. In 1872 while in Kwihara he confined "incorrigibles" without food for forty hours in a makeshift jail in a room of his house.[68] The defense of the massacres at Bumbireh in the Congo during Stanley's second expedition of 1874–1877 was further evidence not only of his personal style of "exploration by warfare," but also of the prevailing values of the leadership of the Royal Geographical Society (RGS) in the late 1870s.[69] Stanley's brutality went beyond late nineteenth-century norms in East Africa, where customary standards on caravans and the possibilities for desertion protected porters from most abuses.[70]

Like Stanley, the German imperialist and adventurer Carl Peters (who had read Stanley and admired him) was a new kind of explorer, more violent and imperialist in ambition. Peters and his colleagues were on a rapid search for colonies and "a place under the sun" for Germany before it was too late.[71] The method was to secure as many "protection treaties" as possible with African rulers, real or fictitious, through the "exploration" of swathes of territory. Thus, vast colonial possessions were invented on paper. German historian Michael Pesek writes, "Peters' obvious deficiency in knowledge and experience produced a narrative that repeatedly switches between fantasy and observation. It is a narrative full of surreal scenes and dream sequences, of descriptions of burlesque behaviors and hybrid practices."[72] Like Stanley, he soon acquired a reputation for brutality, using his Somali *askari* to "carry out a thorough physical authority over the porter element." According to Peters, "Such African masses of men can only be kept in control by a determination uncompromisingly to carry out one's will in the teeth of all opposition."[73]

*   *   *

There is no doubt that the exploration project facilitated imperialism and colonial conquest and aided the pernicious development of scientific racism and social Darwinism. But for historians, the accumulation of primary material combined with new conceptual tools has ultimately helped make possible new interpretations that restored African agency and placed Africans at the center of their own history.

In retrospect, nineteenth-century scholarship has cast a long shadow. One example illustrates the connections between exploration and the imperial project. The information that explorers gathered about Africa and its peoples overlay a rich body of knowledge derived from other sources, much of it essential to their enterprise but rarely acknowledged. Wisnicki argues that a new phase in scholarship and knowledge production related to cartography and with consequences for the partition of Africa began with Burton and Speke's East African Expedition,[74] one of whose aims was to "fill in one of the more important remaining blanks on the cartographical globe."[75] Yet, beneath the "blanks" (and erased by them) lay accumulated evidence of an earlier knowledge derived from African, Arab, and Indian sources that was represented not only on earlier nineteenth century maps of East Africa drawn by William Desborough Cooley, James M'Queen and the missionaries Rebmann and Erhardt, but also on the first maps published by Speke in 1859. Through a process of appropriation, reorganization, and imposition of the hierarchies of European "objectivity," this earlier non-European knowledge was submerged beneath the products of scientific observation and measurement that was expressed on the revised maps published by Burton in 1859 and 1860.[76] For example, in Burton's maps all direct references to the great network of African and Arab trading routes was removed.[77] Wisnicki concludes that the maps moved away from a cartographical practice that identified indigenous trade routes and thus an African "material reality." The revised maps of the RGS and Burton's *Lake Regions* instead told the story of the East African Expedition by placing its routes over existing trade routes, "and so mark at the minute cartographical level the birth of a new imperial approach to Africa." In this way geographical and cartographical knowledge was reformulated in the second half of the century, beginning with Burton and Speke, to represent potential colonial acquisitions.[78]

The argument is elegantly made, yet it can be shown that the process of erasing indigenous knowledge was not completed so quickly. In April 1879, explorer and geographer Keith Johnston spent some days interviewing African travelers at Dar es Salaam and Kola, thirty-two miles into the interior, about the direction and state of routes through Mahenge towards Lake Malawi. He openly acknowledged the sources of his information. The sketch map that resulted was published in the *Proceedings of the Royal Geographical Society*.[79]

European exploration in East Africa simply cannot be understood without appreciating the preexisting caravan trade, its labor force, and their labor culture. No European expedition could succeed without hiring experienced African managers to organize a caravan along local lines, whether on a small scale as, for example, in Krapf's travels with the Kamba, or on the larger scale of Stanley's second expedition. In fact, the typical European explorer's expedition, despite its unusual aims and sometimes more complete outfitting, did not vary substantially from thousands of trading caravans leaving the Indian Ocean coast for the far interior over the second half of the nineteenth century. It consisted of one to three hundred professional porters and *askari* with their loads of trade goods and supplies, and it marched according to the long established practices and customs of African and Arab travelers. It followed their caravan routes and utilized the infrastructure of caravan travel that they established in the interior. All European explorers were completely dependent on the provisioning systems that African travelers had pioneered and on good relations with other caravan leaders and African political authorities. Explorers and other western travelers who failed to quickly adapt to African methods were diverted from their target or perished en route. The complete failure of F. Falkner

Carter's attempt to substitute Indian elephants for professional porters is one example;[80] the pitiable end of Abbé Debaize's expedition in 1880 is another.[81]

The same could be said for exploration in other African regions. Hugh Clapperton, for example, was escorted across the Sahara by troops of the Pasha of Tripoli to become the first European to reach Bornu and Sokoto.[82] When in the 1850s Heinrich Barth crossed the Sahara to explore Hausaland and Songhai, he did not travel with a large caravan of his own, but was befriended by Africans and became a member of their traveling communities.[83] As Robert Rotberg put it forty years ago, nearly all European explorers in Africa "were led and instructed in the arts of travel by the Africans who headed and helped to organize their journeys." Most explorers were practical men who took advice and recognized the power of African monarchs and chiefs.[84] For Africans the legacy of exploration was a harsh one, given its role in the eventual partition of the continent. Yet deconstructed and read against the grain, the explorers' writings can shine a light on late precolonial African history, paradoxically and ironically undermining the myth of the "Dark Continent" whose map lay elsewhere.

NOTES

1. East Africa is defined here as the territory of modern Tanzania, Kenya, Uganda, and the Great Lakes region, including Rwanda, Burundi, the eastern Congo, northern Zambia, and Malawi.

2. For a wide-ranging introduction see Abdul Sheriff, *Dhow Cultures of the Indian Ocean: Cosmopolitanism, Commerce and Islam* (London: Hurst and Company, 2010).

3. Adrian Wisnicki argues that by Burton and Speke's time the region had "already been mapped, even if only to a limited extent." There had been several ancient attempts to map the sources of the Nile, and modern European mapping of much of East Africa had been underway since the beginning of the nineteenth century. See Adrian S. Wisnicki, "Charting the Frontier: Indigenous Geography, Arab-Nyamwezi Caravans, and the East African Expedition of 1856–59," *Victorian Studies*, 51, 1 (Autumn 2008): 107.

4. The standard account is Abdul Sheriff, *Slaves, Spices and Ivory in Zanzibar: Integration of an East African Commercial Empire into the World Economy 1770–1873* (London: James Currey, 1987).

5. For this early history see the important collection, Richard Gray and David Birmingham, eds. *Pre-Colonial African Trade* (London: Oxford University Press, 1970).

6. As in the guide to caravan travel by Paul Reichard, "Vorschläge zu einer praktischen Reiseausrüstung für Ost- und Central-Afrika," in the *Zeitschrift der Gesellschaft für Erdkunde zu Berlin*, 24 (1889): 1–80. It is notable that the first labor legislation in the new Zanzibar Protectorate (1894) was based almost entirely on the customary standards of African and Arab caravans. See Stephen J. Rockel, *Carriers of Culture: Labor on the Road in Nineteenth-Century East Africa* (Portsmouth, N.H.: Heinemann, 2006), 218–219.

7. Annie Hore, *To Lake Tanganyika in a Bath Chair* (London: Sampson Low, Marston, Searle and Rivington, 1886). Other significant missionary-explorers included the Alsatian Spiritan Alexandre Le Roy, Dr. Ebenezer Southon of the London Missionary Society, and Charles New of the United Methodist Free Churches.

8. This is a well-known story that will not be repeated here.

9. The first European to see Lake Albert.

10. See Roy C. Bridges, "The Historical Role of British Explorers in East Africa," *Terra Incognitae*, 14 (1982): 1–21; F. V. Emory, "Geography and Imperialism: The Role of Sir Bartle Frere (1815–84)," *The Geographical Journal*, 150, 3 (Nov. 1984): 342–350; R. A. Stafford, *Scientist of Empire: Sir Roderick Murchison, Scientific Exploration and Victorian Imperialism* (Cambridge: Cambridge University Press, 1989); R. A. Stafford, "Scientific Exploration and Empire," in Andrew Porter, ed. *The Oxford History of the British Empire: The Nineteenth Century* (Oxford: Oxford University Press, 1999), 294–319; John M. MacKenzie, "David Livingstone and the Worldly After-Life: Imperialism and Nationalism in Africa," in John M. MacKenzie, ed., *David Livingstone and the Victorian Encounter with Africa* (London: National Portrait Gallery Publications, 1996), 201–216; Felix Driver, "Henry Morton Stanley and His Critics: Geography, Exploration and Empire," *Past and Present*, 133 (1991): 134–166; Felix Driver, *Geography Militant: Cultures of Exploration and Empire* (Oxford: Blackwell, 2001); Dane Kennedy, "British Exploration in the Nineteenth Century: A Historiographical Survey," *History Compass*, 5/6 (2007): 1890–1891, among others.

11. Oscar Baumann, *Durch Massailand zur Nilquelle: Reisen und Forschungen der Massai-Expedition des deutschen Anti-sklaverei Komites in den Jahren 1891–1893* (Berlin: D. Reimer, 1894).

12. Given limitations of space only the first and the last two of these themes will be discussed here.

13. "Arab" is somewhat of a mutable category in East African history. Most people described as "Arabs" by visiting Europeans were largely of East African ancestry and culture through the maternal line. Arab identities sometimes changed to be more or less inclusive. For the complexities see Norman R. Bennett, *Arab*

Versus European: Diplomacy and War in Nineteenth-Century East Central Africa (New York and London: African Publishing Corporation, 1986); Laura Fair, *Pastimes and Politics: Culture, Community, and Identity in Post-Abolition Urban Zanzibar, 1890–1945* (Athens: Ohio University Press, 2001); Jeremy Prestholdt, *Domesticating the World: African Consumerism and the Genealogies of Globalization* (Berkeley and Los Angeles: University of California Press, 2008).

14. François Bontinck, "La double traversée de l'Afrique par trois 'Arabes' de Zanzibar (1845–1860)," *Etudes d'histoire africaine*, VI (1974): 8.

15. For the full story see Bontinck, "Double traversée" and the sources mentioned there. There is a brief discussion in Sheriff, *Slaves, Spices and Ivory in Zanzibar*, 186–7. Said bin Habib's own short account is in Said bin Habeeb, "Narrative of Said bin Habeeb, an Arab Inhabitant of Zanzibar," *Transactions of the Bombay Geographical Society*, 15 (1860): 146–148.

16. MacKenzie, ed., *David Livingstone and the Victorian Encounter with Africa*.

17. Exeter Hall on London's Strand was the key venue for anti-slave trade meetings.

18. A partial exception is the essay by Jeanne Cannizo, "Doctor Livingstone Collects," in which African peoples are discussed in relation to material culture.

19. Photographs in which Susi and Chuma appear are on pp. 156, 157, 206, 207. The captions on p. 156 include short biographical notes.

20. MacKenzie, "David Livingstone and the Worldly After-Life," 204. See also p. 216 where MacKenzie discusses how the Rev. Horace Waller, one of Livingstone's companions on the Zambezi expedition of 1858–1864, an influential anti-slavery activist, and editor of Livingstone's *Last Journals*, created the myth of Livingstone's last days and death through "a highly elaborated and doctored" rendering of interviews with Susi and Chuma. The larger story is in Dorothy O. Helly, *Livingstone's Legacy: Horace Waller and Victorian Mythmaking* (Athens: Ohio University Press, 1987). Donald Herbert Simpson, *Dark Companions: The African Contribution to the European Exploration of East Africa* (London: P. Elek, 1975) is the only significant secondary source to provide detailed biographical accounts of Susi, Chuma, and many other African caravan leaders, headmen and porters.

21. Livingstone, *Last Journals*, 418 (April 23, 1872); Livingstone to Lord Stanley, Bamberre, Manyema country, November 15, 1870, in *HCPP*, C.598, m.f. 78.621. The Nyamwezi chiefdom of Unyanyembe and its caravan and market town, Tabora, was the most important trading and caravan centre between the coast and the central African lakes.

22. Livingstone, *The Last Journals*, 196 (November 2, 1867).

23. Selemani bin Mwenye Chande, "Meine Reise," in C. Velten, trans. and ed. *Schilderungen der Suaheli* (Göttingen, 1901), 48; Selemani bin Mwenye Chande, "Safari yangu," in C. Velten, ed. *Safari za Wasuaheli* (Göttingen, 1901), 54.

24. Hore, *To Lake Tanganyika in a Bath Chair*, 152–153; Murphy to Sir B. Frere, Zanzibar, March 7, 1874, VLC 3/4, Royal Geographical Society. See also Rockel, *Carriers of Culture*, 116.

25. See Livingstone, *Last Journals*, 457 (September 8, 1872). For caravan women see Rockel, *Carriers of Culture*, 117–130.

26. There is a mine of information in Richard F. Burton, "The Lake Regions of Central Equatorial Africa," *Journal of the Royal Geographical Society*, 29 (1859): 1–464; Burton, *The Lake Regions of Central Africa* (London: Longman, Green, Longman, and Roberts, 1860).

27. Secondary works include S. C. Lamden, "Some Aspects of Porterage in East Africa," *Tanganyika Notes and Records* 61 (Sept., 1963): 155–164; Robert J. Cummings, "A Note on the History of Caravan Porters in East Africa," *Kenya Historical Review* 1, 2 (1973): 109–138; Simpson, *Dark Companions*; Allen Isaacman and Barbara Isaacman, *Slavery and Beyond: The Making of Men and Chikunda Ethnic Identities in the Unstable World of South-Central Africa, 1750–1920* (Portsmouth N.H.: Heinemann, 2004); Ruth Rempel, "Exploration, Knowledge, and Empire in Africa: The Emin Pasha Relief Expedition, 1886–1892" (PhD Thesis, University of Toronto, 2000); Rockel, *Carriers of Culture*, and other works by the author cited here. Catherine Coquery-Vidrovitch, and Paul E. Lovejoy, eds. *The Workers of African Trade* (Beverley Hills, Calif.: Sage, 1985) is useful for comparison.

28. Cornelia Essner, "Some Aspects of German Travellers' Accounts from the Second Half of the 19th Century," *Paideuma* 33 (1987): 200; quoted in Rockel, *Carriers of Culture*, 5. There was often praise as well.

29. John Hanning Speke, *Journal* of the Discovery of the Source of the Nile (Edinburgh: William Blackwood, 1863), 553–555; Oscar Baumann, *Durch Massailand zur Nilquelle* (Berlin: D. Reimer, 1894), 370–377. Another porter list, with names only, was published in Henry M. Stanley, *How I Found Livingstone* (London: Sampson Low, Marston, 1872), liii. Rotberg published Thomson's porter muster roll in Robert I. Rotberg, *Joseph Thomson and the Exploration of Africa* (London: Chatto and Windus, 1971), 306–314. Numerous unpublished muster rolls have survived. See Stephen J. Rockel, "Relocating Labor: Sources from the Nineteenth Century," *History in Africa*, 22 (1995): 447–454, and Rockel, *Carriers of Culture*, chapter 7, for discussion.

30. Tim Jeal, *Stanley: The Impossible Life of Africa's Greatest Explorer* (London: Faber, 2007). Further, the book is replete with factual errors concerning African geography, history, and social and political organization.

31. An unsupportable assertion in this author's view. Earlier but more nuanced judgments of the achievements and mode of exploration of European explorers in Africa are to be found in Robert I. Rotberg, ed., *Africa and Its Explorers: Motives, Methods, and Impact* (Cambridge, Mass.: Harvard University Press, 1970). Wisnicki, in "Charting the Frontier," makes a compelling argument for the seminal importance of the East African expedition of Burton and Speke, 1856–1859.

32. A. G. Hopkins, "Explorers' Tales: Stanley Presumes—Again," *Journal of Imperial and Commonwealth History*, 36, 4 (2008): 679. Yet the gap between the literature on exploration, imperialism, and East African history is narrowing,

especially in the work of Robert Rotberg, Roy Bridges, Dane Kennedy, R. A. Stafford, Michael Pesek, this author and, despite the above criticism, John MacKenzie.

33. In a fine study, Dane Kennedy tackles some of these issues and argues that Burton was a pioneer cultural relativist and thus, despite his evident racism, was particularly perceptive concerning social and cultural practices in Africa and elsewhere. See, *The Highly Civilized Man: Richard Burton and the Victorian World* (Cambridge, Mass.: Harvard University Press, 2005). In later life Burton developed a more nuanced view of race and African qualities and abilities.

34. Stephen J. Rockel, "Slavery and Freedom in Nineteenth Century East Africa: The Case of Waungwana Caravan Porters," *African Studies* 68, 1 (2009): 89. For elaboration, see the introduction to Rockel, *Carriers of Culture*, 3–23.

35. See Owen J. Kalinga, "The Balowoka and the Establishment of States West of Lake Malawi," in Ahmed Idha Salim, ed. *State Formation in Eastern Africa* (Nairobi: East African Publishing House, 1984), 36–52; Rockel, *Carriers of Culture*, 43–44.

36. Rockel, *Carriers of Culture*, 83–85, 164–179. Most of the evidence comes from European caravans, yet the customary standards expected by porters are highlighted both in their acceptance by foreigners and in the breach.

37. One *doti merikani* was four yards of unbleached New England calico. The *doti merikani* assumed all the characteristics of a cloth currency by the third quarter of the nineteenth century, having a fixed value according to the distance from the coast. See Rockel, *Carriers of Culture*, 211–228, for a discussion of porters' wages.

38. For trading practices see Burton, "Lake Regions"; *Lake Regions*; Mtoro bin Mwinyi Bakari, *The Customs of the Swahili People*, trans. & ed. J. W. T. Allen (Berkeley, Los Angeles, London: University of California Press, 1981); for joking relationships, Rockel, *Carriers of Culture*, 199–208 and sources mentioned there.

39. Rockel, *Carriers of Culture*, 148–153.

40. Rockel, *Carriers of Culture*, 69–72.

41. C. T. Wilson, "From Kagei to Tabora and Back," *Proceedings of the Royal Geographical Society* N.S. II (1880), 619; quoted in Rockel, *Carriers of Culture*, 72; O. F. Raum, "German East Africa: Changes in African Tribal Life Under German Administration, 1892–1914," in Vincent Harlow and E. M. Chilver, eds., *History of East Africa* Vol. II (Oxford: Oxford University Press, 1965), 169; also quoted in Rockel, *Carriers of Culture*, 73.

42. Burton noted the importance of various caravan officials and is an essential source on caravan organization. See also Rockel, *Carriers of Culture*, 73–74.

43. For loads see Rockel, *Carriers of Culture*, 103–117.

44. For life in camp see Rockel, *Carriers of Culture*, 141–148.

45. For details see Edward A. Alpers, "The Coast and the Development of the Caravan Trade," in I. N. Kimambo and A. J. Temu, eds., *A History of Tanzania* (Nairobi: East African Publishing House, 1969), 35–56; Sheriff, *Slaves, Spices and Ivory in Zanzibar*, 176–177; Rockel, *Carriers of Culture*, 49–52.

46. See Rockel, "Slavery and Freedom in Nineteenth Century East Africa"; Jonathon Glassman, *Feasts and Riot: Revelry, Rebellion, and Popular Consciousness on the Swahili Coast, 1856–1888* (Portsmouth, N.H.: Heinemann, 1995), 61–62; Jan-Georg Deutsch, *Emancipation Without Abolition in German East Africa c.1884–1914* (Oxford: James Currey, 2006), 40–41; Rüdiger Seesemann, "African Islam or Islam in Africa?" in Roman Loimeier and Rüdiger Seesemann, eds., *The Global Worlds of the Swahili: Interfaces of Islam, Identity and Space in 19th and 20th Century East Africa* (Berlin: Lit Verlag, 2006), 239–240; Prestholdt, *Domesticating the World*, 140–141.

47. C. T. Wilson and R. W. Felkin, *Uganda and the Egyptian Sudan* (London: Sampson Low, 1882), vol. I, 14.

48. Deutsch, *Emancipation Without Abolition*, 40–41; Seesemann, "African Islam or Islam in Africa?" 239–240; Rockel, "Slavery and Freedom in Nineteenth Century East Africa."

49. John Hanning Speke, "On the Commerce of Central Africa," *Transactions of the Bombay Geographical Society* XV (1860): 142.

50. Speke, *Journal*, xxvii.

51. For example, the list of porters in Speke, *Journal*, 553–554; the appended list in Rotberg, *Joseph Thomson*, 306–314, and for a later decade the lists in Notebook, "Stanley's Expedition," in the House of Wonders Museum, Zanzibar. Many of the porters of Stanley's Emin Pasha Relief Expedition are referenced here. See also Rempel, "Exploration, Knowledge, and Empire in Africa."

52. For two such urban centres see Stephen J. Rockel, "Forgotten Caravan Towns in Nineteenth Century Tanzania: Mbwamaji and Mpwapwa," *Azania* 41 (2006): 1–25.

53. Walter and Beverly Brown, "East African Towns: A Shared Growth," in W. Arens, ed., *A Century of Change in East Africa* (Geneva: Mouton, 1976), 183–184.

54. This paragraph is based on Rockel, "Forgotten Caravan Towns."

55. A recent book points to the increasingly multi-ethnic populations of caravan towns in Zanzibar's mainland hinterland. See Marek Pawelczak, *The State and the Stateless: The Sultanate of Zanzibar and the East African Mainland: Politics, Economy and Society, 1837–1888* (Warszawa: Instytut Historyczny Uniwersytetu Warszawskiego, 2010).

56. Mzee Ramadhani Abdallah. Interview: Mbwamaji, June 29, 2005.

57. Catherine Coquery-Vidrovitch, *The History of African Cities South of the Sahara: From the Origins to Colonization* (Princeton N.J.: Markus Wiener Publishers, 2005), 213–214.

58. Wisnicki, "Charting the Frontier," 115, 117, 119.

59. Stephen J. Rockel, "Caravan Porters of the *Nyika*: Labour, Culture and Society in Nineteenth-Century Tanzania" (PhD Thesis, University of Toronto, 1997), chapt. 2, appendices; Pawelczak, *The State and the Stateless*.

60. Helge Kjekshus, *Ecology Control and Economic Development in East African History* (London: Heinemann, 1977), 121–122.

61. The development of the main caravan routes is discussed in Rockel, "Caravan Porters of the *Nyika.*"

62. For a detailed discussion of authority, discipline, punishments, and resistance see Rockel, *Carriers of Culture*, ch. 6.

63. As in Jeal, *Stanley*, 12–15, 220–228, 382, and *passim*.

64. For example, when Tippu Tip's father married a daughter of Chief Fundikira of Unyanyembe sometime in the early 1850s.

65. See Rockel, "Forgotten Caravan Towns," for examples from Mpwapwa and beyond.

66. Stairs Diary, Sept. 10, 1888, quoted in Rempel, "Exploration, Knowledge, and Empire," 204.

67. Henry M. Stanley, *In Darkest Africa* (London: Sampson Low, Marston, Searle and Rivington, 1890), 24.

68. Rockel, *Carriers of Culture*, 178; Norman R. Bennett, ed., *Stanley's Despatches to the New York Herald, 1871–1872, 1874–1877* (Boston: Boston University Press, 1970), 61, 62, 63, 64; Henry M. Stanley, *How I Found Livingstone* (London: Sampson Low, Marston, 1872), 116; Stanley, December 30, 1874, January 24, 1875, February 6, 1875, July 4, 1875, and July 5, 1875, in R. Stanley and A. Neame, eds., *The Exploration Diaries of H.M. Stanley* (London: W. Kimber, 1961), 37, 50, 55, 86–87; Stanley, *Through the Dark Continent*, vol. 1, 209; Frank McLynn, *Stanley: The Making of an African Explorer* (Chelsea, Mich.: Scarborough House, 1990), 137.

69. Driver, "Henry Morton Stanley and His Critics," 150–155, *passim*.

70. For brutal punishments and failure to provide adequate rations in Stanley's expeditions, see Rockel, *Carriers of Culture*, 165, 174, 175–7, 195; Rempel, "Exploration, Knowledge, and Empire in Africa."

71. Michael Pesek, "The Boma and the Peripatetic Ruler: Mapping Colonial Rule in German East Africa, 1889–1903," *Western Folklore*, 66, 3/4 (Summer 2007): 233–257.

72. Pesek, "The Boma and the Peripatetic Ruler." For a rich discussion of similar scenes and sequences of exploration in central Africa see Johannes Fabian, *Out of Our Minds: Reason and Madness in the Exploration of Central Africa* (Berkeley, Los Angeles and London: University of California Press, 2000).

73. Carl Peters, *New Light on Dark Africa* translated H. W. Dulcken (London: Ward, Lock and Co., 1891), 58. During the 1890s British travelers Ewart S. Grogran and Arthur H. Sharp as well as the scientist J. E. S. Moore had similar approaches to the management of their porters. See Rockel, *Carriers of Culture*, 173–174.

74. Wisnicki, "Charting the Frontier," 107ff.

75. Wisnicki, "Charting the Frontier," 107.

76. Wisnicki, "Charting the Frontier."

77. Wisnicki, "Charting the Frontier," 127. This is ironic, given that Burton spent a great deal of time in East Africa collecting geographic information from African, Arab, and Indian informants.

78. Wisnicki, "Charting the Frontier," 128.

79. Keith Johnston, "Native Routes in East Africa, from Dar es Salaam towards Lake Nyassa," *Proceedings of the Royal Geographical Society*, N.S. I, 7 (July 1879): 417–422, map opp. 480. Johnston led the RGS expedition until his death, when Joseph Thomson took command.

80. L. K. Rankin, "The Elephant Experiment in Africa: A Brief Account of the Belgian Elephant Expedition on the March from Dar-es-Salaam to Mpwapwa," *Proceedings of the Royal Geographical Society*, N.S. IV, 5 (1882): 273–289.

81. The cleric, whose porters had to carry twelve large boxes of fireworks, several boxes of brandy, two loads of penny popguns, two suits of armor and a "hurdy gurdy," was abandoned by his men and died at Ujiji.

82. Dixon Denham, Hugh Clapperton, and Walter Oudney, *Narrative of Travels and Discoveries in Northern and Central Africa in the Years 1822, 1823 and 1824* (London: John Murray, 1828), vol. I, 51–52.

83. Anthony Kirke-Greene, "Heinrich Barth: An Exercise in Empathy," in Rotberg, *Africa and Its Explorers*, 13–38.

84. Robert I. Rotberg, "Introduction," *Africa and Its Explorers*, 8, 9.

9

THE EXPLORATION OF CENTRAL ASIA

GORDON STEWART

European explorers in Central Asia had a unique problem: Marco Polo. In the case of exploration of the polar regions, or the interior of Africa or South America, or a new continent like Australia, explorers were either in lands empty of humans or entering territory unknown to Europeans. For these regions of the world, narratives of adventurous explorers matching their skills and endurance against formidable challenges amidst unfamiliar landscapes were routine. Explorers were bringing new knowledge back to Europe. But in Central Asia it was different, because Marco Polo had already been there. The problem went well beyond Marco Polo's famous journey, for the network of ancient trade routes linking the Mediterranean to China—collectively called the Silk Road—meant that there were many written accounts of travels through Central Asia.

Apart from this preexisting European knowledge, there was an extensive Chinese literature of travel and exploration about the deserts, closed basins, mountain ranges, oases, and trade routes of Central Asia. (See Figure 9.1.) These "western regions" had been known to the Chinese at least since the time of the Han dynasty (206 BCE–220 CE). Under the emperor Wu Ti, who came to power in 140 BCE, a number of missions and military expeditions had been dispatched as far west as the Pamirs beyond the last oasis city of Kashgar, and over the passes into Ferghana (which became famous for the celestial horses supplied to the imperial court). The Chinese did not exercise sustained control of these regions after the Han and Tang (618–907 CE) eras but in the 1700s the Qing emperors sent formidable armies westwards and reestablished Chinese authority in all the territory north and south of the Tien Shan range, and further south into Tibet. Although Chinese control weakened again in the 1800s and a local Tajik adventurer like Yakub Beg

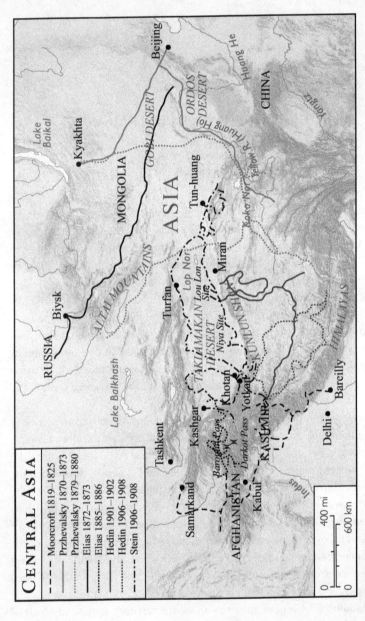

Figure 9.1 Map of Central Asia

could establish himself as a regional ruler in Kashgar between 1864 and 1877, the Chinese reasserted their power in the 1880s and 1890s and created the imperial province of Xinjiang. Their hold on the entire region endures to this day (in spite of separatist regimes during the civil wars of the 1920s and 1930s, and of current Uigher and Tibetan unrest). All European exploration in Central Asia took place in China's imperial backyard.

This meant there were written Chinese accounts from early times. Two of the best known of these were written by Chinese Buddhist pilgrims—Faxian (391–414 CE) and Xuanzang (603–688 CE)—who traveled across deserts and mountains to the holy land of India.[1] A seventh century Chinese text lists over fifty pilgrim-travelers who made this arduous journey. These accounts were available to Western explorers. In 1906 when Aurel Stein, a Hungarian-born British explorer, left Kashgar and headed into the Taklamakan desert, the baggage loaded on his eight camels included the French translation of Xuanzang's route descriptions.[2] This Chinese source proved to be an invaluable guide for Stein on all his expeditions

The existence of this thick layer of prior discovery, and of readily available travel narratives, gave a distinctive cast to European exploration in Central Asia. No raw geographical discoveries could be triumphantly presented to European audiences. This distinctiveness was captured by Sir Henry Rawlinson in the course of his presidential address to the Royal Geographical Society (RGS) in 1871. This was the heyday of European exploration with Britain's Royal Geographical Society in the vanguard. The Society, founded in 1831, was "a sort of scientific broker of nineteenth century British imperial expansion" as it sponsored, promoted, and publicized exploration round the world.[3] The RGS kept itself at the center of things through its prestigious journal and the annual awarding of medals to foreigners and Englishmen alike for achievements in scientific and geographical discovery. Rawlinson acknowledged that "the best known geographical exploits were connected with Arctic exploration on the one hand, and with African discovery on the other" and proceeded to identify what was distinctive about Central Asia:

> Geographical research in Asia does not lead to the same large and brilliant results as in Africa or Australia. There are in the former continent no great discoveries to reward exploration; no important physical features to be determined; no rivers, lakes, or mountains to be introduced for the first time into the maps. All that is left for the most successful inquirer is to verify a few doubtful points of Geography, or to fill in topographical details of more or less extent and consequence. Yet, is the East so rich in associations of the past,

so mixed up with the material interests of the present, that the mere gleanings, as it were, of Asiatic travel command often more attention than do the full harvest of discovery in other places.[4]

This authoritative description of the characteristics and limitations of Central Asian exploration is perhaps too sweeping, and was spoken just before the great outburst of significant archaeological and geographical discovery led by Nicolas Prejevalsky (1839–1888), Sven Hedin (1865–1952), Aurel Stein (1862–1943) and others in the late nineteenth and early twentieth centuries. But Rawlinson's main point was plausible—that exploration in Central Asia was different largely because of the fabled images it evoked in the West. Accounts of Central Asian travel often romanticized the East and linked themselves to Marco Polo.

Even serious scientific figures like the Swedish explorer Sven Hedin who made his reputation by his mapping expeditions in the Taklamakan and Lop Nor deserts as well as northern and western Tibet, and who was the first European to discover the sand-buried cities, fell into this narrative mode. When describing his first success during his 1895 Taklamakan expedition, he dramatized the moment in this almost conventional way: "When Marco Polo made his famous journey through Asia in 1274 the sleeping city had already lain a thousand years unknown and forgotten in its desert. It was to slumber another six hundred and fifty years more before ghosts of its past were raised to life and their ancient documents and letters made to shed new light on bygone days and mysterious human fates." Hedin also heard tales from locals about spirits and demons who lured travelers to their deaths in the trackless dunes: "This is exactly the same story that Marco Polo told, six hundred and fifty years ago, when he travelled along the edge of the desert of Lop situated further east."[5]

In the travel narratives by writers less renowned than Hedin the conjuring up of historical associations was commonplace. The books of two women travelers in the 1920s and 1930s illustrate this pattern. Ella Christie's *Through Khiva to Golden Samarkand* (1925) opened by quoting John Milton's "sonorous chords" on Tamerlane's throne at Samarkand in what was then Russian Turkestan. When Rosita Forbes wrote of her foray into Central Asia, which began in Kabul, she opened her chapter on the stupendous Buddhist sculptures in the Bamyan valley by recalling the description of Xuanzang who had passed along the same trails in 632.[6]

There was a danger of course that if these historical evocations were pushed too far all modern efforts would appear to be merely pale imitations of Marco Polo and his predecessors. There was a delicate tension between the evocation of past explorers and the praising of current ones. The working out of these tensions was nicely illustrated in the case of Mildred Cable, who spent her career as a missionary in the Chinese towns lying on the edge of the Gobi but combined her religious work with exploration. During her stint at Suchow she claimed to have discovered the grave of the Portuguese Jesuit explorer Benedict de Goes. In 1603, Goes had set out from Lahore in the Mughal empire, crossed the high Pamir, followed the oases towns along the edge of the Tarim basin and reached Suchow two years later. This journey had been significant in the annals of European exploration because it confirmed that the fabled land of Cathay was indeed China. Mildred Cable's connection with this achievement enabled British writers to use her as an example of ongoing British prowess in the field of exploration. Cable and other workers in the China Inland Mission were lauded as typical British missionary-explorers. As *The Times* obituary of Cable put it, the women and men of the China Inland Mission

> were not only missionaries but explorers. Each time they returned to England, scientific societies and universities asked them to lecture on their findings. Although they had only one aim on their journey—to spread the message of Christianity—yet they gathered a great deal that was of unique interest to the geographer, the archaeologist, the philologist and the student of human nature.[7]

Sir Percy Sykes in his *Quest for Cathay* (1936) even described Cable "as an equally intrepid traveler as Goes," thus putting her on the same level as the first European to have made the overland journey from India to China.[8] In such ways did the modest achievements of modern part-time explorers like Mildred Cable vicariously gain prestige from associations with their more renowned predecessors in Central Asian discovery.

Following in the footsteps of famous predecessors was one way in which exploration narratives set in Central Asia could be attractively framed, but there were parts of Central Asia that were as unknown to Europeans as parts of Africa, Australia, and South America. Rawlinson was correct in the general sense that there were no unknowns in terms of major rivers or mountain ranges but there were huge swathes of territory that were unmapped and therefore still unknown, even beyond such places as the Taklamakan and Lop Nor deserts. The Russian explorer Nicolas Prejevalsky was awarded the Founder's Medal of the RGS in 1879 "for successive expeditions and route surveys in Mongolia and the high plateau of northern Tibet." In addition to gaining a reputation by adding new geographical knowledge, he discovered a new species of wild horse that was named in his honor.[9] Large sections of the Kun Lun range that divided Tibet from the Tarim basin were unknown to Europeans. Explorers who could make scientific maps of such mountain regions were celebrated by geographical societies in St. Petersburg, Berlin, Paris, and London.

In these untouched areas of Central Asia, explorers' accounts shared many similarities with the first European journeys to the interior of Africa or to the polar regions—above all in the sense that virgin territory was being "conquered" by Europeans or "unveiled" to European eyes. When Sven Hedin ventured into the Taklamakan he wrote exultantly: "I was monarch of all I surveyed!" His pleasure was heightened as he "wandered through nameless regions where no European had set foot." Hedin, like many other travelers, was determined to penetrate the forbidden country of Tibet, closed to Europeans since the 1790s. He described the mountains of western Tibet as a large blank spot on the map and he set out in spite of sustained Tibetan opposition to bring that part of the world into the European world of maps and geographical knowledge. He noted that "the consciousness of being the first white man to traverse this region gave me an indescribable feeling of satisfaction. I felt like a powerful sovereign in his own country. There are bound to be future expeditions . . . but the discovery is mine. That fact will never be forgotten."[10]

In addition to these unmapped regions of Central Asia, there was one geographical challenge that did not fit into Rawlinson's picture. That challenge was Chomolungma, the highest mountain in the world, situated on the southern extremity of Central Asia. It was named Everest by the British and the attempts to climb it bore some similarities to polar exploration. It was not known whether humans could survive at such high altitudes; the routes had to go through the "forbidden" land of Tibet; and access even to the base of the mountain had to be discovered by the first expedition in 1921. Because it lay along the northern border of the British raj, because of looming international competition, and because they held a belief in their exemplary role as explorers, the British were determined to conquer this "third Pole" of the world. From 1921 to 1953 they mounted a series of expensive expeditions. To enhance the seriousness of purpose, and to fit the Everest attempts into the traditional concerns of scientific exploration, every expedition had a scientific dimension to it. Each weighty volume describing the early attempts on Everest had appendices on topics like botany and geology to make clear that this was not simply a climbing jaunt. In this aspect, the Everest expeditions were linked to the work of botanical explorers such as Joseph Hooker in the 1840s, and George Sherriff in the 1930s and late 1940s.[11]

In the aftermath of the disappearance George Leigh Mallory and Andrew Irvine during the 1924 Everest expedition ("one of the most compelling mysteries in the history of exploration"), Frank Smythe, the British mountaineer and writer, compared them to the noble self-sacrificing Scott in Antarctica. As he looked westward toward Everest while on Kanchenjunga in 1930, he ruminated about death in harsh and remote places: "Nature decrees that man shall ever war against the elemental powers of her Universe. If man were to acknowledge defeat, he would descend in the scale of life and sink once more to the animal. But there has been given to him that 'something' which is called the 'Spirit of Adventure'. It was this spirit that sustained Captain Scott and his companions, and Mallory and Irvine."[12] When exploration narratives involved Central Asia's inaccessible mountains and deserts, they had many resonances with tales of heroic exploration by white men in other parts of the world. In a small but revealing aside, John Hunt, the leader of the successful British attempt in 1953, compared the Everest expeditions to British feats of exploration elsewhere in the colonial world. "Organizing a major expedition," he explained, "whether it be to the Himalaya, the polar regions, or darkest Africa, is a formidable business."[13] Imperial nostalgia about exploration lingers on in our own postcolonial times. In his unapologetically jingoistic description of the first expedition to cross the Taklamakan desert from west to east, aptly titled *Conquering the Desert of Death* (1995), Charles Blackmore contrasted the sturdy British with the weak Chinese. This 1993 expedition was a joint one with Chinese and Uigher members as well as British, but Blackmore had no doubt that "the British have the advantage of history as a race renowned for tackling some of the world's greatest challenges in exploration."[14]

In their magisterial account of Himalayan climbing and exploration historians Maurice Isserman and Stewart Weaver draw attention to another significant feature of the Everest expeditions. Their use of corporate sponsors marks a "shift from the traditional idea of exploration in search of resources to the modern idea of exploration itself as a resource, a marketable product available for investment."[15] This was already underway to some extent long before the Everest expeditions—Stein, for example, wore "hygienic wool" underwear made by the Jaeger Company and stocked up on Cadbury's chocolate bars—but the use of product endorsement by the British Everest expeditions certainly highlighted this new development. While the Taklamakan crossing of 1993 ended with Blackmore giving the traditional lecture at the RGS (with Sir Wilfred Thesiger, famous for his own desert journeys in Arabia, sitting in the front row) the expedition had begun by lining up corporate sponsors.[16]

The most remarkable feature of exploration in Central Asia was the dramatic way in which exploration and archaeology were brought together. The peak moment came in the 1890–1930 period with the discovery of sand-buried cities that had been flourishing settlements along the branch of the ancient Silk Road that ran along the southern edge of the Taklamakan desert. This desert was the dominant geographical feature of Central Asia. Rivers, like the Tarim and Khokand, formed from the glaciers and snow-fields of the Pamir and Kun Lun ranges had allowed human settlements to thrive, but as the river flows gradually declined towns were abandoned to the sand. These lost cities captured the imagination of the West, not only because they were bound to contain hidden treasures, but they would also reveal how Buddhism had moved from India to China. When Sven Hedin stumbled across the first buried city in 1896, the competition began. During the early twentieth century, as renowned writer Peter Hopkirk put it, "in the remote and unexplored deserts of Chinese Central Asia, a great international race took place for the long lost treasures of the ancient Silk Road."[17] The most successful of the archaeologist-explorers was Sir Aurel Stein. In four expeditions stretching as far east as the Buddhist caves at Dunhuang he made his name as the leading expert on the buried cities.

The buried cities discoveries in the 1890–1920 years seem to represent modern exploration in its best light, as well-informed experts from Britain, France, Germany, Russia, and the United States systematically scoured the region for ancient sites lost to history for a thousand years. This was a new and romantic chapter in the Silk Road story, confirming Rawlinson's general observation about the appeal of Central Asian exploration. But there was also a negative side. Discovery of the lost cities exposed the relationship between exploration and the plundering of antiquities. From all these international expeditions to the sand-buried cities and temples of a once flourishing Buddhist civilization, "archaeologists from seven nations removed, literally by the ton, huge wall paintings, sculptures, priceless manuscripts and other works of art and shipped them home."[18] The sites were ransacked for objects that now stock the great museums of Europe and North America. Aurel Stein comes top of the list of offenders. During his fourth expedition the local Chinese authorities in Khotan finally attempted to stem the flow by simply forbidding him to dig. Stein had also been in touch with Langdon Warner, a director of Harvard's Fogg Museum, whose 1924–1925 expedition had removed, among other objects, a bodhisattva statue from Cave 328 at Dunhuang (the empty space is still shown to today's tourists). Warner wrote to Stein that he felt no hesitation in doing so: "I believe that neither you nor your patron saint, Hiuen Tsang [Xuanzang], would disapprove of my vandalism." As Susan Whitfield, Director of the International Dunhuang Project at the British Library, has pointed out, Stein was viewed, because of his own record and his connections with Americans like Warner, "as an imperialist thief for generations of Chinese scholars."[19]

This episode in Central Asian exploration opens up one of the most lively debates in the contemporary world about the role of explorers in helping to stock western museums during the imperial era.[20] Many of the expeditions that brought back artifacts were run by knowledgeable scholars whose goal was to recover lost history. Had they not done this, so the defense case runs, the objects would have been scattered or destroyed or sold into dubious markets. There were simply no viable authorities on the ground, so the argument continues, with the will or resources to protect the sites and their treasures. Warner, for example, claims that he had no intention of removing any objects from Dunhuang until he arrived there and was appalled to see "the caves scarred by the graffiti of several hundred White Russian cavalrymen."[21] Stein saw his work as rescuing irreplaceable manuscripts and murals that would otherwise have been destroyed or lost or scattered into the hidden byways of the private market for antiquities. His careful removal, and the subsequent meticulous cataloging by the British Museum, preserved these treasures for an international audience. The prosecution's response is that these explorers used their privileged position as Europeans and Americans to ride roughshod over whatever regional authority existed and manipulated difficult local conditions to their own advantage.

Stein's case is an iconic one for weighing the rights and wrongs of imperial archaeology and exploration. As Susan Whitfield notes in *Aurel Stein on the Silk Road* (2004) the issues are more complicated than they at first seem. The local Islamic cultures were not sympathetic to Buddhist remains, and the Chinese themselves were an imperial presence, certainly in the regions west of Dunhuang. Moreover, empires can have unexpected outcomes—British rule in India during this period meant that many of the finds remained in an Asian setting. Almost three fifths of Stein's finds from his first expedition are on display in the National Museum in New Delhi, nearer to the birthplace of Buddhism than had they been sent to European or American museums.[22] During these archeological explorations along the old Silk Road both plundering and rescuing took place. Meng Fanren, an eminent Chinese scholar, perhaps captures the inescapable ambivalence surrounding this type of archaeological exploration when he laments the damage done "at the hands of Western colonial powers" in the Silk Road sites of Xinjiang while acknowledging that "the publications of Stein and others . . . are now the primary sources of information."[23] The counterfactual question remains worth pondering—what would have happened to the sites if these archaeological explorers had not done what they did?

The compelling story of the sand-buried ruins also raises questions about who deserves credit for "discovery." This is not to deny the enormously learned, and physically courageous, exploits of the likes of Stein and Hedin but to broaden the context beyond the myth of the solitary heroic explorer that was so widespread in nineteenth century Europe and North America. Many of the sites had been described by the Chinese pilgrim travelers back in the fifth and sixth centuries before the desert took over, and there was always information available among local populations. Hedin honestly acknowledged these two existing sources after he had found the first traces of a buried city by noting that "the ancient Chinese geographers, as well as present-day natives living on the edge of the desert, were now vindicated." In his *Riddles of the Gobi Desert* (1933) he again acknowledged that he was "walking in the tracks of innumerable fore-runners." But while Hedin conceded this preexisting knowledge he could not help relapsing into the posture of the heroic white man uncovering the lost sites: "never had a white man set foot in this part of the world before. Every step was a new conquest for human knowledge."[24]

In this kind of narrative, "human knowledge" means "European knowledge." When the American geographer Ellsworth Huntington turned up at Khotan in 1905 in pursuit of his buried ruins he inquired about a guide. He was told: "Oh, Ibrahim Beg, the Master of Canals, is the man you want. He went with the other sahib [Stein] and knows all the ruins everywhere."[25] So in the narratives of Stein, Hedin, and Huntington local guides were mentioned, but often in a passing way that simply added some local color to the achievements of the European and American explorers.

The relationship of local guides to European explorers is a vexed one in general not only in this example from Central Asia. Outside the polar regions, guides were usually essential to success. The very first British foray north of the Himalayas—a mission sent by Warren Hastings to Tibet in 1774—depended on the expertise of Purangir Gosain, a local merchant and member of the Gosain sect, who made regular trips between Calcutta and towns in southern Tibet. He carried letters from the Panchen Lama to Warren Hastings and accompanied the British emissary, George Bogle, on his journey to Shigatse. In his letters and journals, Bogle paid generous tribute to Purangir but this essential figure only appeared, if at all, in the margins of published books on this early British contact with Tibet.[26]

The issue flared up in a slightly different form during the British Everest expeditions, most notably in the aftermath of the successful climb in 1953.

The Sherpas had been part of all the British attempts and some of them became accomplished high altitude climbers, so much so that in the final assault it was the Sherpa Tenzing Norgay who accompanied the New Zealander Edmund Hillary to the top of the world. In Nepal, Tenzing was hailed as a national hero (although the Indians claimed him too); in Britain he was feted but presented more as a loyal member of the team. Peter Hansen and other scholars have brought the voices of Tenzing and other Sherpa porters and climbers into accounts of these European expeditions in the Himalaya and Karakoram mountains during this imperial phase of "conquests." In their detailed account of this pioneering era of Himalayan mountaineering, Isserman and Weaver bring out the contributions of experienced Sherpa guides such as Ang Tharkay.[27] As in this example, the recent scholarship on exploration has done a much better job of recognizing the role of local informants, guides, and coworkers.

The issues at stake in the debate about the relationship of local guides and intermediaries to European exploration is even more dramatically highlighted by the dispatching of Indians as British agents northward into Tibet and Chinese Turkestan in the middle decades of the nineteenth century. These Indian mapmakers and spies were disguised as pilgrims or merchants. The first of the "pundits," as they came to be known, was Abdul Hamid (Mohammed-i-Hameed) who set out from Leh for Yarkand in 1863 dressed as a simple *munshi* (a teacher or learned one). Such men as Hamid and others, like the cousins Nain Singh, Kisten Singh, and Mani Singh, were given technical and scientific training at Dehra Dun, the headquarters of the Survey of India, before being sent over the mountains to gather topographical information and political intelligence. A recent analysis has argued that while these men could be viewed as merely human calculating machines, and thus another example of the European science establishment subordinating colonial subjects for their own ends, they were much more than that. According to Kapil Raj in *Relocating Modern Science. Circulation and the Construction of Knowledge in South Asia and Europe 1650–1900* (2007) the pundits "shaped the very nature of the knowledge they produced." The pundits were recognized individually in official correspondence, and Kapil Raj notes that Thomas Montgomerie of the Royal Engineers and the Survey of India elevated the collaboration of the early pundits "from the rank of a simple instrument, a 'docile body', to that of a peer." Pundits such as Kisten Singh and Abdul Subhan were also part of official expeditions such as Thomas Forsyth's diplomatic mission to Yakub Beg in 1873, and Stein always praised the work of the surveyor and mapmaker Ram Singh who went along on his expeditions. In 1877 Nain Singh was awarded the prestigious Patron's Medal of the RGS in recognition of "his great journeys and surveys in Tibet and along the Upper Brahmaputra during which he determined the position of Lhasa and added largely to our knowledge of the map of Asia." This recognition of Nain Singh, argues Raj, "can be taken as much to be a sign of recognition of the individual to whom they were awarded as reinforcement of the legitimization of the knowledges and techniques mobilized to acquire them."[28]

While the pundits were recognized by European scientific societies, these intrepid explorers remained marginal figures for European public audiences. They were described as "adventurous explorers" who exhibited "great pluck and endurance" in articles in the RGS journal, but even when they were praised the phrasing kept them at a certain distance from European achievement. For example, when Henry Rawlinson, president of the RGS at the time, summed up one of Montgomerie's pundits (known as "the Havildar" because of his rank), he spoke of this "bold, energetic and well-trained officer" but then added "he owed his safety to a combination of boldness and discretion which is very rare in an Asiatic."[29] So the pundit explorers, in spite of their considerable achievements, and in spite of the individual recognition they did receive, were often described in public accounts simply as brave, competent subordinates. However, they were professional explorers in the sense that they were trained and paid to do nothing else but explore Tibet and Chinese Turkestan. They received a pension when they retired. They are the first and only example of exploration as a salaried profession.

A key difference between the pundit explorers and their European counterparts was their lack of opportunity to publish popular narratives of their achievements. Because of the secret nature of their work they could not write for European, or even Indian, audiences in the same way that European travelers could produce appealing adventure stories about Central Asia for a broad public readership. When they did write for publication, as in the case of Sarat Chandra Das in his *Contributions on the Religion and History of Tibet* (1882), their approach was more restrained and reflected a perspective in which they were, as fellow Asians, writing about sophisticated neighboring cultures and religions rather than telling an exotic tale for Westerners.[30]

The case of the pundits raises general questions about exploration and espionage. The Russian expansion into the khanates between the Pamirs and the Caspian Sea and the British concern for their position in India led to a contest between these two great powers for influence in Central Asia, the so-called Great Game.[31] The pundit agent-explorers were part of the effort to gain intelligence about these contested borderlands but numerous British officers and agents were also engaged in this game. Geographical and scientific exploration was often mixed up with spying. This mixture has led many scholars to conclude that there was always something nefarious about European exploration. Even such apparently objective scientific pursuits of making maps and ascertaining geological facts facilitated colonial intrusions and the exploitation of resources. Those charges may well be true, but Central Asia shows that these features connecting exploration to empire to were not unique to Europeans.

In his account of the Qing conquest of Central Eurasia in the 1700s, Peter Perdue has made a comparative commentary on explorers and travelers in this region.[32] He agrees that mapmaking was never simply a neutral scientific enterprise but was a practical manifestation of European enlightenment methods of scientific observation being used to develop control over non-European territories and peoples. This is certainly a reasonable reading of the evidence during the imperial era. Even in the case of unpeopled Antarctica the maps and other scientific work of explorers were used by European states to lay claim to new territory. In the case of Central Asia most explorers and travelers were involved in mapmaking and imperial espionage to a greater or lesser extent. This was quite explicit, for example, in the case of Francis Younghusband whose epic overland journey in 1886 from Peking to India ended with the perilous crossing of the Mustagh pass in the Karakoram mountains. Younghusband was an officer in the Indian Army at the time and subsequently became a major player in the Great Game and the leader of the British march to Lhasa in 1904.[33]

As Perdue notes, much recent scholarship on this matter "has left the impression that only western Europeans pursued cartography as part of their imperial projects." The industrial-scientific basis of western European states by the late 1700s and 1800s was seen to be the key factor in this orientation to the rest of the world. Perdue points out, however, that "other agrarian empires of Eurasia, especially Russia and China, also promoted surveying on large scale." The work of Matthew Edney on the role of the Great Trigonometrical Survey of India is often cited as an example of this tight nexus between mapmaking and imperialism. Perdue remarks that Edney's description of British imperial aims shows striking parallels to those of the Qing empire.[34]

Perdue cites the example of the Manchu envoy Tulisan who traveled to the country of the Torghuts in 1712–1715 and whose narrative was published in 1723. He concludes that the Chinese, Russian, and British were all "sending their envoys, merchants and travelers on missions of exploration. Like their contemporaries the Qing emissaries combined strategic, geographical and commercial objectives." Perdue compares Tulisan to John Bell, a Scottish doctor employed at the court of Peter the Great, who accompanied a Russian mission across southern Siberia to Peking in 1719, and to the Russian Ivan Unkovski, who was sent on a mission to the Zunghar Mongols in 1722–1724. In each case, the reports of these Chinese, Russian, and British emissaries "combine exploration, geographical discovery, intelligence gathering, diplomatic interviews, and personal reactions to the landscape."[35] The first British exploration of Tibet during the mission of George Bogle to Shigatse in 1774 illustrated the general pattern. Bogle reported on potential invasion routes, collected trade information, commented on flora and fauna, and he and Hastings hoped to open up Tibet to British eyes in the same way that Captain Cook was opening up the Pacific.[36] Exploration and imperialism were always imbricated, but the writings of these explorers are so rich and their perspectives so varied that it seems needlessly reductionist to view them as one-dimensional agents of empire.

Exploration in Central Asia also contributed to the opening up of fundamental questions about the nature of history and the fate of human societies. Much of the most appealing work in world history in recent years has focused on environmental factors as shapers of human history. Emblematic of this trend has been the best-selling books by Jared Diamond, *Guns, Germs and Steel* (1998) and *Collapse: How Societies Choose to Fail or Succeed* (2005). In Central Asia this issue was raised in dramatic form by the discovery of the sand-buried cities, for here were settlements that had flourished as late as the 800s yet had disappeared. Environmental factors seemed the most likely explanation. The disappearance of the oases towns seemed directly tied to the dwindling water supply from the glaciers and snowfields of the surrounding mountains. So alongside the romantic response to these newly discovered buried cities (exemplified in Hedin's comment that he felt like "the prince in the enchanted wood having wakened to new life the city which has slumbered for a thousand years"[37]) there was also a hard scientific question of how this momentous change had happened.

Some of the explorers themselves thought about this matter. Aurel Stein speculated that the glaciers formed in the last Ice Age were slowly diminishing and that this centuries-old natural phenomenon explained the gradual drying up of the river beds that fed into the Taklamakan.[38] A more elaborate theory was developed by the American geographer Ellsworth Huntington who made Central Asia his natural laboratory for history in a similar way to Jared Diamond's use of the Pacific islands. Based on observations made during his expedition in 1906–1907 Huntington developed "the hypothesis of pulsatory climatic changes" that had shaped world history. Huntington is now discredited by geographers because of the racist and deterministic nature of his theory, but he was a product of his time when it was common in the United States and Europe to think in debased Darwinian terms of race hierarchies. He thought, for example, that Kashmiris who went to English-style schools in British India would be improved from their natural craven state: "To be sure they are still cowardly but there has begun to be a school spirit which makes them ashamed to show their fears." After his journey to Central Asia he wrote a book "to illustrate the geographic relations between physical environment and man, and between changes in climate and history."[39]

Huntington argued from his Central Asian example that human societies had been shaped by climate. Favorable climatic zones, including the one in which Russia, Germany, France, England, and the United States were located, had produced nations "possessing a high degree of will-power and energy and capacity for making progress and for dominating other races." While Huntington's conclusions have been rightly condemned, subsequent generations of scholars have made more complex and multi-factor arguments about the dynamic interaction among physical environments, climate, and human history. David Christian's work on Central Asia's role in world history is a good example, as is Perdue's on the environmental factors that shaped Chinese and Russian expansion in Siberia and central Eurasia.[40] Some critics of geographic-environmental approaches to history, most notably the renowned world historian William McNeill in his commentary on Diamond's assumptions about historical change, have warned that environmental approaches have their own flaws.[41] Geography and environment are fundamental shaping factors but if they are given too much play then human agency and human cultures as shapers of history are pushed to the margins. The debate about environmental change and the fate of human societies has enormous resonance in our own age of global warming. The discovery of the sand-buried cities in Central Asia was one fascinating starting point for making us aware of these momentous issues.

Beginning with the accounts by early Chinese Buddhist pilgrims, there have been more than two thousand years of narratives about travel and exploration in Central Asia. Those narratives encompass all the features of exploration beyond the discovery and mapping of new geographical spaces—promotion of empire, espionage, the search for commercial opportunities and natural resources, the insistent pressure from national rivalry, the hidden role of local guides, and the everlasting human search for individual celebrity. The two aspects of exploration in Central Asia that stand out from exploration in other parts of the world are the discovery of the ancient Silk Road sites and the work of the pundits, the world's first and only full-time professional explorers. The Silk Road archaeological-explorers bring out all the issues at stake in the current global debate about who owns the world's antiquities; the pundit-explorers are a compelling example of the complicated roles played by subaltern professionals in the imperial era. In spite of the ghostly presence of Marco Polo, the subsequent exploration of Central Asia has produced a rich harvest of narratives. As Sir Henry Rawlinson pointed out as far back as 1871, many of these accounts evoke romantic and exotic images of the region for Western readers, but the narratives also reveal the wide range of approaches that inform exploration literature—and shed light on issues that are shaping our world today.

NOTES

1. "Journeys of the Buddhist Pilgrims to India," in Owen and Eleanor Lattimore, eds., *Silks, Spices and Empires. Asia Seen Through the Eyes of its Discoverers* (New York: Delacorte Press, 1968), 35–53.

2. Susan Whitfield, *Aurel Stein on the Silk Road* (Chicago: Serindia Publications, 2004), 9, 19, 46, 52.

3. Maurice Isserman and Stewart Weaver, *Fallen Giants. A History of Himalayan Mountaineering from the Age of Empire to the Age of Extremes* (New Haven, Conn., and London: Yale University Press, 2008), 36. Dane Kennedy, "British Exploration in the Nineteenth Century," *History Compass* 5/6 (2007): 1886–1890. Felix Driver, *Geography Militant: Cultures of Exploration and Empire* (Oxford: Blackwell, 2001) *passim* and review of Driver book in *Journal of European Studies* vol. 31 (2001): 112–113 by Denis J. B. Shaw.

4. Sir Henry Rawlinson, "Anniversary Address," *Proceedings of the Royal Geographical Society*, vol. 16, no.4 (1871–1872): 331. Delivered on the fortieth anniversary of the founding of the RGS.

5. Sven Hedin, *My Life as an Explorer* (New York: Kodansha, 1996 [1925]), 139, 330.

6. Ella Christie, FRGS, *Through Khiva to Golden Samarkand. The Remarkable Story of a Woman's Adventurous Journey Alone through the Deserts of Central Asia to the Heart of Turkestan* (London: Seeley, Service & Co., 1925), 5. Rosita Forbes, *Forbidden Road. Kabul to Samarakand* (New York: E. P. Dutton & Co., 1937), 91.

7. "Miss Mildred Cable. A Missionary in Central Asia," *The Times* [London], May 2, 1952, 8.

8. Brigadier-General Sir Percy Sykes, KCIE, CB, CMG, Gold Medallist of the Royal Geographical and Royal Empire Societies, author of *A History of Exploration*, etc. *The Quest for Cathay* (London: A. C. Black, 1936), 262.

9. Lieutenant-Colonel Nicolas Prejevalsky, *Mongolia, the Tangut Country, and the Solitudes of Northern Tibet being a Narrative of Three Years' Travel in Eastern High Asia* (London: Simpson Low, Marston, Searle & Rivington, 1976) 2 vols., vol. II, 170. Several recent expeditions have failed to find any survivors of this breed.

10. Hedin, *My Life as an Explorer*, 196, 516.

11. Lieutenant-Colonel C.K. Howard-Bury, DSO, *Mount Everest. The Reconnaissance* (London: Edward Arnold, 1922), 281–350, with sections on natural history, geology, and the mammals, birds, and plants collected, as well as the scientific equipment used by the party. See too Lucile Brockway, *Science and Colonial Expansion: the Role of the Royal Botanic Gardens* (New York: Yale University Press, 1979), 84–86, 92–99, and Gordon T. Stewart, "Tenzing's Two Wrist-Watches: the Conquest of Everest and Late Imperial Culture in Britain,' *Past & Present*, No.149 (November 1995): 170–185. Kenneth Mason, *Abode of Snow. A History of Himalayan Exploration and Mountaineering* (London: Rupert Hart Davis, 1955), 42, 81.

12. Frank Smythe, *The Kanchenjunga Adventure* (London: Victor Gollancz, 1930), 16–17. The comment in parenthesis is by Jon Krakauer, author of *Into Thin Air* and *Into the Wild* on the cover of Conrad Aker and David Roberts, *The Lost Explorer. Finding Mallory on Mount Everest* (New York: Simon & Schuster, 1999).

13. John Hunt, *The Ascent of Everest* (London: Hodder and Stoughton, 1953) 21, 249.

14. Charles Blackmore, *Conquering the Desert of Death. Across the Taklamakan* (London: Tauris Parke, 2008 [1995]), 27.

15. Isserman and Weaver, *Fallen Giants*, 119.

16. Blackmore, *Conquering the Desert of Death*, xxi, 31. Thesiger made his reputation as an explorer with his travels in the empty quarter of Arabia in the late 1940s and among the marsh Arabs of southern Iraq in the 1950s. Wilfred Thesiger, *Arabian Sands* (New York: Dutton, 1959) and *The Marsh Arabs* (New York: Dutton,1964).

17. This is Peter Hopkirk's phrasing in Hedin, *My Life as an Explorer*, xvii. Hopkirk is the author of several fine books on exploration in Central Asia, including *Trespassers on the Roof of the World. The Secret Exploration of Tibet* (London; John Murray, 1982), and *Foreign Devils on the Silk Road: the Search for the Lost Cities of Central Asia* (London: John Murray, 1980)

18. Peter Hopkirk, "Prologue," in Hedin, *My Life as an Explorer*, xvii.

19. Whitfield, *Aurel Stein on the Silk Road*, 99, 101.

20. Hugh Eakin, "Who Should Own the World's Antiquities," *New York Review of Books* vol. 56 (May 14, 2009): reviewing James Cuno, ed., *Whose Culture? The Promise of Museums and the Debate over Antiquities* (Princeton: Princeton University Press, 2008).

21. Whitfield, *Aurel Stein on the Silk Road*, 72, 99.

22. Ibid., 79.

23. These are the words of Meng Fanren in his Preface to the Chinese edition of Stein's *Serindia. Detailed Report on Exploration in Central Asia and Westernmost China* (Oxford: Clarendon, 1921). Whitfield, *Aurel Stein on the Silk Road*, 128, 136.

24. Hedin, *My Life as an Explorer*, 188, 196; Hedin, *Riddles of the Gobi Desert* (New York: Dutton, 1933), 5.

25. Ellsworth Huntington, *The Pulse of Asia. A Journey in Central Asia Illustrating the Geographic Basis of History* (Boston: Houghton Mifflin, 1907), 171.

26. Schuyler Camman, *Trade through the Himalayas. The Early British Attempts to Open Tibet* (Princeton, N.J.: Princeton University Press, 1951), 30; Gordon T. Stewart *Journeys to Empire. Enlightenment, Imperialism and the British Contact with Tibet 1774–1904* (New York: Cambridge University Press, 2009), 47–49.

27. Isserman and Weaver, *Fallen Giants*, 232, 281–294. Peter H. Hansen, "Partners: Guides and Sherpas in the Alps and Himalayas 1850s–1950s," in Jaś Elsner and Joan-Pau Rubies, eds., *Voyages and Visions: Towards a Cultural History of Travel* (London: Reaktion, 1999), 210–231 and "Vertical Boundaries, National Identities: British Mountaineering on the Frontiers of Europe and the Empire, 1868–1914," *Journal of Imperial & Commonwealth History*, vol. 24 (January 1996): 48–71. Peter H. Hansen and Gordon T. Stewart, "Debate: Tenzing's Two Wrist-Watches: The Conquest of Everest and Late Imperial Culture in Britain 1921–1953," *Past & Present*, No. 157 (November 1997): 159–190.

28. Kapil Raj, *Relocating Modern Science. Circulation and the Construction of Knowledge in South Asia and Europe 1650–1900* (London: Palgrave Macmillan, 2007), 185, 203, 221. Kenneth Mason, *Abode of Snow. A History of Himalayan Exploration and Mountaineering* (London: Rupert Hart Davis, 1955), 92

29. T. E. Montgomerie, RE, FRGS, "A Havildar's Journey through Chitral to Faizabad in 1870," *Proceedings of the RGS* vol. 16, no. 3 (1871–1872): 259; Sir H. C. Rawlinson. "Anniversary Address," ibid., vol. 16, no 4 (1871–1872): 339.

30. Sarat Chandra Das, *Contributions on the Religion and History of Tibet* (New Delhi: Manjusri Publishing House, New Delhi, 1970 [1882]); Raj, *Relocating Modern Science*, 203.

31. Peter Hopkirk, *The Great Game. The Struggle for Empire in Central Asia* (New York: Kodansha, 1992); Karl Ernest Mayer, *Tournament of Shadows: the Great Game and the Race for Empire in Central Asia* (Washington D.C.: Counterpoint, 1999).

32. Peter C. Perdue, *China Marches West: The Qing Conquest of Central Eurasia* (Cambridge, Mass.: Harvard University Press, 2005), 213–222.

33. Patrick French, *Younghusband. The Last Great Imperial Adventurer* (New York: Harper, 2004 [1994]); Anthony Verrier, *Francis Younghusband and the Great Game* (London: Jonathan Cape 1991); Stewart *Journeys to Empire*, 139–186.

34. Perdue, *China Marches West*, 443–454. Matthew H. Edney, *Mapping an Empire. The Geographical Construction of British India 1765–1843* (Chicago: University of Chicago Press, 1997).

35. Perdue, *China Marches West*, 213–214, 219–222, 410.

36. Stewart, *Journeys to Empire*, 26–27.

37. Hedin, *My Life as an Explorer*, 188.

38. Aurel Stein, "Innermost Asia. Its Geography as a Factor in History," *The Geographical Journal,* vol. LXV (June 1925): 472–501.

39. Ellsworth Huntington, "Problems in Exploration—Central Asia," *The Geographical Journal* vol. XXXV (1910): 406–411, and *The Pulse of Asia: A Journey in Central Asia Illustrating the Geographic Basis of History* (Boston: Houghton Mifflin, 1907), vii–xxiii, 359–385.

40. David Christian, "Inner Asia as a Unit in World History," *Journal of World History* vol. 5 (September 1994): 173–211; Perdue, *China Marches West*, 1–51

41. William McNeill, "History Upside Down," *New York Review of Books* vol. 44 (May 15, 1997): 48–50.

10

THE HISTORIOGRAPHY OF ANTARCTIC EXPLORATION

STEPHANIE BARCZEWSKI

Antarctica represents a unique subject within the history, and historiography, of exploration. The historian of exploration Stephen J. Pyne has written of the distinctiveness of Antarctic exploration:

> Not even the Arctic offered a comparable degree of alien-ness. On the interior ice terranes there are no ecosystems or permanent human societies. Humans must confront an entirely physical universe one to one . . . without intervening biological communities or indigenous cultures.[1]

As Pyne indicates, every other part of the world has a history, and thus an historiography, that reflects its evolution separately from its encounters with foreign explorers. Antarctica, however, had no indigenous population, and indeed no population at all prior to the arrival of British and American sealers on its surrounding islands in the 1780s. No human being set eyes, much less foot, on the Antarctic continent until the early 1820s, and even today, when Antarctica is more densely populated than it has ever been, its only inhabitants are the researchers who live at the stations maintained by various countries, who total a mere 5000 people in the summer and 1000 in the winter. (See Figure 10.1.)

This lack of a human presence is paralleled by a relative dearth of attempts by professional scholars to record Antarctica's history. In contrast to the countless works on the political, military, social, cultural, intellectual, economic, religious, gender, and environmental histories of the rest of the world, there are only a handful of texts focusing on the Antarctic, where most of the categories listed above are irrelevant. Instead, writing about the history of the continent has remained largely the province of biographers

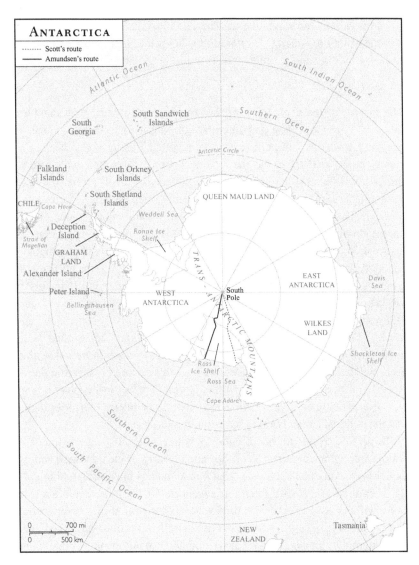

ANTARCTICA
- .... Scott's route
- ——— Amundsen's route

Atlantic Ocean

South Indian Ocean

Southern Ocean

South Sandwich Islands

South Georgia

Antarctic Circle

Falkland Islands

South Orkney Islands

South Shetland Islands

CHILE Cape Horn

Deception Island

Strait of Magellan

GRAHAM LAND

Alexander Island

Peter Island

Bellingshausen Sea

QUEEN MAUD LAND

Weddell Sea

Ronne Ice Shelf

TRANS-ANTARCTIC MOUNTAINS

WEST ANTARCTICA

South Pole

EAST ANTARCTICA

Davis Sea

WILKES LAND

Shackleton Ice Shelf

Ross Ice Shelf

Ross Sea

Cape Adare

Southern Ocean

South Pacific Ocean

0   700 mi
0   500 km

NEW ZEALAND

Tasmania

Figure 10.1 Map of Antarctica

and popular authors who have focused almost exclusively on the "Heroic Age" of Antarctic exploration in the early twentieth century. But despite these limitations, the historiography of Antarctic exploration deserves inclusion in the historiography of exploration of the rest of the world. Dozens of countries have taken an active interest in Antarctica over the last two centuries, and at present no less than fourteen nations claim or reserve the right to claim various territories there.[2] There is thus a strong case to be made that the history of Antarctic exploration is uniquely global in scope and that historical writing about it thus reflects uniquely global concerns.

* · *   *

The history of the exploration of the Antarctic is suffused with complex motives. There was, first and foremost, the quest for scientific and geographic knowledge, but political and strategic factors have also been constantly at work. Peter Beck, the leading historian of Antarctica's role in international politics, writes that "although many scientists prefer to ignore the political exploitation of Antarctic research, this attitude is both naïve and unrealistic on account of the uneasy relationship-cum-alliance of science and politics in Antarctica."[3] In tracing the historiography of Antarctic exploration, this essay will link the way in which authors, both popular and scholarly, have written about the continent's past not only to the events with which Antarctica was directly involved, but also to broader developments in world politics. Although the forms of Antarctic history, dominated by biography and chronological narrative, have remained relatively static, the manner in which they reflect the contemporary geopolitical context has been anything but. Though reference to more general works will be made, this essay will focus on the treatment of three Antarctic explorers in particular—Robert Falcon Scott, Richard Byrd, and Ernest Shackleton—each of whom can be used to illustrate the relationship between the relevant historiography and the political and cultural climate that produced it.

To be sure, Antarctic historiography is not an exclusively postmodern realm offering no illumination of the actual history of the continent and its exploration. Antarctica is a place that human beings have struggled mightily to explore, often with fatal consequences. Of the three explorers this essay will discuss in detail, two died while on expeditions to the Antarctic; Byrd is the sole exception who died of natural causes at an advanced age. This attempt to analyze historical writing about their accomplishments in cultural context is in no way meant to diminish what they achieved. It is intended, however, to recognize that Antarctic historiography, because it tends to concentrate on a handful of events and figures, and because it usually is constructed from a very limited range of sources—often the account of a single person—tends to be even more subject than other areas of the historiography of exploration to the prevailing winds of political and cultural trends.

But that is to put the end at the beginning. The earliest phase of writing about the exploration of Antarctica lasted from the late nineteenth century until the end of the First World War. The stirrings of interest were initially faint, as the Arctic continued to receive the lion's share of attention. Typical was *The Polar World*, published in London by the German author George Hartwig in 1869, in which only five of the forty chapters were devoted to the Antarctic regions.[4] But in the first decade of the twentieth century, as the race for the South Pole intensified, a bevy of nations, including Britain, Belgium, Norway, Germany, France, Sweden, Australia, and Japan, all sponsored Antarctic expeditions. This significantly increased popular interest in the continent. In *The Romance of the South Pole* (1900), the first work to focus exclusively on the Antarctic, the journalist George Barnett Smith noted that "so much heroism has been devoted to polar exploration in the North . . . that far less attention has been paid to the discoveries in the South Polar regions. . . . Happily a change is coming over popular feeling on this question."[5] Barnett Smith's use of the term "romance" in his title is indicative of the fact that the public expected Antarctic exploration to be heroic and adventurous but not too dangerous, and certainly not deadly.

The growing interest in the Antarctic must be gauged in light of the still-prevalent imperialist attitudes of many of the countries that became actively involved in the exploration of the continent. As nations scrambled to claim territory all over the globe, Antarctica was seen as a possible site for future colonization; the fact that it possessed no obvious economic or strategic value made it no different from many other places that were avidly sought after by the powers of Europe, America, and Asia.[6] Accompanying this was a belief in Social Darwinism, which asserted that to the strongest nations would go the greatest spoils. Seen from this perspective, victory in the competition to claim colonies became proof positive of a country's worth. As the polar historian Beau Riffenburgh writes, "Since continued expansion represented a means to achieve or maintain moral, racial, spiritual and physical supremacy, exploration thus became an instrument not only to justify imperial or nationalist political doctrine, but to embody the supposed collective cultural superiority of a nation."[7]

The British, determined to maintain their political, economic, and imperial supremacy in the face of challenges from Germany, America and other nations,, were particularly focused on Antarctic achievement. Barnett Smith asked, "Will Great Britain be content to see the glory attaching to the discovery of the South Pole pass to other nations? We hope and believe not. By doing she would do much to forfeit the position of the first maritime nation in the world, which she has held for centuries."[8] This theme became even more prevalent after 1909, when Robert Peary, an American, won the race to the North Pole. In his *Heroes of the Polar Seas* (1910), the popular author John Kennedy MacLean lamented that the British had "dropped" Arctic exploration following the Nares expedition of the 1870s, when "this country seems to have suddenly concluded that the glory of planting the national flag at the summit of the earth was not worth the expenditure of additional lives and treasure." But in the case of the South Pole, "The way is still open, and the honour of being first there has now become a matter of international competition."[9] Even a more scholarly author such as the Scottish geographer Hugh Robert Mill joined in the prevailing patriotism. At the conclusion of his essay on the history of Antarctic exploration that prefaced Shackleton's *The Heart of the Antarctic*, Mill wrote, "The enthusiasm and devotion of an individual has once more vindicated the character of the British nation for going far and faring well in the face of difficulties before which it would have been no dishonour to turn back."[10]

As Barnett Smith, MacLean, and Mill demonstrate, from a British perspective, the imperatives of contemporary national rivalries demanded that the South Pole be reached first by a British explorer.[11] The South Pole was the only remaining "blank spot" on the map, and the British regarded it as theirs to claim, a natural extension of their still-growing Empire. That Antarctica had become a site for imperial conquest was recognized by Mill in his *Siege of the South Pole* (1905), the only major scholarly work of the era. The "motive to Antarctic exploration," Mill wrote, had grown to be "a burning question in the struggle of rival Powers for commercial and political supremacy," as well as "a force in empire-building."[12] Three years later, the sector of Antarctica from 20 to 80°W was claimed by the British as an extension of the Falkland Islands Dependency.[13]

In 1912, however, the failure of Robert Falcon Scott to beat the Norwegian Roald Amundsen to the South Pole complicated the imperial triumphalism of the desired British narrative of Antarctic exploration. Scott's failure made it all the more necessary for British authors to promote their nation's previous polar accomplishments. In *A Book of Discovery* (1912), the popular historian M. B. Synge wrote:

> An American had placed the Stars and Stripes on the North Pole in 1909. It was a Norwegian who succeeded in reaching the South Pole in 1911. But the spade-work which contributed so largely to the final success had been done so enthusiastically by two Englishmen that the expeditions of Scott and Shackleton must find a place here.[14]

In Britain, Scott's "heroic failure" in coming second to the Pole and dying nobly on the way back transformed Antarctic historiography. Instead of a chronicle of adventure and derring-do, it became a story of explaining and justifying personal and national defeat, starring Scott as its tragic hero.

* * *

The interwar period saw a significant increase in international competition over Antarctica. The British government responded by attempting to assert control over the entire continent through the gradual extension of its territorial claims; most of the "scientific" expeditions that were mounted in the subsequent decades were in fact thinly veiled efforts to validate these assertions of sovereignty. By the mid-1930s, the British claimed two-thirds of Antarctica, but the other interested nations did not silently acquiesce.[15] In 1924, France seized control over Adélie Land, which had first been discovered in 1840 by the French explorer Jules Dumont d'Urville, while Norway, eager to protect its whaling interests, protested British claims to territory discovered by Norwegian explorers. Most ominously, in 1938 the Germans mounted the Ritscher expedition, which sought to expand the Nazi regime's ever-increasing territorial ambitions to the Antarctic.[16] The biggest challenge to British aspirations in Antarctica, however, came not from European rivals, but from South America, as Argentina and Chile announced territorial claims that overlapped with Britain's. The Argentines had long opposed Britain's efforts to extend the Falkland Islands Dependency, and in 1927 they made their own claim to South Georgia Island, a British possession since the late eighteenth century.

This complex geopolitical context clearly influenced writing about Antarctica in the interwar period. It was no accident that in his history of Antarctic exploration published in 1930, the American writer and film-maker Francis Trevelyan Miller titled his chapter on the period after Amundsen had reached the Pole, "The War for the Possession of Antarctica."[17] But because British authors continued to dominate the field, it was their perspective that was most frequently expressed. Scott therefore loomed large in interwar Antarctic historiography. In 1922, Apsley Cherry-Garrard, a member of the *Terra Nova* expedition, published his account of the ill-fated expedition, *The Worst Journey in the World*, which quickly became a classic work of exploration literature. There were also a handful of scholarly efforts, including the Irish writer Stephen Gwynn's hagiographic biography of Scott in 1929 and J. Gordon Hayes's *The Conquest of the South Pole* (1932), an examination of the entire history of Antarctic exploration. For the most part, however, the field remained the province of popular writers, who were united in their lavish praise of Scott. Their volumes included Harold Avery's *"No Surrender!": The Story of Captain Scott's Journey to the South*

Pole (1933), Martin Lindsay's *The Epic of Captain Scott* (1933), Howard Marshall's *With Scott to the Pole* (1936), and Wilfrid Bruce's *Captain Scott* (1937). Lindsay's description was typical:

> Scott will always be remembered. But not because he was a great explorer, nor because he reached the Pole, nor yet again because he died a heroic death. His name lives because he was a great and noble man.[18]

These authors frequently compared Scott to the heroes of old, not only Franklin and Ross but also Drake and Nelson, as if to assure a nervous nation that their character, strength, and moral fiber had survived over the centuries. Other frequently identified "British" Antarctic heroes of the interwar period included the Australian Douglas Mawson, whom Trevelyan Miller praised for having spent a "lifetime . . . adding new domains to the British Empire," and Sir Hubert Wilkins, who in 1928 became the first person to explore Antarctica by air.[19]

The most dramatic feat of Antarctic exploration of the interwar period, however, was accomplished not by a Briton but by an American, when Admiral Richard Byrd flew to the South Pole and back in 1929. Once again, the British had been beaten in the race to accomplish an important polar feat. Byrd's nationality, however, posed an entirely different set of questions and attracted an entirely different set of responses from those generated by Amundsen's conquest of the South Pole. Byrd was the first of the new, privately-funded, more media-savvy generation of explorers. He did not "discover" anything, but that was the point. Stephen Pyne writes that during the Heroic Age:

> It was as though the object was not to struggle to advance a goal, but to discover a goal that would justify struggle. . . . Modernism dissolved many of the scientific and cultural ties that had sustained [the traditional] mode of geographic exploration. No longer did visits to remote tribes, jungle-covered ruins or wind-swept deserts seem to answer fundamental questions. . . . Exploration suffered a crisis of identity and purpose.[20]

More specifically, the interwar years saw a shift in the balance of power away from Europe and its far-flung territorial empires, and across the Atlantic towards the emerging American superpower. From the perspective of the British government, this shift was in some ways threatening, but also comforting, as America, with its large population and immense industrial capacity, seemed to offer an invincible ally against Axis fascism and Soviet communism. The complexity of Anglo-American relations in this period was manifested in the interactions of the two countries in the Antarctic. In an era of Wilsonian anti-imperialism, the American government refused to recognize any of Britain's extensive territorial claims unless a strict standard of "effective occupation" was met, an impossibility in the harsh conditions of the Antarctic. The nobler impulses of the Wilsonian moment, however, soon gave way to more hardheaded strategic considerations, and the United States began to seriously consider claiming its own Antarctic territory in the late 1930s, though the Second World War intervened before any action could be taken.[21]

Byrd's flight served as a harbinger of a new age of Antarctic exploration, one which the British no longer dominated. His achievement marked the third time in the twentieth century that the British had to concede polar victory to another nation, and the second time to an American. On the surface, Byrd's blatantly patriotic promotion of his polar exploits seemed likely to offend British audiences. He named his Antarctic base "Little America" and deliberately positioned it to provide access to unexplored areas of the continent that might be ripe for American claims.[22] In addition, the fiercely competitive Byrd was reluctant to give credit to the British pioneers of Antarctic exploration.[23] Nonetheless, he was embraced as a hero in Britain as well as in America. "The achievement of Admiral Byrd brings world supremacy to America," wrote Trevelyan Miller, before proclaiming that Byrd had "discovered and surveyed more new territory than any other [Antarctic] exploring party on record."[24] The popular author Bertie Webster Smith also had high praise for Byrd in his *To the South Pole* (1936). He outlined the contributions to the knowledge of the Antarctic made by previous explorers, but declared emphatically that "Byrd's work was the most important."[25] Nor was the more scholarly J. Gordon Hayes immune to Byrd's heroic allure. "The name of Richard Evelyn Byrd," he wrote, "shines brightly even in the galaxy of brilliant Americans to whom he belongs."[26]

The willingness of the British to praise an American explorer marked the first indications of a shift in the strategic contours of global power, in which the old European-dominated international system gave way to the bipolar world of the Cold War. The British elevation of Byrd to the highest levels of heroism, which continued after the Second World War, represents a concession to this new reality. In 1957, Kenneth M. King included him alongside Benjamin Franklin, George Washington, Abraham Lincoln, Mark Twain, and Henry Ford in his *Six Great Americans*.[27] At a time when any lingering Anglo-American rivalry had all but surrendered to the exigencies of wartime alliances and postwar rebuilding, it is not surprising that Byrd enjoyed such a lofty reputation on both sides of the Atlantic. Byrd's British biographers typically traced his ancestry back to the family of prominent planters established by the colonist William Byrd in Virginia in the seventeenth century, thereby emphasizing his British bloodline and suiting British class-based conceptions of what a hero should be. Byrd thus became a representative of the common heritage and shared values of Britain and the United States, a living symbol of the spirit of cooperation that had won the war. His hagiographic reception reflects a context in which Britain and the United States were close allies in the Cold War, a conflict that played out all over the globe, including the Antarctic. Even though the Soviet Union had no legitimate claim to territory there, the Soviet government sent a declaration to the American, British, and Argentine governments in 1950 that used Fabian Gottlieb von Bellingshausen's ostensible "first sighting" of 1820 as the basis for the establishment of Russian interest in the region.[28] For their part, the Americans dispatched a series of military expeditions to Antarctica in this period, including Operation Highjump in 1946–1947, which with its 4700 participants was the largest exploration effort ever undertaken on the continent.[29]

* * *

At the same time as it became a pawn in the strategic rivalries of the Cold War, however, Antarctica also maintained a place in the history of the British Empire. The Falkland and South Sandwich Islands and South Georgia Island remained as colonies even as Britain relinquished most of its other territorial possessions. In 1955, the British launched the Commonwealth Trans-Antarctic Expedition, which used Sno-Cat motorized vehicles to achieve what Ernest Shackleton had failed to do on the *Endurance* expedition of 1914–1916: crossing the Antarctic continent via the South Pole. The choice of nomenclature was significant: whereas the name of Shackleton's venture had been the *Imperial* Trans-Antarctic Expedition, the name of this expedition was intended to display a new spirit of egalitarianism and cooperation among the former members of the Empire. Comprised predominantly of New Zealanders, the Ross Sea support team was led by Sir Edmund Hillary, five years after his triumphal ascent of Mount Everest.

The Everest story provides an interesting parallel to the postwar trajectory of British Antarctic historiography. Although Everest was chalked up as a victory, the triumphal tone of the celebrations occluded the changes that had occurred in the nation's status as a great power since the beginning of the twentieth century. Neither of the two climbers who reached the top was in fact British, an issue that has occasioned a spirited debate between two British imperial historians in the pages of the academic history journal *Past and Present*. Gordon Stewart contends that in Edmund

Hillary's case this was dealt with fairly easily, by transforming Hilary into a "Commonwealth subject."[30] Peter Hansen, on the other hand, claims that Hilary's incorporation into "British narratives" as "an example of the continuing partnership and loyalty to the Commonwealth of independent peoples" was more contested.[31]

In some ways, a similar phenomenon occurred in British Antarctic historiography in the years after 1958, which focused on the Commonwealth Trans-Antarctic Expedition as the long-awaited victory in Antarctic exploration that Britain so richly deserved. But the presentation of the Commonwealth expedition as a "British" triumph could not entirely conceal the dramatic changes in the Empire that had occurred since the Second World War. While the official, "master" narrative presented the expedition as a great achievement made possible by the harmonious spirit of cooperation between the British and New Zealand teams, the reality was different. Hillary was a far greater celebrity at the time than the expedition's British leader, Vivian Fuchs, and received a disproportionate share of public attention as a result. He was initially only supposed to lay a series of supply depots on the Ross Sea side of the expedition's route, before turning back well short of the South Pole. But equipped only with converted Massey-Ferguson tractors rather than Sno-Cats, he achieved his objectives easily and continued to the Pole, which he reached sixteen days before the British team. The expedition, which had been intended to reflect a new spirit of camaraderie among the former members of the British Empire, ended up being a little *too* egalitarian. Hillary's temerity in stealing a march for the second time on his former rulers was difficult to ignore, for this time he not only reached the goal first, but also beat an Englishman in the process.

At the same time, the British effort to maintain their grasp on their Antarctic possessions was met with hostility from the Argentine and Chilean governments, which sought to oust them from the region with increasingly aggressive diplomatic maneuvers and occasional military intervention. For its part, the United States found itself in the awkward position of being allied to both sides; further complicating matters was the American government's "continuing vacillation" on making Antarctic territorial claims of its own.[32] The American desire to prevent Soviet interference and resolve the growing tensions among its allies pushed policymakers in Washington in the direction of seeking an international solution to the "Antarctic problem" that would ultimately result in the Antarctic Treaty of 1959.

The postwar era thus opened a new phase of Antarctic history and historiography. By the 1960s, the anxieties created by the rapid collapse of the British Empire and increasing doubts about Britain's importance in the new world order focused on Robert Falcon Scott, loser of the race to the Pole, who had traditionally been interpreted as representing the values of the political and social elite, values that were traditionally perceived as having contributed to the maintenance of Britain's military and imperial hegemony. That hegemony was now endangered, and along with it Scott's status as a hero.[33] In the 1960s and 70s, biographies of Scott by Reginald Pound and David Thomson depicted a moody, indecisive, and insecure man who was ill-suited for polar leadership. Thomson went so far as to attack the entire British effort to reach the South Pole first as a desperate stab to maintain imperial greatness by a nation whose power was ebbing:

> The several British attempts on the South Pole spoke with unequivocal earnestness of the need to stamp a British imprint on the most inaccessible part of the earth. There was disappointment, envy and grumbling at unsportingness when a Norwegian flag was found stuck in the snow, and there are all manner of flags in the grim portraits of the British party second at the Pole: flags from school and colleges, national flags, pennants given by queens, flags to honour the wind. Had the British been there first, with smiles on their burned and shrivelled faces, the South Pole would have been made a pretty scene of chivalrous bunting, like a fete in an English cathedral city on a cold June day.[34]

Criticism of Scott reached its apex in 1979, when Roland Huntford published his dual biography *Scott and Amundsen*. Viewing Scott as "a suitable hero for a nation in decline," Huntford saw his undeservedly lofty stature as a clear reflection—and in some ways as a progenitor—of Britain's decline as a major power.[35] Appearing at the end of a decade—the 1970s—in which Britain's decline as a political, economic, military, and imperial power became an unavoidable reality, *Scott and Amundsen* suited the contemporary mood. In such a climate, it was all too easy to dismiss Scott as an effete, weak-willed exemplar of the national malaise that had engendered Britain's twentieth-century decline.

Beyond the British context, the attacks on Scott must also be viewed in light of a climate that was generally hostile to the type of Antarctic exploration that he represented. The signing of the Antarctic Treaty in 1959 by the twelve nations (later joined by eight others) considered to be actively involved in Antarctica transformed the continent from a site of international competition to one of cooperation. Suddenly, the older style of explorer, with his desire to plant the flag everywhere he went, seemed out of sync with the times. On the other side of the Atlantic, Byrd came to be treated with equal hostility as Scott. The 1970s saw three American biographies that collectively presented him as "cold, aloof, rabidly ambitious, manipu-lative, cowardly and deceitful."[36] Antarctic exploration, it seems, had sud-denly become as unfashionable as Empire.

*   *   *

By the 1990s, however, Scott-bashing had given way to Shackleton-mania, as Ernest Shackleton suddenly zoomed to the forefront of Antarctic her-oism and historiography. He was the subject of a blockbuster museum exhibition that traveled the globe, a BBC miniseries starring Kenneth Branagh, and a best-selling book by Caroline Alexander.[37] Five new biog-raphies, including one by Huntford, appeared between 1985 and 2003.[38] By this time, the cultural climate in both Britain and the United States had created an atmosphere that was more favorable to heroes. Emerging from the era of post-Vietnam, post-imperial malaise that had so tarnished Scott, an Anglo-American culture suffused with disillusionment suddenly regained some of the confidence it had lost. Shackleton fit this era per-fectly. He was strong and masculine, and, unlike Scott, *succeeded*, at least in not getting anyone, including himself, killed. "Heroic failure" was not a concept that appealed in an America trying to recover from the humili-ations of Vietnam and the Iran Hostage Crisis, nor in a Britain trying to move past the trauma of postindustrial economic collapse and decoloni-zation. In Britain, the key event of the era was the Falklands War, which reminded the nation of its imperial and specifically of its Antarctic his-tory. What better hero at such a time than a man who had played such a prominent role in determining that history? With Scott largely discredited, Shackleton was a logical choice.

It was in the Blair and Clinton eras, however, that Shackleton truly became the new *beau ideal* of the polar explorer. For all his rugged mas-culinity, there were a number of factors that complicated his role as a cul-tural hero in Thatcher's Britain. In particular, his moral reputation, fairly or unfairly, had never conformed to the Iron Lady's carefully constructed sense of "Victorian values," and his Irish birth was a further handicap in a nation whose government was less than sympathetic to Celtic cultural diversity within the United Kingdom and the political agenda of Irish repub-licanism. But in the Blair era, Shackleton's concern for his men showed that he was a tough guy with a soft heart, just as a New Labour-ite should be. His Irishness, meanwhile, became something to be celebrated rather than ignored as new, less Anglocentric relationships with the non-English nations of the British Isles were sought. Finally, the fact that Shackleton was better known for rescuing his men on the *Endurance* expedition than for any territorial achievement made it far easier to endorse him as the perfect polar hero for a postcolonial age.

*   *   *

Viewed with hindsight several decades from now, I suspect—and in some ways hope—that Shackleton's moment of glory will appear as the last gasp of an outmoded way of writing about Antarctic history by focusing on the feats or failures of individual explorers and the Heroic Age. In some ways, that future is already here, with movement away from the biographical and narrative accounts that have previously dominated the field and momentum toward the emphasis on cultural history that has come to characterize the study of the British Empire in other parts of the world. The first attempt to examine Antarctic exploration from a cultural rather than traditional perspective was Max Jones's *The Last Great Quest: Captain Scott's Antarctic Sacrifice* (2003). Instead of yet again recounting the history of the *Terra Nova* expedition, Jones focuses on the question of "why did the death of five men in the Antarctic cause such a sensation ninety years ago, not only in Britain but around the world?"[39] He provides nuanced answers to this question that not only go beyond the narrow, technical issues that have traditionally obsessed polar historians, but also reveal much about British culture in the decades following the Great War.

Jones's work was followed by my own *Antarctic Destinies: Scott, Shackleton, and the Changing Face of Heroism* (2007), which compares the evolving reputations of Scott and Shackleton and attempts to answer why the latter has waxed while the former has waned by examining how the cultural context surrounding them has changed, in both Britain and the United States:

> Shackleton remained in Scott's shadow for decades, . . . his own accomplishments barely recalled or credited. In more recent years, however, the tide has turned. In the late twentieth century, Shackleton came to be regarded as the greater leader, the greater explorer and the greater hero, while Scott was denigrated as a bungler, a martinet and, ultimately, a failure. . . . What happened to bring about this dramatic reversal in the reputations of the two men? Since it occurred well after their deaths, it can have little to do with their own characters or achievements. Instead the explanation lies in how our perceptions and interpretations of their characters and achievements have changed.[40]

In some ways, however, these works represent less of a departure from the conventional concerns of Antarctic historiography than they might initially appear. The *Last Great Quest* was as much an attempt to overturn the arguments of Scott's numerous recent detractors, particularly Roland Huntford, as it was an examination of Edwardian values. *Antarctic Destinies*, meanwhile, concludes by expressing the hope that "someday we can appreciate both explorers as men, as well as cultural icons."[41]

More recent Antarctic historiography suggests movement in this direction. There have been no further cultural studies, but rather a succession of works along conventional lines that have attempted to resuscitate Scott's reputation. Published in 2003, Ranulph Fiennes's emphatically pro-Scott biography, which refers to Huntford's account as a "travesty," derives its authority from the author's first-hand experience of Antarctic exploration.[42] Two years later, David Crane's more scholarly biography acknowledged that Scott's reputation rose and fell with the fortunes of the British Empire in the twentieth century, but denied that this automatically discounted the heroism of his accomplishments:

> While nothing is more inevitable or healthier than historical revisionism, what has happened to Scott's reputation requires some other label. . . . The historical process that has shrunk the rich, complex and deeply human set of associations that once clustered round his story into an allegory of arrogance, selfishness and moral stupidity is . . . extraordinary.[43]

While both Fiennes and Crane acknowledge that the changing cultural context has been responsible for Scott's declining reputation, they also both utilize a conventional empirical, biographical approach to overcome the effect of these cultural forces. All it takes to correct matters, they both assert, is to present the truth.

These recent works of Antarctic historiography thus continue to focus on the leading lights of the Heroic Age. Perhaps it is time, however, for Antarctic historiography to move past its obsession with individual expeditions and their leaders and to take a new look at what those explorers found so compelling about the continent: the natural environment. Such an approach was pioneered by Francis Spufford in his *I May Be Some Time: Ice and the English Imagination* (1997), which attempts to provide an "imaginative history of polar exploration," both Arctic and Antarctic, by tracing the evolution of English fascination with the coldest places on earth from the eighteenth century to the present:

> Polar history, as it is usually written, is technical history. It recounts a sequence of expeditions. There is a degree of variety in the chosen starting point . . . but a great constancy of focus and emphasis thereafter . . . . But there is a second kind of polar history, largely uncharted; an intangible history of

assumptions, responses to landscape, cultural fascination, aesthetic attraction to the cold regions.[44]

Or perhaps it is time to leave the human focus behind altogether, for Antarctica is a land where exploration may tell us more about the rest of the world than it does about the place actually being explored. In an age in which the effects of global warming are most visible in the polar regions, the environmental history of the Antarctic is crying out for serious scholarly attention. In *The Coldest March: Scott's Fatal Antarctic Expedition* (2001), Susan Solomon uses meteorological data collected by the *Terra Nova*'s scientists to argue that Scott's tragic fate may have been determined by unusually cold weather rather than his ineptitude.[45] Her book was thus in many ways yet another intervention into the post-Huntford debate over Scott's reputation. Beneath the surface, however, *The Coldest March*'s focus on climatic conditions may offer a new way forward for Antarctic historiography. Perhaps it is time to stop worrying about whether Scott or Shackleton, or Byrd or Amundsen, was the greater hero, and time to start worrying about what the history of environmental change in the Antarctic means for all humanity.

NOTES

1. Stephen J. Pyne, "Heart of Whiteness: The Exploration of Antarctica," *Environmental Review* 10:4 (1986): 238.

2. The nations currently claiming territory in the Antarctic are: the United Kingdom, New Zealand, France, Norway, Australia, Chile, and Argentina. Brazil maintains a "zone of interest" which is not a formal claim, and Ecuador, Peru, Russia, Canada, Uruguay, and the United States all reserve the right to make claims at some point in the future. Most of these nations, however, are signatories to the Antarctic Treaty of 1959, which prohibits any future territorial claims.

3. Peter Beck, *International Politics of Antarctica* (London and Sydney: Croom Helm, 1986), 29.

4. G. Hartwig, *The Polar World: A Popular Description of Man and Nature in the Arctic and Antarctic Regions of the Globe* (London: Longmans, Green and Co., 1869).

5. George Barnett Smith, *The Romance of the South Pole: Antarctic Voyages and Explorations* (London: T. Nelson and Sons, 1900), 9–10.

6. Antarctica has substantial deposits of coal, manganese, iron, copper, lead, uranium, and other minerals. Joseph S. Roucek, "The Geopolitics of the Antarctic: The Land Is Free for Scientific Work but its Wealth of Minerals Has Excited Imperialist Claims," *Journal of Economics and Sociology* 45:1 (1986): 71.

7. Beau Riffenburgh, *The Myth of the Explorer: The Press, Sensationalism and Geographical Discovery* (London and New York: Belhaven, 1993), 2.

8. Barnett Smith, *The Romance of the South Pole*, 234.

9. John Kennedy MacLean, *Heroes of the Polar Seas* (London: W. & R. Chambers, 1910), 378.

10. Hugh Robert Mill, "Introduction: South Polar Exploration in the Last Hundred Years," in Ernest Shackleton, *The Heart of the Antarctic: Being the Story of the British Antarctic Expedition 1907–1909* (London: William Heinemann, 1909), xxxviii.

11. As Robert David writes, "Paradoxically the exploration of the uninhabited continent of Antarctica was the antithesis of everything that economic imperialism and 'civilising mission' ideology stood for, but it more than made up for Britain's diminished role in the Arctic." Robert David, *The Arctic in the British Imagination, 1818–1914* (Manchester: Manchester University Press, 2000), 237.

12. Hugh Robert Mill, *The Siege of the South Pole* (London: Alston Rivers, 1905), 1.

13. Beck, *The International Politics of Antarctica*, 28.

14. M. B. Synge, *A Book of Discovery* (London: T. C. and E. C. Jack, 1912), 536.

15. Beck, *International Politics of Antarctica*, 29.

16. See Colin Summerhayes and Peter Beeching, "Hitler's Antarctic Base: The Myth and the Reality," *Polar Record* 43:1 (2007): 1–21.

17. Francis Trevelyan Miller, *Byrd's Great Adventure: With the Complete Story of All Polar Explorations for One Thousand Years* (London: Stanley Paul, 1930), 298.

18. Martin Lindsay, *The Epic of Captain Scott* (Edinburgh: Peter Davies Limited, 1933), 169–172.

19. Trevelyan Miller, *Byrd's Great Adventure*, 369.

20. Pyne, "Heart of Whiteness," 239.

21. Beck, *International Politics of Antarctica*, 30.

22. Warren R. Hofstra, "Richard E. Byrd and the Legacy of Polar Exploration," *Virginia Magazine of History and Biography* 110:2 (2002): 141.

23. Robert N. Matuozzi, "Richard Byrd, Polar Exploration and the Media," *Virginia Magazine of History and Biography* 110:2 (2002): 213.

24. Trevelyan Miller, *Byrd's Great Adventure*, 375.

25. B. Webster Smith, *To the South Pole: The Story of Antarctic Exploration* (London and Glasgow: Blackie & Son, 1936), 201–203.

26. J. Gordon Hayes, *The Conquest of the South Pole: Antarctic Exploration, 1906–1931* (London: Thornton Butterworth, 1932), 53.

27. Kenneth M. King, *Six Great Americans* (London: Hamish Hamilton, 1957).

28. Beck, *International Politics of Antarctica*, 40. See also Walter Sullivan, "Antarctica in a Two-Power World," *Foreign Affairs* 36:1 (1957): 154–166.

29. Ronald E. Doel, "Constituting the Postwar Earth Sciences: The Military's Influence on the Environmental Sciences in the U.S.A. After 1945," *Social Studies of Science* 33 (2003): 639.

30. Gordon Stewart, "Tenzing's Two Wrist-Watches: The Conquest of Everest and Late Imperial Culture in Britain 1921–1953," *Past and Present* 149 (1995): 187–188.

31. Peter H. Hansen, "Debate: Tenzing's Two Wrist-Watches: The Conquest of Everest and Late Imperial Culture in Britain 1921–1953," *Past and Present* 157 (1997), 167.

32. Beck, *International Politics of Antarctica*, 39. See also Jason Kendall Moore, "Maritime Rivalry, Political Intervention and the Race to Antarctica: U.S.-Chilean Relations, 1939–1949," *Journal of Latin American Studies* 33:4 (2001): 713–738.

33. "Hero or fool," writes Stephen J. Pyne, "attitudes toward Robert Scott seem to reflect the contemporary state of British self-esteem and change with each generation." Pyne, "Heart of Whiteness," 231.

34. David Thomson, *Scott's Men* (London: Allen Lane, 1977), 1–2.

35. Roland Huntford, *Scott and Amundsen* (London: Hodder and Stoughton, 1979), 560.

36. Lisle A. Rose, "Exploring a Secret Land: The Literary and Technological Legacies of Richard E. Byrd," *Virginia Magazine of History and Biography* 110:2 (2002): 175.

37. Caroline Alexander, *The Endurance: Shackleton's Legendary Antarctic Expedition* (New York: Alfred A. Knopf, 1999).

38. Roland Huntford, *Shackleton* (London: Hodder and Stoughton, 1985); Kim Heacox, *Shackleton: The Antarctic Challenge* (New York: National Geographic, 1999); Paul I. Sipiera, *Ernest Shackleton: A Life of Antarctic Exploration* (Dubuque, Iowa: Kendall Hunt, 2001); Christopher Edge, *Shackleton: A Beginner's Guide* (London: Trafalgar Square, 2002); and George Plimpton, *Shackleton* (New York: DK Publishing, 2003).

39. Max Jones, *The Last Great Quest: Captain Scott's Antarctic Sacrifice* (Oxford: Oxford University Press, 2002), 9.

40. Stephanie Barczewski, *Antarctic Destinies: Scott, Shackleton and the Changing Face of Heroism* (London: Continuum, 2007), xii–xiii.

41. Barczewski, *Antarctic Destinies*, 311.

42. Ranulph Fiennes, *Captain Scott* (London: Hodder and Stoughton, 2003), 2.

43. David Crane, *Scott of the Antarctic* (London and New York: Harper Perennial, 2006), 10.

44. Francis Spufford, *I May Be Some Time: Ice in the English Imagination* (London and Boston: Faber and Faber, 1996), 6.

45. Susan Solomon, *The Coldest March: Scott's Fatal Antarctic Expedition* (New Haven, Conn., and London: Yale University Press, 2001).

INDEX